# Open the Door
# Let's Explore
# More!

## by Rhoda Redleaf
### illustrated by Stéphanie Roth

 Redleaf Press
St. Paul, Minnesota

© 1996 Rhoda Redleaf
All rights reserved.

Illustrations by Stéphanie Roth

Published by:   Redleaf Press
                a division of Resources for Child Caring
                450 North Syndicate, Suite 5
                St. Paul, MN 55104

Distributed by:  Gryphon House
                P.O. Box 207
                Beltsville, MD 20704-0207


Library of Congress Cataloging-in-Publication Data

Redleaf, Rhoda
    Open the door, let's explore more! : field trips of discovery for young
children / Rhoda Redleaf: illustrated by Stéphanie Roth.
      p      cm
    Includes bibliographical references.
    ISBN 1-884834-13-2
    1.School field trips.     I.Title
LB1047.R394  1996
371.3 8—dc20

                                          96-14294  CIP

# Contents

# Acknowledgments

It is impossible to give full credit to everyone who has in some way contributed to this book. Many of its ideas and activities are adaptations of things I've learned from others in workshops, courses, and observations in over 35 years as an early childhood educator. This book includes a revision of the earlier *Open the Door Let's Explore*, and I wish to acknowledge and thank my colleagues who contributed either directly or indirectly to that edition, especially David Allen, Laurel Goulding, Ardis Kysar, Beth Overstad, Susan Middleton, Zona Ivory, Jane Heille, and my children, Karen and Eric. Any acknowledgment of that earlier publication must include in memoriam recognition of Deb Fish, who prodded me into writing it and presided over and nurtured the development of our then fledgling press. How proud she would be of this revision and of the outstanding work of our present-day press.

In addition, I would like to acknowledge and thank those most closely involved in the production of this book. My daughter, Karen, admirably rescued her computer illiterate mother, laboring long and hard and battling untold computer demons to transcribe my chaotic scribbling into the disk format publishers now require. Copy editor Rosemary Wallner did an amazing job of transforming my overly long or confused sentences and imperfect composition into the logical, succinct, and highly readable final text. The design team of Ronna Hammer and Paul Woods did a beautiful job of formatting and structuring my very long manuscript into this attractive and accessible book. Stéphanie Roth's wonderful illustrations add the perfect touch of whimsy, adventure, and fun. Working with press director Eileen Nelson is always a joy. Her knowledge and skill inspire complete confidence that her final editorial judgments will be perfect.

I would also like to thank the nursery school and child care directors and child development instructors who shared their ideas and suggestions with me. Special thanks to Lynn Galle and her staff for assistance with current safety procedures and policies, and for her other suggestions.

Thanks also to the librarians and staff of the White Bear Lake branch of the Ramsey County, Minnesota, Public Library. They were most helpful in assisting me in finding books. I know that the hundreds of books I plowed through and checked out several times a week greatly increased their workload for several months, but they always welcomed me with enthusiasm and interest in my work.

Thanks to my grandchildren, Nathaniel, Benjamin, Brian, and Jonathan, who accompanied me on so many of these excursions and to Adam and Isabel who will provide a continuing opportunity for me to explore the world through the eyes of children. My granddog (Karen's) Whiskey provided the inspiration for at least one finger play and several references to pets.

And finally, thanks to my husband, Paul, for his constant support and encouragement, and his "professional" management of our household during the months of my intense efforts to meet deadlines.

# Introduction

The smell of the air after a rain.
The feel of a woolly sheep.
The sounds of an airport.
The sight of a shadow on a sunny wall.
The taste of a crisp, red apple.

These are small, everyday things we want children to know about, experience, and appreciate. In our eagerness to expose young children to the wonders of our technological society, however, we may overlook the learning potential of common, ordinary, everyday experiences. In *Open the Door Let's Explore More!*, I hope to open up a world of these experiences to parents, providers, and children.

The most important learning task facing young children remains that of making sense of their world—and adults are the tour guides. Adults provide the bridges from the known to the unknown for the children they teach.

When we as adults explore something new—whether it be a new country or location—we rely on knowledgeable tour guides to point things out and give just the right amount of information to stimulate our interest and curiosity. In the same way, we can enhance children's explorations of the new (and not so new) sites in their world. The trick is to provide just the right amount of information, questioning, and stimulation.

In the midst of my work on this book, I visited Denmark. Because it was only a short trip, I did not plan to visit any preschools despite their reputation for excellence. As it turned out, I didn't need to arrange a visit—throughout the three weekdays I was there, the preschoolers visited me every place I went. At a train station, a group was waiting for a train to take them to see the newly purchased house of one of their teachers. At a castle, very young preschoolers romped in the castle's great hall and fondly peered at the statues of three small but fierce lions—the royal family's insignia. I encountered another group at an outdoor fountain as they admired the sculptures and orifices spouting water, and so it went. I was in a field trip proponent's paradise.

I saw groups walking or on buses and trains everywhere. It was early October and most people in northern climates take advantage of the outdoors as long as they can—and from the rosy cheeks I saw everywhere, these children spend a lot of time exploring outdoors. The public transportation system in Denmark is outstanding, which certainly facilitates going places. But more impressive was seeing the educational philosophy of the importance of doing in action.

This book contains a wealth of ideas and activities—use it as a resource, picking and choosing what's best for your group. Modify activities based on your group's interest and location. Repeat trips to focus on another aspect. Ask parents to talk about their experiences with the places your group wants to visit. This book will provide the basics; use your knowledge of the children in your care to create fun-filled explorations.

I hope someday I will see as many groups of American preschoolers everywhere I go—and not just in the children's museums or zoos, but appreciating all the resources our communities have to offer.

Rhoda Redleaf

# How to Use This Book

In this book's first chapter, "Experience and Learning," you'll find general information about how children learn—which will set the stage for the trips that follow. This chapter also includes planning suggestions and helpful hints.

The trips themselves are separated into two parts: "A World of Walks" and "Your Community." The suggested activities help to make the trip a focal point in an integrated learning process, rather than an added-on activity of unclear relevance.

Each field trip begins with an overview and purpose statements. The "Before the Walk" (or "Before the Trip") section includes discussion topics, activities, and books to read that will start children thinking about the topic. This section also includes a list of words, randomly selected, that are associated with the field trip. Choose six or seven words from that list to emphasize and explain. The words you choose will vary depending on the children's age and vocabulary: a three year old will be learning basic names and descriptive words; a five year old will be learning technical terms and words related to concepts. For older children, write down the words on small pieces of paper so they can begin to recognize them. Consider presenting some words in a variety of languages. If you have children who speak different languages, the translations should reflect those languages. Ask parents or older children to translate a few of the most common words on the list. Using words in more than one language helps bridge language barriers, makes children more comfortable in a multilingual environment, and supports language learning!

A "Things to Bring" section lists supplies (such as paper and pencils, a camera, and bags for collecting things) that you and your group might need for the field trip.

The "On the Walk" (or "On the Trip") section lists questions to ask, points to wonder about, and experiments to try.

The "After the Walk" (or "After the Trip") section provides many follow-up activities. Children can study found specimens with a magnifying glass, construct a mural using pictures from magazines, complete experiments, or use dramatic play to reenact the activities they've just seen.

When you take a trip not in this book, use the same basic planning process used here. Consider your purpose, choose the vocabulary to emphasize, plan how to introduce the trip, look for opportunities along the way to enhance learning, and schedule follow-up activities to reinforce learning.

To round out the experience, you'll find original and traditional finger plays and songs, as well as a "Resources" section. All are meant to enhance learning and provide variety to the activities—before, during, and after the field trip.

The books in the Resources sections contain a mix of old and new titles. Some of the older titles have become classics and may even have current reissue dates. A few that are dated still have useful information and are included for their historical value or uniqueness. Because of a shortage of good books on a few of the topics, some of the books included are not preschool-level books. Use these books for their pictures and general information and adapt as needed. (They are listed in a separate section titled "Other Good Resources.")

All of the books and videos listed should be available at your local library. Your library and librarian can be invaluable resources when you are planning a trip. Use them whenever possible.

The appendixes at the back of the book include forms, lists, and general resources that you can use in any way you wish. You may copy them to give to parents or use in your own planning.

# Experience and Learning

# Field Trips: An Approach to Learning

Excursion tours, car trips, and cruises give adults an opportunity to see for themselves something they have heard or read about. Field trips serve similar functions for children, and more. They give children an opportunity to see something for themselves—sometimes even before they have seen or read about the place—ultimately learning more than if they just looked at pictures or talked about it. Children learn to make sense of the world around them through many different experiences. The greater the quantity and variety of experiences, the greater the learning potential.

While books, pictures, filmstrips, videos, and TV provide information, they are all only two-dimensional and secondhand, and are no substitutes for the real thing. Young children have limited experiences and understanding of the world, and do not have the background or skill to use secondhand sources of information effectively. Think of the difference between seeing a picture of an ice-cream sundae and eating a real one. If you have only seen pictures or heard about ice cream, your notion of what it is will be different than if you have eaten the real thing.

The same principle is true for all concepts that children are learning. Children need to use all their senses to gain an undistorted view of the world. The more exposure children have to firsthand experiences, the richer their understanding becomes. A look at the world through the eyes of a child can help parents and providers find valuable material for learning right under their noses.

Take the first field trip around a familiar room. This trip offers any child, from infant to preschooler, a chance to notice and learn the names of all the things in the room. Look at furniture, pipes, heat registers, and wall and floor composition, in addition to toys. For a baby, mention simple words such as *chair*, *table*, and *window*. For older children, provide more details such as *rocking chair*, *leather chair*, *round table*, *dining room table*, and *windowsill*.

For the next trip, further explore the home or building, perhaps visiting the kitchen to explore the appliances and pipes, and going down to the basement to see where those pipes go. In a school or center, children could visit the office area to look at the machines, special furniture, or equipment.

3

After looking closely at rooms within the house or building, explore the neighborhood. Every neighborhood contains opportunities to explore and learn if you become alert to the things you take for granted. There are many common and obvious things that children have never had explained to them, such as the way sidewalks are made, how puddles are formed, where water goes, and how trees grow and change.

From the immediate neighborhood, move to the larger community and its services and resources. Look for a service station, grocery store, or other general shopping area within walking distance. If you need to, use transportation (public, car pool, or school bus) to explore the community.

Think about the parts of your community that are most readily available. You might overlook the possibility of public transportation, but going on a bus is itself an exciting experience for many children. In making choices, weigh safety, convenience, and monetary factors.

You can visit the same site many times, but for a different purpose each time. Each visit becomes a unique experience because of that different purpose. Take a trip to the grocery store to see how grocers organize and arrange food; return to observe what other employees do and how the store works. During a third visit, you can put these observations to use and have the children shop for a cooking project. Revisiting a site allows the children to gain more mature insights because of what has been learned in the interim.

Excursions offer many opportunities to name objects and activities, which will in turn have the immediate impact of enlarging children's vocabularies. In our eagerness to give information, however, it is easy to overlook the value of asking questions such as, "I wonder what that squirrel is doing?" or "What do you suppose is in that package the mail carrier is delivering?" This questioning approach develops the children's curiosity and problem-solving skills. By offering children clues to use in their guesses (such as the size of the package), you demonstrate a logical thinking technique. This approach is worth using, even though it may produce silly answers from some children.

To maximize the value of a field trip, carefully plan preparatory and follow-up experiences so that the new knowledge can become integrated with what the child already knows.

Tell children about the trip and the things they can expect to see. Rehearse the trip, thus making them more self-assured. After the trip, provide opportunities to use new concepts, and let the children state in their own words what they have experienced. Listen to what the children say and how they react to the experience. Don't be surprised if they are impressed with something you might not have noticed.

A field trip is not just a trip to the zoo in a bus or car, although that is certainly one type of trip—too often the only type we think of. A field trip is more a frame of mind, an approach to an experience either indoors or out, which focuses attention on inquiry:

- on noticing things in more or less detail depending on the child's age;

- on comparing or contrasting new things to known or familiar objects or experiences;
- on wondering how things get to be where and what they are; and
- on enjoying and learning from our environment.

From this point of view, it becomes clear that field trips have a valuable role to play in helping children learn. They help children:

- develop an awareness of surroundings and sharpen observation skills;
- correct misunderstandings and gain new information;
- build vocabularies through concrete experience;
- join in group discussions stimulated by the field trip experience;
- create new ideas for use in dramatic play;
- increase their understanding of seasonal changes and the role of nature;
- find collections of things to study or use for art projects;
- observe the way people live and work and how the community functions;
- get exercise needed for growing bodies and minds;
- become aware of the scientific method of inquiry; and
- have fun.

## What Does Learning Have to Do Field with Trips?

Children naturally seek out experiences that will expand their understanding of the world and themselves. They are learning all the time, from everything around them. Their thoughts develop from their interactions with people, objects, and events. Through numerous and varied direct experiences, children learn to make sense of the world. This active physical and mental involvement works to enhance children's ability to pay attention, remember, and ultimately, understand their world as well as the things they encounter in it.

The early learning process can be divided into four components: perception, language, memory, and logical thinking. These components continually interact and reinforce each other.

1. **Perception**. The learning process begins with direct sensory experiences. To learn about something, children must be able to perceive it—to take it in through their senses. From infancy on, children look at, listen to, touch, smell, and taste the things in their environment in order to learn about them. As they get older, children push, pull, twist, manipulate, and actively explore things for the same reason. There are a multitude of things in the environment and no one can pay attention

to everything at once. To learn, the child must selectively pay attention to some things and ignore others.

The events most likely to capture a child's attention are those with which the child is somewhat familiar. If a new experience is unrelated to what the child already understands, the child may ignore it. Young children and adults frequently pay attention to different features of a situation. You can help children sort out the important and unimportant features of a learning situation and supply the names of patterns or events. Rather than giving children lots of information, you can teach them to be observant by asking pertinent questions and helping to focus their attention.

2. **Language**. Language is not essential to learning or thinking, but it can aid the process. The development of language helps a young child think; and developing new ways of thinking helps the child learn language. When learning the name of an object, the child is forced to attend to the features that distinguish that object from others. Young children first learn to understand words that name specific objects or actions. Words that represent concepts or conditions (*big*, *round*, *soft*), rather than objects, present more difficulty to the child and only become understood through repeated exposure to those concepts in a variety of contexts. Hardest of all are the words that are used to relate objects to each other, such as *underneath*, *behind*, and *over*. Children who have learned the names for relationships are better prepared to solve problems than other children.

You can aid this process by providing children with many opportunities to talk and listen. Supply new vocabulary and encourage children to generalize and state things in their own words. Provide good examples of language every time you speak to children.

3. **Memory**. Memory affects learning. Learning of new information is related to what the child already knows. Children compare new information with things they already know, evaluate the new information, and store it in memory for further use. The more children understand, the more new information they can learn and remember. Generally speaking, older children have better memory skills than younger children and can therefore learn and retain more readily. Because young children have a limited ability to absorb and recall new information, repetition can be in the form of repeated exposure to the same new material in several different forms or ways.

Young children generally remember more if they are actively involved in what is to be learned. Encourage children to recall new experiences by pretending to be something they have seen, felt, heard, touched, or smelled. Children also remember new information better if it is organized in some manner. In short, you can best facilitate the development of memory by encouraging children to actively explore the world around them. Present new information to them in small doses, repeat it in a variety of contexts, and provide bridges that link new and old information.

4.  **Logical Thinking**. Children can, and do, learn without any formal teaching. The rate of the development of logical thinking varies, depending on the child and the experiences the environment offers. But all children progress through stages of thinking in the same sequence.

    This popular theory, developed by Jean Piaget, suggests that young children are unable to comprehend logical principles. Piaget believes that older children do not simply know more than younger children; they think in different ways. Children learn best when they are ready to learn, and understanding develops from the active manipulation of materials and the observation of resulting changes. Piaget does not believe it is possible to speed up the development of logical thinking, but his theory suggests that offering a variety of opportunities to practice new concepts will enhance a child's breadth and depth of understanding at each stage.

    You can help children organize what they know into logical groupings. Specific skills develop slowly, as the children experience and practice them and use them in their world of play.

Direct experiences (such as field trips) with real things in the outside world play an important role in this continually interactive process of children's learning. But the extent to which these experiences become effective teaching tools will be dependent on the way you structure and interpret them.

As the children walk along, it is important to:

- emphasize the sensory experiences around them by touching the grass and bark, smelling the flowers, listening to the cars and the wind;

- name the things they are seeing—such as the colors and shapes of different leaves, the parts of a house, the signs along the road—and talk about them in detail;

- help the children recall the things they have seen before and talk about how these relate to things they are seeing now, such as shrubs that resemble an evergreen tree they have seen, or a collie who has longer hair and is bigger than the poodle they know; and

- encourage thinking about how and why things happen by wondering what the squirrels are doing running up and down the oak tree and why so many leaves pile up on the ground in the fall.

The learning process is greatly influenced by a child's attitudes and feelings. Children who have had some successes and feel self-confident will be more able to cope with new learning situations. Relationships with others also influence feelings about learning. Children who feel they are liked and valued as people will want to become involved in learning. You can support children's learning by paying attention to their efforts, treating their questions with respect, and giving encouragement and approval. You can help children learn to cope with disappointment, frustration, and failure, since true learning will always include periods of failure on the road to mastery.

## Questions to Ask Yourself When Planning Field Trips

Any experience a young child has will make a deeper impression and last longer if you reinforce it. Asking yourself the following questions will help you make the trip more meaningful and enjoyable, and the children will be more easily guided. When preparing for a trip, ask yourself:

> What things are the children already familiar with which relate to the new ideas, concepts, and experiences?
>
> How can they act out or dramatize the experience before and after the trip?
>
> What opportunities will I have, or can I make, to talk about the experience before, during, and after the trip?
>
> How can I encourage the children to talk about the experience before, during, and after?
>
> In what ways can I expect the children to show their interest, reactions, or excitement on this particular trip? What can I do to reinforce these feelings?
>
> What secondary images (such as photographs, television, videos, movies, books, displays) are available to reinforce the experience?
>
> What new social experiences will the children have, and how can I plan to make them healthy experiences?
>
> What kinds of sensory experiences are available on this field trip?
>
> What related experiences can I plan before and after the trip?

Although you probably can think of one or two potential learning experiences for every trip, many more hidden possibilities usually exist; and some child is bound to bump into one. Prior thought will help prepare you to respond immediately to the child's discovery in a manner that builds on spontaneous interest.

## Hints for Happy Trips

1.  Make preparations for each trip beforehand through the use of books, pictures, films or filmstrips, songs, finger plays, and group discussions. Let children hear and become familiar with the words associated with the trip and the types of things they will see. A good planning technique is to take a few minutes to write down all the words you can think of that are associated with the trip site. Choose a dozen or so that you are going to emphasize before the trip, during the trip, and afterward. Announce the trip close to the day you will be taking it because of young children's limited understanding of time.

2.  Dramatize, through a rhythmic activity or homemade story, the actual process of going on a trip. Detail such things as getting onto a bus or into a car, sitting on the bus, looking out the window, getting off the bus, holding partners' hands, walking in a group to the destination, meeting the people at the trip site, hearing noises, going back to the bus, and returning to the school or home. This trial run helps the chil-

dren understand what will happen and makes the actual process more meaningful. It also reduces the anxiety involved in leaving a familiar setting and going to an unknown one.

3. When visiting a special place, plan the trip carefully with the person in charge. Visit the site ahead of time and learn the type of information the children will be told and what they will see. Find out what you can do and what the resource person at the site will do. If appropriate, alert that person to the nature of young children. Make sure the information is age-appropriate and that children will be able to see things in small groups. Discourage people from giving long lectures to young children. Notice the physical setup (such as where the bus should stop or you should park, what door to come in, bathroom locations, and places for regrouping or snacking). The more familiar you are with the site, the more you can help make the introduction and onsite comments suitable for your group. If possible, take a few photos of the site to show to the children as you discuss your impending visit.

4. Plan your route (with maps for other drivers), timetable, strategy for moving children from one area to another, who will ride with whom, and who is responsible for which children *in advance*—communicate this information to the other adults and the children. Note good meeting spots and where people should go in case of an emergency. (See the "Orientation List for Volunteers" in the appendix, which can either be photocopied as it appears or rewritten in a letter format.)

5. Let parents know about the trip both before and after. Send out permission slips and a note about the proposed trip and its date and time. (See the "Sample Notification and Permission Slip" in the appendix.) After the trip, reinforce the experience with a newsy note home on what the children have seen. Encourage parents to come along on trips, as this helps them learn what to point out to children. It also helps the child feel more secure, and allows the parent a meaningful way of helping and participating in the child's experience.

6. Remember that children who are anxious in a new situation and accept change reluctantly are apt to find a trip frightening, or may not want to go. Such children need extra support, comfort, and individual attention on trips. These children should be with the teacher, provider, or a familiar adult. Consider inviting parents of these children to help ensure a smooth experience, especially in the beginning. Tell volunteers to watch for signs that a child is becoming anxious and to physically comfort that child. It is not a good idea to undertake trips of any distance the first few weeks the children are with you. Give them time to become thoroughly familiar with their new setting and with you before venturing too far away. Whenever possible, it is always helpful to have extra adults with you.

7. Trips provide a wealth of new experiences, but new experiences can sometimes be frightening even to the most well-traveled child. Whenever possible, anticipate sounds and situations that might frighten the children. Prepare them by talking about the potentially frightening thing and dramatizing it in advance. For example, "Some animals make loud noises. Let's all 'oink' as loud as we can to see what it might sound like at the farm." These things can be done in the home or classroom and again en route to the site. Discuss what to do if the sound occurs (such as cover ears, laugh, or jump three times). All of these activities will prevent tears and fright, which could mar the trip. Although it is not possible to guess ahead of time what may frighten a particular child, it is worthwhile to identify some potentially frightening aspects and think of ways to prepare the children for them.

8. After a trip, allow plenty of time for discussion as well as a dramatic play situation related to the trip. Children assimilate new knowledge by using it in play. Thus, follow-up activities become an important part of the learning that can occur through field trips. Try to bring something back from each trip to use in follow-up activities. Keep souvenirs, brochures, postcards, or pictures to refresh the children's memories. Bring a camera and take photos of the children during the trip to display on a bulletin board or use in a homemade story about your trip.

## Safetyproofing Your Field Trip

1. Undertake trips only after you have established good group control and children have learned to remain with the group. Before taking your first neighborhood excursion, plan one or two trial runs. Return immediately if any children run ahead of the group.

2. Plan trips for the middle of the week to allow planning with children and return of permission slips. Avoid taking trips on Mondays, when children are apt to be tired from the weekend and not completely re-oriented to the group. Also avoid Fridays, when follow-up activities are not possible. Plan excursions for the morning when children are less tired, if possible.

3. If necessary, arrange for extra help on the trip. When establishing the adult-child ratio, consider the ages of the children and their personalities. Keep in mind that children can get much more out of a trip if they can talk about it with an adult and get answers to their questions. Suggested ratios are:

   - for two year olds: one adult to two children
   - for three year olds: one adult to four children
   - for four and five year olds: one adult to five children

Know your group and plan for extra help if you have many children who need extra support.

If your group is large, plan to have one adult who is not responsible for any children. That person can supervise the logistical arrangements at the site and take care of things such as snacks and personal belongings. This person could also cope with any sudden emergencies without endangering supervision of the total group, and could be the group photographer.

4. Give all trip assistants a copy of the "Orientation List for Volunteers" and a trip information sheet (both found in the appendix). Let them know the specific purpose and objectives of this trip, and what they will be seeing en route. This will help them talk about the trip with the children. Orient the adults to safety procedures and remind them to

   - be conscious at all times of the number of children they are responsible for and count noses frequently.

   - concentrate on the children in their care and avoid being distracted by conversations with other adults.

   - never leave children alone or send them ahead of the group for any purpose. If necessary, the whole group goes into the bathroom together.

   - take the children to the bathroom before leaving on a trip and, if necessary, before leaving the trip site.

   - carefully supervise toileting in public places.

   - be sure everyone understands directions. It is best if they are in writing. Plan meeting places at the site and places for regrouping.

5. Establish simple safety rules that are well-known to the adults accompanying them. Help children learn these rules by rehearsing or playing them out several days before a trip. Review them immediately before departing. Some sample safety rules:

   - Always wait for the adults before crossing streets or going into buildings.

   - Everyone holds hands near hazards.

   - Always walk and never run on trips.

   - Everyone needs to sit down on the bus or in the car and fasten their seat belt (or be in a car seat).

   - For groups of ten or more: "A leader in the front and a leader in the back and all the children in between." This makes a nice chant to use as you walk along.

6. Check insurance policies to make sure they include coverage during excursions away from your home or school and en route. Also check your coverage for volunteers accompanying the group and for anyone providing transportation. Be sure all drivers have extra liability insurance (extra coverage may be relatively inexpensive).

7. Take along a first-aid kit on all trips. Tape an index card of emergency numbers to the top (including paramedics and the poison control center). Be sure the kit includes materials for cleansing scrapes and bruises, plenty of bandages, plastic gloves, syrup of ipecac, and an instant cold pack. Take along the parent permission slips (they include the phone numbers where parents can be reached in an emergency) or make a list of phone numbers for the kit. Include a cellular phone or change for phone booths.

8. Take medications for children with allergies on all trips. Be sure you know if any of the children are allergic to bee stings and have appropriate treatment.

9. Be sure all children are wearing tags that include the name and phone number of the school or provider. For large groups, color code the tags so children and their group leader have tags of the same color. Do not put children's names on the tags.

   For the benefit of any extra helpers, use a sticker identification system. Put individual stickers on each child's tag. Give the leader a list with the stickers and the accompanying name. Encourage leaders to learn each child's name by playing name games such as: I see a bunny and Pearl is her name, I see a puppy and Sudan is his name.

10. Take an emergency bag of tricks for special situations. Items for this bag include: several sets of extra clothes, safety pins, tissues, money, storybooks, and a box of graham crackers or raisins for an extra snack in case of unexpected delay. Include instant playthings packed in individual plastic bags such as crayons, small spiral notebooks, small pleated muffin paper cups, one-foot pieces of yarn, pipe cleaners, packing pellets, and toothpicks. Put a disposable camera in your bag of tricks in case the regular camera was forgotten.

11. If a snack is to be served on the trip, plan it carefully for ease of serving. Fresh fruits, such as apples or bananas, are easier to serve than juice and crackers. Carry snacks in disposable bags so your load will be lighter on the return trip; use the empty bags to collect treasures on the trip. If the trip is during lunchtime, pack lunches in individual disposable paper bags. If lunches are sent from home, put names on the bags. Discourage carrying anything that must be cared for and returned, such as lunch boxes or thermos bottles. Provide beverages for the group. Be sure to bring paper cups, napkins, and a can opener if you are serving juice. A damp cloth in a plastic bag or moist towelettes come in handy. Food should not be served in moving vehicles.

12. If a large group is traveling by bus, have someone drive a car to the trip site that you can use in the event of an emergency or mechanical trouble with the bus.

13. When walking with very young children or in hazardous situations, you could use a knotted or looped walking rope as an added precautionary measure. Have each child hold onto a knot or loop on the rope.

14. If you have one, take along a cellular phone even on walks. It is always reassuring to know you can call for help from anywhere without having to leave the children.

15. Never leave a child alone or allow anyone to leave your group for any reason.

## What Would You Do?

*You are visiting the local television station and an emergency news announcement delays the program you are scheduled to visit. What would you do? Some ideas:*

- Take an informal tour around the waiting area or the outside of the building.
- Sing songs, do finger plays, or read a story from your emergency bag of tricks.
- Pretend you are putting on a TV show and have the group participate.

*You are en route home and your vehicle has a flat tire. What would you do? Some ideas:*

- If the location is safe, let the children watch the changing of the tire.
- If the group must wait for help, locate a safe area nearby or keep the children in the vehicle. Sing songs, do finger plays, or read stories. Have a snack in your emergency bag of tricks.

*As you approach the chicken coop at the farm, one of the children becomes very frightened and won't go any closer. What would you do? Some ideas:*

- Stay with the child yourself or assign someone else to remain with the child. Don't force the child to go closer. Practice making chicken sounds and wonder if there are eggs to see. Offer encouragement. If the child is willing, suggest going closer, taking a peek, and leaving quickly.
- Allow the child to remain at a comfortable distance. Avoid all shame and coaxing, but let the child know it is okay to come closer when he or she feels ready.

*You have just left for a neighborhood walk after carefully instructing the children to stay together. Two children run ahead of the group. What would you do? Some ideas:*

- Immediately end the walk. This is a good time to firmly establish the rule of not running ahead. Control on trips is essential and establishing good control requires strong reinforcement.

- When back at school or home, practice walking together as a group. When the group learns to walk together, take another walk. If the children stay together, be sure to acknowledge their learning to stay together.

- When you return from the next walk, express your appreciation of their responsible behavior. Tell them you liked the way they took care of themselves by staying together, and that now the group can go on more outings.

- Write a story about both walks: about the time your group had to come back and the next time. Write and illustrate a simple list of procedures for going on walks. Include: we stay together, we hold hands, and we stop at the corner.

## A Word about Trips and Toddlers

The trips and activities in this book are generally geared for preschool and young school-aged children; they offer a broad range of ideas and activities. Use them selectively according to age and interests of the children involved.

The same principles used throughout this book also apply to planning trips for toddlers. Toddlers love to go places and can certainly do so with the same type of careful planning to make sure the trip is geared to the pace and interest level of toddlers. For example, you can adapt the trip to a school by emphasizing only a few words such as *auditorium*, *stage*, *trophy*, *gym*, and *locker*. Allow ample time to look at the school trophy display; provide many chances to climb up and down the steps to the stage in the auditorium; sing songs on the stage and parade around it; walk up and down the aisles several times; visit the gym and run around it; peer in some lockers, watch them open and close, and see the locks on them; and look again at the trophy case before leaving. The emphasis would be on repeating the same activities a couple times rather than exploring the whole building. The trip might move at a slower pace, but allow time for physical activity. Keep explanations short and focus on a few new words with concrete examples of what they mean.

Planning for safety is especially important with toddlers. If one or two toddlers are in a small mixed-aged group, they should be in a stroller or holding an adult's hand while walking. For traveling with a group of toddlers, a walking rope is a big help. This knotted or looped rope with a knot or loop for each toddler to grasp provides security for the children and adults. Adults should carry all supplies in backpacks so both hands are free.

Practice trip procedures each time you take a walk. Plan brief outings to practice using your walking rope, following directions, and staying together. Decide on a word that tells everyone to immediately stop and listen. The word could be *freeze*, *statue*, *hands up*, or anything that becomes automatic for the group. When children hear that word. they should immediately freeze, make a statue, or stop and put their hands up.

Follow all the suggested procedures found elsewhere for supervising and planning trips. As you walk along, sing songs to familiar tunes, changing the words to describe where you are going and what you will do. Be flexible and ready to allow for exploration of things that attract the children's attention. Remember, the process of exploring is just as worthy as the destination. Enjoy that process and your toddlers will too.

# A World of Walks

# After-a-Rain Walk········

Children are fascinated with water, and it offers many opportunities for play and experimentation—especially after a rainstorm. As you and the children walk outside after a storm, you can

- notice the effect of rain on trees, plants, sidewalks, and things left outdoors;
- learn about puddles and where they collect;
- observe where water goes and how it moves;
- float twigs in little rivulets of water, and experiment with sinking and floating;
- observe worms;
- think about what rain does for the neighborhood and plant life; and
- look for a rainbow.

Give some special thought and preparation to puddles—especially if your area has just had a large downpour and big puddles have formed. Be sure children have rubbers or boots to wear, since puddles seem to invite children to splash. If walking in puddles is not appropriate, discuss ahead of time how far away from puddles children should stand.

Depending on the weather and other conditions, let the children take off their shoes and socks to feel water on the grass and wade in puddles on smooth sidewalks.

## Before the Walk

### WORDS TO LEARN AND USE

rain ● thunder ● lightning ● clouds ● fog ● damp ● drizzle ● shower ● rainbow ● puddle ● moisture ● evaporate ● absorb ● earthworm ● mud ● sewer ● drain ● storm ● umbrella ● raincoat ● water repellent ● soak ● monsoon ● arroyo

### TALK ABOUT IT

The amount of rainfall is responsible for how an environment looks. Ask the children about the look of their neighborhood. Is it lush and green or warm and dry? Find out how much rainfall your area receives in a year. Let the children figure out why their neighborhood looks the way it does.

Talk about why it rains. Wonder what happens if there is no rain or not very much rain. Talk about deserts and other places that do not get much rain. Talk about things that grow where it is very wet and things that grow where it is dry. Make a picture chart that ranges from desert cactus scenery to lush rain forest.

### Read a Story

Read the story *Mushroom in the Rain,* by Mirra Ginsburg, and lead a discussion about how rain affects things. Act out or use a flannelboard to illustrate the story. Open an umbrella and pretend it's a mushroom. Have the children act out the animal parts. Find out how many children can fit under the umbrella. Plan to look outside for places where animals can get out of the rain.

### Do and Experiment

Experiment with water using an eyedropper and a variety of materials such as stones, feathers, grass, and leaves. Drop water on each object and observe what happens. What happens to the water and the materials? Ask the children what they've noticed about rain; what happens to trees, grass, and the pavement? Write down a list of questions about rain to investigate on your walk.

paper and a pen or pencil to record observations ● objects for floating and sinking experiments (such as small toy boats, leaves, stones, rocks, twigs, bottle caps, pennies, nails, Styrofoam craft foam) ● towels to wipe hands and feet ● plastic or paper bag for collecting things ● a camera

## On the Walk

### OBSERVE

Look at and touch trees and bushes. Notice how they appear and feel. Shake some branches to see what happens.

Look for spots where puddles have collected. Why did they collect where they did? How long do the children think the puddles will last?

Notice where water is flowing. Are there any hills or indentations where the water is going? What direction is it flowing?

### USE YOUR SENSES

Notice the air—take some deep breaths and sniffs. How does the air feel? Is it cool, hot, muggy, humid, fresh, windy, or sunny? What did the air outside feel like while it was raining? How is the air different now?

Look at and touch cars, grass, dirt, sidewalks, and things left outside (such as playground equipment, toys, and a sandbox) to see what evidence is left of the rain. Dig in the dirt to find out how wet it is on top and further down. Look for places where there is no evidence of any rain having fallen. Why isn't that place wet?

### EXPERIMENT

Look for places where the water is flowing. What makes the water move? Put some twigs in the flowing water to see what happens. Put a large rock in the twigs' path. Can you stop the water? If possible, watch the water flow down the sewer. Where does the water go from there?

Look for worms and observe them. Dig in the dirt to see if there are any worms. Are there more worms on the sidewalk or in the dirt? What happens to the worms left on the sidewalk?

Float the objects you brought along in the puddles and little streams formed after a rain. Notice which things float and which don't. Collect the things that float in one container, and the things that don't in another. Guess what makes things float.

### TALK ABOUT IT

Ask the children about the things they notice. What questions do they have about rain and water?

What happens if there is too much rain to be soaked into the ground? Think about the streams and rivers the rain goes into. Talk about the way it rains—a nice shower or a heavy downpour—and how that affects what happens to the rain on the ground. Talk about floods, which occur when there is too much rain.

# After the Walk: Follow-up Activities

### TALK ABOUT IT

Talk about the walk and write down the things the children remember and mention.

Discuss rain and storms. Make a book about weather.

### CREATE A RAINY DAY MURAL

Talk about the rain's cycle: how it falls into a river, is evaporated into clouds, and falls down again as rain. Make a large rainy day mural using a variety of materials: cotton balls for clouds, tinfoil for raindrops, clear plastic for puddles, green and blue yarn for rivers, silver cording for lightning, fabric or oilcloth for raincoats and umbrellas, and foam packing squiggles painted brown for worms. Read *Rain,* by David Bennett, for wonderful pictures and explanations of rain and storms.

### EXPERIMENTS TO TRY

Put water in a pie tin and let it sit out for a few days. Observe what happens. Discuss evaporation. Return to an outdoor puddle later in the day or the next day. What happened to the puddle?

Make your own rain. Heat water in a tea kettle until it boils. Hold a cold plate over the spout so steam hits the plate. When many drops have formed on the plate, let the children feel the plate. Talk about how it feels. When the plate becomes really full of drops, what do the drops do? Notice how the steam over the pot resembles a cloud. The book *How's the Weather?*, by Melvin and Gilda Berger, has pictures illustrating this experiment.

Drop water from an eyedropper onto different fabrics. Talk about absorption and water repellent. Discover which fabrics offer protection from water and would make a good raincoat or umbrella.

Fill baby food jars half full with dry materials, such as sugar, sand, and dirt. Add a layer of water, put the cap on, and shake. Observe what happens. Let the jars stand awhile and observe them again. Try many different dry materials and types of dirt and discuss which ones hold water the longest. Which ones would be best for plants?

Write a story about your experiments with water, letting the children tell you their observations and conclusions. Include the results of the floating and sinking experiment you did outside.

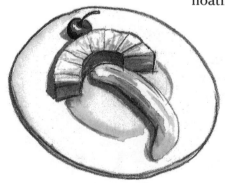

### UMBRELLA SALAD

Eat an umbrella salad for lunch or snack. For each plate, cut a slice of canned pineapple in half. Make a stem by cutting a banana in half and slicing it the long way. Put a maraschino cherry on top of the pineapple (in the center) to decorate the umbrella.

## PRO AND CON CHART

Make a pro and con chart about rain. Have children finish the sentences "I like rain because" and "I don't like rain because."

## BUOYANCY/FLOATING DEMONSTRATION

Use the following demonstration to discuss the concept of floating. Fill a large lightweight container up to the brim with water. Set the container inside a flat pan.

Tie a rope around a rock and immerse it in the container so the water overflows into the pan. Put the rock on one side of a balance scale and the pan of overflowed water on the other side and weigh them.

When an object weighs more than the same amount of water, it sinks. When an object weighs less than the same amount of water, it floats. When the object weighs the same as the amount of water it displaces, it floats halfway down, producing "neutral buoyancy."

Repeat this experiment with a piece of wood, a stick, and a piece of Styrofoam craft foam.

# Related Trip Ideas to Explore

lakes ● streams and rivers ● waterfalls ● water treatment facility ● reservoirs ● water towers ● fountains ● dams ● canyons or arroyos ● areas that show the effects of water erosion

# Songs, Poems, and Finger Plays

## RAIN AND THUNDER

*(to the tune of "Frere Jacque")*
Rain and thunder, rain and thunder,
Boom, boom, boom; (Clap hands)
Boom, boom, boom. (Clap hands)
See the flash of lightning,
Oh, my, it is frightening,
Boom, boom, boom; (Clap hands)
Boom, boom, boom. (Clap hands)

### RAIN IS FALLING

*(to the tune of "Twinkle, Twinkle, Little Star")*
Pitter, patter, little drops,
Rain is falling, never stops.
On the windows and the roofs,
Like the sound of little hoofs.
Pitter, patter, splash the drops,
The raining noise never stops.

## A RAIN STORY

"Pitter, patter, pitter, patter," hear the raindrops say.
(Drum fingers on table or floor)
But if a sunbeam should peep out, they'd make a rainbow gay.
(Touch fingers overhead to make rainbow)

"Rumble, rumble, rumble, rumble," hear the thunder say.
(Move knuckles back and forth on table or floor)
Soon the clouds will be all gone, and we'll go out to play.
(Move hands behind back)

### THUNDER

Black clouds are giants, hurrying across the sky
And they slip out bolts of lightning, as they go racing by.
When they meet each other, they shake hands and thunder,
How-do-you-do, how-do-you-do,
HOW-DO-YOU-DOOOOOOO.

## Resources

Bennett, David. (1988) *Rain*. New York: Bantam Books.

Brandt, Keith. (1982) *What Makes It Rain: The Story of a Raindrop*. Mahwah, NJ: Troll Associates.

Branley, Franklyn. (1983) *Rain and Hail*. New York: Crowell.

Broekel, Ray. (1982) *Storms* (New True Book Series). Chicago: Childrens Press.

Cole, Sheila. (1991) *When the Rain Stops*. New York: Lothrop.

Foster, Joanna. (1969) *Pete's Puddle*. San Diego: Harcourt Brace.

Ginsburg, Mirra. (1990) *Mushroom in the Rain*. New York: Aladdin Books.

Lynn, Sara. (1994) *Rain and Shine*. New York: Thomson Learning

Markle, Sandra. (1993) *A Rainy Day*. New York: Orchard Books.

Martin, Bill Jr. (1988) *Listen to the Rain*. New York: Henry Holt.

Ryder, Joanne. (1977) *A Wet and Sandy Day*. New York: Harper & Row.

Schlein, Miriam. (1964) *The Sun, the Wind, the Sea, and the Rain*. New York: Abelard-Schuman.

Schmid, Eleanore. (1989) *The Water's Journey*. New York: North-South Books.

Shulevitz, Uri. (1969) *Rain, Rain Rivers*. New York: Farrar, Straus & Giroux.

Tresselt, Alvin. (1946) *Rain-Drop Splash*. New York: Lothrop.

Wyler, Rose. (1989) *Raindrops and Rainbows*. Englewood Cliffs, NJ: J. Messner.

## OTHER GOOD RESOURCES

Berger, Melvin and Gilda. (1993) *How's the Weather?* Nashville: Ideals Children's Books.

*Which Way Weather?* (video). (1994) Bo Peep Productions.

# Animal Life Walk·············

Children are curious about small animals and their comings and goings. Taking an animal life walk can help children learn to identify small animals and common birds. On these excursions children can also

- observe an animal's characteristics and how it behaves;
- see where an animal lives;
- observe how animals eat and gather food;
- notice if an animal stays by itself or is found in a group;
- observe how animals approach others and what their favorite activities might be; and
- look for clues of an animal's presence.

There may also be opportunities to pet or touch neighborhood pets, but use caution in approaching any unknown animals. Allow children who are frightened of animals to remain at a safe distance. Encourage them to watch the animal, but don't force any close encounters. Never pet unknown animals, because any sized animal can present some hazards. If a neighbor or person walking a dog says it's okay to pet an animal and that the pet is child friendly, it's usually all right to do so. Never approach a dog when it's growling. Use encounters with small stray animals to teach safety in approaching animals.

## Before the Walk

### WORDS TO LEARN AND USE
animal ● living ● mammal ● pet ● dog ● puppy ● cat ● kitten ● rabbit ● squirrel ● gerbil ● mouse ● mole ● raccoon ● duck ● fur ● hair ● warm-blooded ● species ● vertebrate ● invertebrate ● bird ● reptile ● amphibian ● frog ● tadpole ● nest ● skeleton ● eyes ● legs ● wings ● tail ● mouth ● ears ● paws ● egg-laying ● live-bearing ● life cycle

### TALK ABOUT IT

Ask the children if they have any pets, and let them tell everyone about their pet. Where does the pet stay? What does their pet eat? Do their pets go outside? If so, what do they do when there? Talk about other animals besides pets that might be found outside. Wonder what they eat, and if they have special living arrangements. Make a list of all the different types of small animals you might see on a walk.

### MAKE BINOCULARS

Make binoculars by stapling together two empty toilet paper rolls. For decorated tubes, color the tubes or cover them with contact paper. Create a carrying strap so that children can wear the tubes like binoculars. Punch a hole on the outside edges of each tube and thread yarn or ribbon through them. Tie the ends of the thread or ribbon together, allowing enough length to go around a child's neck and hang like binoculars. Use the binoculars to look for birds or other small animals on your walk. Watch children carefully whenever they wear the binoculars around their neck.

### LOOK AT PICTURES

Use magazines or books to find pictures of birds and mammals. Notice some of the animals' identifying characteristics. The New True Books, First Look At Books, and First Discovery Books all have beautiful pictures (see Resources). Encyclopedias are also excellent sources of pictures. Talk about the types of birds or small animals you might find in your neighborhood at this time of year. Plan to look for animals at another time of year as well.

### THINGS TO BRING

paper and a pen or pencil to record observations ● bread crumbs ● small bags of birdseed ● binoculars ● small animal and small bird guides ● plastic or paper bag for collecting things ● a camera

## On the Walk

### OBSERVE

Look for pets. Do you see any pets besides cats and dogs? Are the animals running free, on a leash, in a fenced-in area, or tied up? Think about why the pets are penned up or leashed. What are they doing? Notice the sizes of the animals, and decide if any of them are still young (puppies or kittens). Notice the different ways the animals move and behave.

Look for other forms of animal life besides pets, such as squirrels, rabbits, birds, and moles. Notice their body parts, how they move, and how they eat. What are they doing? Put bread crumbs near the animals to help facilitate your observations.

Look for signs of animal life even when you can't see the animals. Look for doghouses, holes in trees, birds' nests, and mole holes. Look for footprints and tracks in the mud or snow.

Watch at bird feeders to see if many birds come and go. If there are trees near the feeders, are there birds in them? Watch the birds through the binoculars.

## USE YOUR SENSES

Listen for the sounds the animals make. Have the children close their eyes and listen. Can they tell what animals might be around from the sounds they hear?

Listen for sounds other than vocalizations associated with animal life, such as rustling of bushes or trees, pecking on wood, or flapping of wings.

If you're near a pet that can be touched, feel the different textures of the body covering. Talk about what makes the animal feel the way it does.

## IDENTIFY

Name as many different kinds of creatures as you can. Try to identify them as members of a specific category, such as birds, but also as a specific kind of bird, such as robin. Look through the picture guides of birds or animals to help you in the identification process.

Call attention to body parts and features that can help you make identifications. For birds, look for coloring; markings; shape of head, body, wings, and bill; eye rings; and stripes. For dogs, notice general size; length of legs and hair; shape of head, ears, and body; facial features; tail; coloring; and markings. For other small animals, notice likenesses and differences in ears, tails, and facial features.

Compare the number of legs, type of covering (fur, hair, skin, or feathers), sizes, movement, and behavior of several different animals. Don't forget to observe the large-sized animals we call people.

## SPECULATE

Wonder where the different creatures live at different times of year. What do they do in the wintertime? Do they need shelter all the time, or just while they have babies? Wonder if they live in families or groups of their own. How do they feed their babies?

Think about what foods the creatures eat and wonder how they find their food. Do they have trouble finding food at some times of the year, and what do they do about it? Can we help?

How do the creatures protect themselves from each other? Do they fight or bother each other?

Plan to observe animal life at different seasons of the year to gather more information on these questions.

# After the Walk: Follow-up Activities

### TALK ABOUT IT

Talk about the things you observed on your walk, and make some generalizations about the creatures in your neighborhood. For example: All the dogs are on leashes; all birds around the area are called pigeons; or there are lots of different kinds of birds.

Look at books and review some basic categories of animal life so the children get some notion of classification and differentiation among classes of animal life. Think about which grouping various animals—such as reptiles, frog families, and rodents—belong in.

Talk about what functions the creatures you have observed serve. Cats catch mice, and dogs can help protect people or work on farms. They are pets for people to love. What roles can you think of for birds, squirrels, and other creatures? Think about their roles in spreading plants and trees, eating pests, and helping gardens. Are there some creatures that seem to be mostly pests, useful only for their fur skins, or as part of the food chain? What harm can animals cause?

### MAKE LOTTO GAMES

Using a variety of animal seals or pictures from wrapping paper, make animal lotto games. Use them to play games for small groups or as a sorting activity for individual children.

### MAKE MATCHING GAMES

Cut out pictures of animals and animal homes. Let the children match the animal to its home.

Mount pictures of animals, such as birds, mammals, and reptiles, on tagboard. Draw or cut out other pictures of animal body parts such as bills, tails, wings, and facial features. Mount these on small cards. Have children match the body part to the appropriate animal.

### ANIMAL STORIES

Make up a large storybook about pets. Include information about pets from babyhood to old age. Include pictures and comments about puppies in a litter, how puppies behave, and how mature and old dogs behave. At each stage of development, include anecdotes about the children's own pets that are at that stage. Magazine ads for dog food or other animal products often use pictures of animals at different stages. Have different sections in the book show different types of pets.

Write stories about the small animals you observed and how they behaved. What did you see them doing, what did they eat, how did they look and move? Let the children tell you what to write about each animal. If you get lots of information, you may want to copy it into separate books about each creature.

## CREATIVE DRAMATICS

Make a variety of animal headbands such as rabbit ears. Have the children wear the headbands and imitate the actions of the animals: rabbits hopping, dogs running, or frogs jumping. Many of the picture books found in the Resources section are ideal for dramatization.

Set up an animal fair using a variety of paper bag costumes for the children to wear. Design different settings for the animals. Chairs or boxes can be used as cages or habitats.

Some children can pretend to be the animals, while others come to watch the animals or feed them.

## BOOK DISPLAY

Set up a table display with lots of books containing animal pictures. Read animal stories. Let the children dramatize some of the stories, such as the "Angus" or "Mousekin" stories (see Resources).

Make up your own stories about imaginary pets and the antics they might get into.

## SOMETHING-FOR-THE-BIRDS, BIRD FEEDER NO. 1

In a large bowl, have children mix together one part margarine to one part peanut butter. Twist wire around a pinecone to form a loop for hanging. Spread the peanut butter mixture over the pinecone with a knife. Roll the pinecone in birdseed or cereal crumbs. Hang outside.

## SOMETHING-FOR-THE-BIRDS, BIRD FEEDER NO. 2

Poke a pair of holes near the top of a paper cup; tie string or wire to these holes to use for hanging. Poke another pair of holes near the bottom; insert a pencil or twig through the holes so the birds can use it as a perch. Poke other holes in the sides of the cup above the perch.

Fill the cup with a mixture of peanut butter, bread crumbs, birdseed, and apple bits. Hang outside.

## ANIMAL CATEGORY GAME

Cut several 8-by-10-inch sheets out of tagboard. On each sheet, draw a large picture of a setting where creatures might be found, such as a yard, woods, house, farm, swamp, or zoo. Cut out pictures of the creatures that might be found in those settings. Have children sort the pictures according to where the animals, insects, or birds might be found.

Locate a hamster, guinea pig, rabbit, or other small animal from a zoo's visiting animal program, or ask parents if they could bring in small pets from home. You could also purchase a small animal from a pet store and have your class take care of it. (Guinea pigs are easier for children to handle and care for than some other animals. They are also easier to find if they get out of their cage.)

## Related Trip Ideas to Explore

bird food store ● pet store or pet supply center ● pet section of the grocery store ● kennel ● veterinarian's office

## Songs, Poems, and Finger Plays

### OH, DID YOU HEAR?

*(to the tune of "The Muffin Man")*
Oh, did you hear the doggies bark?
The doggies bark, the doggies bark?
Oh, did you hear the doggies bark
When you went out today?

Oh, yes, we heard the doggies bark
The doggies bark, the doggies bark.
Oh, yes, we heard the doggies bark
And this is what they say: (make dog sounds).

Additional verses:
Oh, did you hear the kittens mew?
Oh, did you hear the birdies sing?
Oh, did you hear the froggies croak?

### I'D LIKE TO BE

I'd like to be a bunny
And hop and hop all day. (hop)
I'd like to be a little pup
And run and run and play. (run)
I'd like to be a birdie
And fly and fly so high. (imitate flying)
I'd like to be a buzzy bee
And buzz and swoop and fly. (make a buzzing
    sound and swoop hands)
I'd like to be so many things
That I see out my door. (look outside)
But really I'm a little child
Who sits down on the floor. (sit down)

### THE LITTLE SQUIRREL

The little squirrel with a bushy tail
Goes scampering all around.
And every day he stores away
The nuts that he has found.
Whiskey, frisky, hippety-hop,
Up he goes to the treetop.
Whirly, twirly, round and round,
Down he scampers to the ground.

### IF I WERE A BIRD

If were a bird, I'd sing a song
And fly around the whole day long. (flap arms to fly)
And when night comes, I'd go to rest
Way up in my cozy nest. (rest head on arms)

### A BACKYARD STORY

The squirrel keeps climbing all over the yard,
Plotting and planning what he will try:
To get food from the bird feeder, he really works hard
While the family dog keeps a watchful eye.
At his post by the tree, the dog stands guard;
Hoping to catch that squirrel by and by.

## Resources

Arnosky, Jim. (1993) *25 Birds Every Child Should Know.* New York: Bradbury Press.

Bailey, Jill, and David Burnie. (1992) *Birds.* New York: Dorling Kindersley.

Bare, Colleen Stanley. (1991) *Busy, Busy Squirrels.* New York: E. P. Dutton.

Day, Jennifer. (1975) *What Is a Bird?* New York: Golden Press.

Dorros, Arthur. (1991) *Animal Tracks.* New York: Scholastic.

Dunn, Judy. (1984) *The Little Puppy.* New York: Random House.
———. (1980) *The Little Rabbit.* New York: Random House.

Eisler, Colin. (1988) *Cats Know Best.* New York: Dial Books.

Esme, Eve. (1973) *Birds.* New York: Grosset & Dunlap.

Flack, Majorie. (1971) *Angus and the Cat.* New York: Doubleday (also available in Spanish).
———. (1930) *Angus and the Ducks.* New York: Doubleday.

Florian, Douglas. (1980) *A Bird Can Fly.* New York: Greenwillow Books.

Gallimard, Jeunesse. (1992) *Cats* (First Discovery Series). New York: Scholastic (also in the series: *Birds*).

Gibbons, Gail. (1993) *Frogs.* New York: Holiday House.

Kuhn, Dwight. (1993) *My First Book of Nature: How Living Things Grow.* New York: Scholastic.

Lane, Margaret. (1971) *The Beaver.* New York: Dial Books.
———— (1981) *The Squirrel.* New York: Dial Books.

Lavies, Bianca. (1989) *Tree Trunk Traffic.* New York: E. P. Dutton.

Lepthien, Emilie. (1994) *Rabbits and Hares* (A New True Book). Chicago: Childrens Press.
———. (1992) *Woodchucks* (A New True Book). Chicago: Childrens Press.

Lionni, Leo. (1967) *Fredrick.* New York: Pantheon.
———. (1985) *Fredrick's Fables.* New York: Pantheon.

Martin, Linda. (1994) *Watch Them Grow.* New York: Dorling Kindersley.

Miller, Edna. (1981) *Mousekin's Fables.* Englewood Cliffs, NJ: Prentice-Hall.
———. (1990) *Mousekin's Frosty Friends.* New York: Simon & Schuster.

Patent, Dorothy Hinshaw. (1989) *Singing Birds and Flashing Fireflies.* New York: Franklin Watts.

Pfoog, Jan. (1976) *Kittens Are Like That.* New York: Random House (also available in Spanish).

Rylant, Cynthia. (1993) *Everyday Pets.* New York: Bradbury Press.

Selsam, Millicent, and Joyce Hunt. (1984) *A First Look at Mammals.* New York: Macmillan (also in the series: *Birds, Cats,* and *Dogs*).
———. (1989) *Keep Looking.* New York: Macmillan.

Sill, Catherine. (1991) *About Birds.* Atlanta: Peachtree Publications.

Snow, Pegeen. (1984) *A Pet for Pat.* Chicago: Childrens Press.

Thayer, Jane. (1981) *Clever Raccoon.* New York: William Morrow.

## OTHER GOOD RESOURCES

Leach, Michael. (1984) *Rabbits.* London: Adam & Charles Black.

Bailey, Jill. (1987) *Discovering Rats and Mice.* New York: Bookwright Press (also in this series: Squirrels, Rabbits and Hares, and Frogs and Toads).

*Doing Things* (video). (1988) Bo Peep Productions.

*Pets* (See How They Grow Videos). (1993) Sony Kids' Video.

# Bugs-Around-Us Walk····

Most parents and providers have experienced a young child arriving at home or school with some kind of bug in hand. Many children are delighted to hold a ladybug or caterpillar. This walk helps children learn proper ways to collect and care for bugs and prevent squishing them. Bug walks can also help children

- learn about different kinds of bugs;
- learn about the characteristics of insects, spiders, and other small creatures;
- observe their ways of behaving and working;
- observe where some insects live and learn about their life cycles; and
- learn which insects to avoid to be safe.

So many different types of insects exist; you can plan many walks to observe them under different conditions. Spread your bug watching throughout the year. Some insects, such as bees, are busy working in the spring, but are more troublesome in August or September. Worms are easiest to find and watch in rainy seasons. Spiders may be more plentiful in dry weather.

## Before the Walk

### WORDS TO LEARN AND USE

insect ● worm ● spider ● ladybug ● bee ● ant ● butterfly ● caterpillar ● moth cocoon ● change ● metamorphosis ● feelers ● chrysalis ● antennae ● invertebrate ● mosquito ● fly ● grasshopper ● colony ● hive ● sting ● anthill ● spider web ● fireflies ● cricket ● life cycle ● eggs ● larva ● pupa

### READ

Read *Inch by Inch*, by Leo Lionni, and ask the children if they have ever seen an inchworm move. Plan to go out and look for one. Talk about the differences between caterpillars, such as the inchworm, and other worms or insects that are wormlike. Explain that caterpillars are a stage in the life cycle of moths and butterflies. Look for one you can bring back and observe.

### MAKE BUG BOXES

Make bug boxes to take on your walks so
the children can collect insects if they wish.

To make a bug box, cut off the top section of a plastic dish detergent bottle. With
scissors, make a few small openings along
the sides of the lower section. Insert the
lower section into a section of nylon stocking—making sure there are no holes in the
part of the stocking that covers the openings in the bottle. Leave about 6 to 8 inches
of stocking hanging loose above the bottle
for the children to hold onto. It is not necessary to knot the stocking at
the top, as long as the children hold the stocking closed. The children can
spread the stocking open, roll it down a bit, and drop the bug inside.

### LOOK AT IT

Look at pictures of insects in books such as *Insects,* by Casey Horton, or
*Bugs,* by Nancy Winslow Parker and Joan Richards Wright. Talk about the
characteristics of insects and spiders, and talk about their differences.
Make a list of the bugs you might see in your area at this time of year.
Books in the Life Cycle Series by Jill Bailey have wonderful clear pictures
of bugs in their habitats and beautifully illustrate each bug's life cycle
(each book is about a different creature). *The World Book Encyclopedia*
also has excellent pictures of insects and spiders, as does *My First Book of
Nature: How Living Things Grow,* by Dwight Kuhn.

### THINGS TO BRING

paper and a pen or pencil to record observations ● food (such as raisins
and crackers) ● magnifying glass ● bug boxes ● plastic or paper bag for
collecting things ● a camera

## On the Walk

### OBSERVE

Keep an eye out for insects. Notice which settings may have more bugs in
them and what type of bugs live there. Under eaves may be good places
to find spider webs and spiders; trees and shrubs may have caterpillars
and beetles; and flowers attract bees. Search the yard for anthills. Can
you see a trail of ants? Attract flies by sitting down and having a snack.

Put out some food to attract insects. Watch how the insects move,
and how they eat or try out the food.

Use the magnifying glass to look on leaves for white or pale-
colored eggs or older stages in the insect's life cycle.

## IDENTIFY

Use the magnifying glass to help identify small creatures. Count legs to help in the identifying process. All insects have six legs, so even though the creature looks like an insect, if it has more than six legs (such as a spider) it is not an insect.

Point out the insect's antennae (or feelers), which grow out of the head, the front part of an insect. Most insects have three pairs of legs, one pair of antennae, and one or two pairs of wings. See how many body parts you and the children can identify. It's easiest to identify parts on ants or ladybugs, which you can hold in your hand, and occasionally on large flies, which may pause on an arm or speck of food. Other identifying characteristics are size and shape of body, wings, and coloring.

## USE YOUR SENSES

Talk about how it feels to hold an insect or have one crawling on you. (Some children may not like the idea and shouldn't be required to hold insects if resistant.) Notice the differences in how insects, worms, and caterpillars feel. Some are smooth, others are rough or furry.

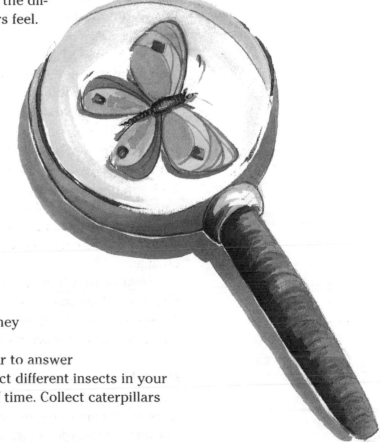

Do any insects make sounds? Listen for crickets, cicadas, or noisy beetles. Can you hear sounds and not find the bug? Do bees really buzz?

## SPECULATE

Wonder about what happens to bugs at different times of the year. Do they go underground, hide in trees, or die when it gets cold? How long do bugs usually live?

How do new bug cities get started? How do the worker insects know what to do when they live in colonies? How can ants carry such heavy loads?

Do insects fight with each other? How do they protect themselves from predators?

Look at insects at different times of the year to answer these questions or think of others to ask. Collect different insects in your bug boxes to observe changes over a period of time. Collect caterpillars to watch their life cycle.

## After the Walk: Follow-up Activities

### TALK ABOUT IT

Talk about the walk and write down the children's observations about bugs. Write down as much information as they remember about the different insects and their characteristics. Without putting too much emphasis on the scientific categorization, point out the different clusters of bugs such as insects, spiders, worms, and caterpillars. Look at books to help you with this type of classification.

Talk about a bug's usefulness. Decide if there are some bugs that are really harmful or just pests. Think about degrees of harm and good. For example, although bees may sting us, they also help the flowers bloom and give us honey. Think about mosquitoes and flies who spread diseases, bite and annoy us, and whose only redeeming feature may be providing food for birds, frogs, and other large creatures. Read the book *Ladybug,* by Emery Bernhard, to learn about the usefulness of these creatures.

### ALL ABOUT LIFE CYCLES

Look at many of the books in the Resources section that show bugs in their habitats, and tell about their life cycles. Put the books out on a display table so the children can look at them. Use the information to create a chart or bulletin board display that illustrates the life cycle of a caterpillar from caterpillar to butterfly or moth. Do the same for other insect life cycles. Make similar picture displays or charts matching bugs to their homes (for example, spiders to webs, ants to anthills, and bees to hives).

### LISTEN AND LEARN

Watch the videotape *Bugs Don't Bug Us,* and let the children dramatize some things about bugs. Can the children move like inchworms or other caterpillars, fly like butterflies, crawl like crawly bugs?

### BUG WATCHING DISPLAYS

Set up displays of the bugs you collected in jars or habitats—use the books in the Resources section for suggestions. Put the displays on the same table as the books. Include magnifying glasses to use for bug watching. Plan how to feed the bugs and decide what you need to bring in to feed them. Write up your observations about the bugs. How do they change?

Set up an ant farm and observe the ants. Write up all of their activities. Insect Lore has many living insect nature kits available; call them at 1-800-LIVE BUG for information. Several catalogs advertise insect-keeping kits and special containers with air holes for keeping bugs.

### MAKE NUMBER LADYBUGS

Make ladybugs and use them to talk about circles and numbers. Cut two large circles out of red or orange construction paper for each ladybug. Cut one of the large circles in half for the wings. Use a brass fastener to attach the wing sections to the circle. The fastener should be large enough to allow the halves to open or close. Cut many small circles out of black construction paper. Paste one black circle to each ladybug for its head. Use the other circles to paste onto the wings, varying the number of circles on each ladybug so that you can use them for number games. Make some ladybugs with the same amount of dots on each wing (from one to five) and some with different amounts on each wing.

Ask the children to find the ladybugs with *five* dots, or find the ladybug with *three* dots on each wing. Have one child place cutout numerals on the body under the wings indicating how many dots are on the wings. Another child looks under the ladybug to see if the number is correct.

## MAKE CREATIVE CREATURES

Have children collect smooth, oval stones (1 1/2 to 2 inches long is ideal). (Talk with the children about where they may collect stones and tell them to always ask first.) Wash the stones in warm soapy water (many children love this part), pat dry, and let stand for a day or two to be sure they have dried completely. Paint the stones to look like various insects. Add bits of pipe cleaners for legs and antennae and paper scraps for wings. Add the stone creatures to your table displays. You can also make bug bodies out of clay, using the same decorations for other body parts.

For inspiration on the look of bug bodies, read *Miss Spider's Tea Party*, by David Kirk. It's a delightful story in verse with highly imaginative bug pictures. Perhaps the children can plan some imaginative activities for their bug creations.

## Related Trip Ideas to Explore

honey farm or beekeeper ● nature center ● special exhibits at natural history museums or zoos ● butterfly collector ● woods or camping areas

## Songs, Poems, and Finger Plays

### THE DADDY LONGLEGS (AUTHOR UNKNOWN)

Said the thousand legged worm (open hands three times: 10 x 10 x 10)
As he gave a little squirm, (squirm around)
"Has anybody seen a leg of mine? (lift leg to one side)
For if it can't be found, (shake head)
Then I will have to hop around (hop on one foot)
On the other nine hundred and ninety-nine." (open hands three times, leaving out one finger the last time)

### CREEPING, CREEPING LITTLE BUG

*(to the tune of "Twinkle, Twinkle Little Star")*
Creeping, creeping little bug
What a heavy load you lug
Working hard the live long day,
Do you every stop to play?
Creeping, creeping little bug
Rest inside the home you dug.

### HERE IS THE BEEHIVE (TRADITIONAL)

Here is a beehive (hold up fist)
But where are all the bees? (make questioning motion)
Hidden away where nobody sees (hold up fist again)
Here they come creeping out of the hive
One, two, three, four, five (open fist—one finger at a time)
Buzz, buzz, buzz. (make hand fly all around)

### ONE LITTLE ANT

*(adapted from "One Elephant Went Out to Play")*
One little ant crept out to play
Out from his little hill one fine day.
He had such enormous fun
He called for another little ant to come.

Two little ants crept out to play
Out from their little hill one fine day.
They had such enormous fun
They called for another little ant to come.

(Hold up fingers for each number or use this
song as a circle game and have one child pick
another for each new number.)

### CATERPILLAR CHANT

Caterpillar, Caterpillar
What can you do?
Spin a cocoon before I'm through.

Caterpillar, Caterpillar
What's happened to you?
Changed to a butterfly that's what I do.

# Resources

Bailey, Jill. (1990) *The Life Cycle of a Grasshopper*. New York: Bookwright Press (other books in this series: *Ant, Bee, Butterfly, Frog,* and *Ladybug*).

Bernhard, Emery. (1993) *Dragon Fly*. New York: Holiday House.
———. (1992) *Ladybug*. New York: Holiday House.

Brenner, Barbara, and Bernice Chardiet. (1993) *Where's That Insect?* New York: Scholastic.

Carter, David. (1992) *Butterflies and Moths*. New York: Dorling Kindersley.

Dorris, Arthur. (1987) *Ant Cities*. New York: Crowell.

Fowler, Allan. (1991) *It's a Good Thing There Are Insects* (Rookie Read About Science Series). Chicago: Childrens Press.

French, Vivian. (1993) *Caterpillar, Caterpillar*. Cambridge, MA: Candlewick Press.

Freschet, Bernice. (1973) *The Ants Go Marching*. New York: Scribner & Sons.

Gallimard, Jeunesse. (1991) *The Ladybug and Other Insects* (A First Discovery Book). New York: Scholastic.

Gibbons, Gail. (1989) *Monarch Butterfly*. New York: Holiday House.
———. (1983) *Spiders*. New York: Holiday House.

Glaser, Linda. (1992) *Wonderful Worms*. Brookfield, CT: Millbrook Press.

Hauser, Judy. (1964) *Bees and Beelines*. New York: Crowell.
———. (1991) *Fireflies in the Night*. New York: Crowell.

Howe, James. (1987) *I Wish I Were a Butterfly*. San Diego: Harcourt Brace.

Kirk, David. (1994) *Miss Spider's Tea Party*. New York: Scholastic.

Kuhn, Dwight. (1993) *My First Book of Nature: How Living Things Grow*. New York: Scholastic.

Lewis, Bianca. (1990) *The Praying Mantis*. New York: E. P. Dutton.

Lionni, Leo. (1962) *Inch by Inch*. New York: Scholastic.

McDonald, Megan. (1995) *Insects Are My Life*. New York: Orchard Books.

McKissack, Patricia and Frederick. (1988) *Bugs*. Chicago: Childrens Press.

Mitgutsch, Ali. (1981) *From Blossom to Honey* (Start to Finish Series). Minneapolis: Carolrhoda Books.

Mound, Laurence. (1993) *Amazing Insects* (Eyewitness Juniors). New York: Knopf.

Parker, Nancy Winslow, and Joan Richards Wright. (1987) *Bugs*. New York: Greenwillow Books.

Pollock, Penny. (1978) *Ants Don't Get Sunday Off*. New York: Putnam.

Porter, Keith. (1990) *Discovering Butterflies and Moths*. New York: Bookwright Press.

Royston, Angela. (1992) *Insects and Crawly Creatures*. New York: Aladdin Books.

Ryder, Joanne. (1994) *My Father's Hands*. New York: Morrow Junior Books.

Sardegna, Jill. (1994) *The Roly Poly Spider*. New York: Scholastic.

Selsam, Millicent, and Ronald Goor. (1981) *Backyard Insects*. New York: Four Winds Press.

Simon, Seymour. (1982) *Pets in a Jar*. New York: Penguin Books.

Watts, Barrie. (1991) *Butterflies and Moths*. New York: Franklin Watts (books in the same series: *Ants, Beetles, Caterpillars, Ladybugs,* and *Spiders*).

## OTHER GOOD RESOURCES

Fioldu, Alice. (1990) *Insects*. New York: Franklin Watts.

Horton, Casey. (1984) *Insects*. New York: Gloucester Press.

Parker, Steve. (1990) *Insects*. New York: Dorling Kindersley.

*Bugs Don't Bug Us* (video). (1991) Bo Peep Productions.

*Insects and Spiders* (See How They Grow Videos). (1995) Sony Kids' Video.

*Tadpoles, Dragonflies, and Caterpillars—Big Change* (video). (1994) National Geographic Kid Videos.

# Garden Walk・・・・・・・・・・・・・・

For many young children, the sudden appearance of yellow flowers in the middle of lawns is one of the most exciting things about spring. Almost all parents and providers have received carefully picked bouquets of dandelions. Children have an interest in growing things; a walk can nurture that curiosity and interest as they look for growing things—from random weeds and wild flowers to carefully planted gardens. Garden walks can also give children opportunities to

- see flowers, flowering shrubs, and vegetables growing;
- learn about the differences between weeds, wild flowers, and other plants;
- smell flowers and maybe pick some;
- learn what plants need to grow and how people care for gardens; and
- identify some common flowers, plants, and vegetables, and learn about their characteristics.

A little sleuthing can help you find gardens to visit. Ask friends, neighbors, and the children's parents if they garden or know of a neighborhood garden your group could visit. Check with garden clubs, the agricultural extension service in your community, community garden projects, or local colleges that may have gardens.

Practice walking carefully around plants so the children will be prepared and not trample people's gardens. Teaching respect and care of growing things is an important part of learning about nature. Other safety considerations include: never putting plants in the mouth unless it is clearly something that is okay to eat, and keeping a safe distance from bees. Be sure you know of any children who may be allergic to bee stings, and have the proper first-aid materials with you.

## Before the Walk

### WORDS TO LEARN AND USE

bulb ● seed ● plant ● leaf ● stem ● root ● flower ● blossom ● fruit ● vegetable ● weed ● bush ● shrub ● hoe ● rake ● trowel ● spade ● shovel ● wheelbarrow ● dandelion ● grow ● bloom ● soil ● shade ● sun ● rain ● grass ● petals ● annual ● perennial ● biennial ● bud ● sprout ● border ● climber ● gardener ● nectar ● germinate ● seedling ● pollinate ● stamen ● pistil ● cutting ● hybrid ● crossbreeding ● rock garden ● window box ● mulch ● fertilizer ● vine

### DO AND EXPERIMENT

Bring in bean seeds, bulbs, grass, and flower seeds. Cut them open and show them to the children. Ask the children what would happen if you planted these seeds. Sprinkle the grass seed in dirt, and keep the dirt moist. Watch it for a few days. Plant the other seeds too, and show the children pictures of plants starting to grow.

Bring in carrots with plant tops. Cut the top off one carrot. Place the top in a small bowl of water. Watch what happens. Take a carrot with you on a walk to see if you can find other plants that look like it.

### READ A STORY

Read *The Carrot Seed,* by Ruth Krauss. Talk about what plants need to grow. Show the children an encyclopedia with pictures of different flowers and gardens. The book *Flowers, Fruits, Seeds,* by Jerome Wexler, also has nice pictures and good explanations. Plan to take a walk to visit a neighborhood garden and look for wild flowers and other growing things.

### THINGS TO BRING

paper and a pen or pencil to record measurements and other observations ● field guide to flowers or seed catalogs with pictures of flowers and other plants ● carrot ● tape measure ● socks ● plastic or paper bag for collecting things ● a camera

## On the Walk

### OBSERVE

As you walk, notice everything that is blooming, and name as many things as you can. This may include shrubs, weeds, and trees, as well as garden plants. Use the guide or catalog to help you identify names.

Call attention to the setting where things are blooming: weeds crop up anywhere; wild flowers may grow in fields or along a roadside; gardens have a more planned look.

Notice the different types of gardens. Do they look formal or informal? Do you see rock gardens, Japanese gardens, hedges, border gardens, window boxes, hanging baskets, trellises with climbing plants or vines?

Notice the arrangements in gardens. Where are different-sized plants placed? Does the garden bed curve? How does it follow the contour of the land? How is the garden area separated from the grass? Are different flowers and plants mixed up or grouped together? Are there differences in flower and vegetable gardens?

Notice the color and appearance of different flowers or plants. Call attention to the parts of the plant. Be sure to tell the children their names, such as stem, leaf, petal, even pistil and stamen, if you can see them. Don't forget to talk about the roots that can't be seen.

Look for other things that may be placed in gardens, such as statues, birdbaths, lights, scarecrows, rocks, stones, or wood chips. Talk about how they look or what purpose they serve.

## Ask

Ask to see the tools people use in the garden. Find out the tools' name and their purpose. If possible, have the gardener show your group how each tool is suited to its task.

Ask what has to be done in the garden regularly to make sure it grows well.

How does the gardener decide where to plant things? Does sun or shade make a difference, or the time of day the bed gets sunshine? Ask if the children can smell the flowers. Can you take some samples or some plant cuttings back with you?

## Compare

Measure the height of different plants with the tape measure. The children can also take hand measures. Measure how far apart the plants grow.

Notice similarities and differences among the groups of flowers. Notice that some flowers may be the same except for their colors, or they may vary in size of blossom or height of plant. Talk about families of flowers or hybrid varieties. Do the same thing for vegetables.

Compare the plants or flowers you see growing in the garden to the carrot and pictures in the guide or catalog you brought along.

Do any of them look exactly the same so that you know it is the same flower or a carrot?

## Speculate

What might be some problems that would interfere with the plants growing well?

What plants might be hurt by strong winds or bad storms?

What happens to plants if there are too many insects or rabbits in the garden? How do gardeners try to protect their plants? Do you see any fences or scarecrows?

How would the garden look if the plants were put too close together or too far apart, or if weeds were not pulled?

How do some plants get started in unusual places where no person planted them? Can bees, birds, and wind be seed carriers?

### COLLECT

Bring back some samples of wild flowers (be sure it is permissible to pick them), all different kinds of seeds or seedpods, and any flowers, vegetables, or slips of plants.

Put the socks you brought over children's shoes and let them walk around for a while. Remove the socks and collect all the things that are sticking to the socks. Are any of them seeds? Take the interesting things back for future projects.

Take photographs of the flower and vegetable gardens you visit, planters, or any other things of interest related to the walk. If possible, take photographs of plants in different stages of development, from stems poking through the ground to petals falling off to the forming of seedpods or berries.

## After the Walk: Follow-up Activities

### TALK ABOUT IT

Talk about the walk and let the children share the things they remembered and liked about the walk. Compose a group thank-you note to the person whose garden you visited, and include the children's comments and some pictures they drew.

Review the names of the parts of plants and the specific common flowers and vegetables you saw. Discuss the differences in wild flowers, weeds, and planted gardens. The book *Weeds and Wild Flowers*, by Illa Podendorf, is helpful in this area.

Make up a story about the trip using the photographs you took along the walk. Mount the pictures on individual pages of a small photo album. Write down the children's comments for each picture and mount those with the picture. Invite your host or hostess from the walk to see the finished product.

### MAKE VEGETABLE SOUP

Bring in a variety of fresh vegetables. Taste some of them raw. Then cut them up to make soup. Also cut and taste any vegetables you brought back from your walk, and add them to the soup. Cook along with other ingredients (such as noodles or seasonings) to make vegetable soup.

Read the folktale *Stone Soup*, by Marcia Brown, or the book *Vegetable Soup*, by Jeanne Modesitt, while the soup is cooking. Ask the children if you should put a stone in your soup too.

## Experiments with Seeds

Read the story *Seeds and More Seeds*, by Millicent Selsam, and try the experiments in that story.

Plant a variety of seeds, including those collected on the walk, in different types of environments. Bean seeds sprout very quickly and are good for watching the growth process. Plant seeds in moist paper towels, sponges, dirt, or sand. Place one paper towel and one sponge in pie tins and another set in glass jars with covers. Keep all seed beds moist.

Observe which ones need more watering and which ones sprout first. Place the seeds in the towels and sponges in such a way that you can see the seeds and watch them as the roots and plants begin to sprout.

Plant a sweet potato by suspending it with the pointed end down in a glass jar. Use toothpicks poked into the sides of the potato to hold it up. Add water until the bottom of the potato is covered. Watch what happens. Avocado pits can be planted in the same way.

Plant flower bulbs according to the directions.

## Table Garden Display

Plant small box gardens in flat plastic containers. Fill three medium-sized containers with dirt. In one container, sprinkle lots of grass seed. In another, plant different vegetable seeds, sowing the seeds in rows and marking each with the name of the seeds planted. In the third container, plant flower seeds in the same way.

Keep a log book on the table and record the growth of each garden. Use a ruler to measure things as they grow. When the grass grows tall, let the children cut it with scissors. It will need cutting on a regular basis, just as a lawn does.

On the table, display pictures of different types of gardens and gardens in different areas, such as desert gardens, cactus gardens, rock gardens, and Japanese gardens. The book *Your First Garden,* by Marc Brown, has directions on growing many types of plants.

## Life Cycle Chart

Make charts of the life cycles of different plants, starting with seeds planted in the ground and ending with the formation of new seedpods. You can make separate charts for flowers and other plants, depending on available pictures.

Good sources of pictures for these charts are elementary school workbooks, especially from first or second grade.

## Flower Arranging

Read about flower arranging in an encyclopedia, and show the children the patterns used to plan flower arrangements. Make arrangements using the flowers you brought back from the walk. See which ones you like best.

Have the children make a variety of flowers out of egg cartons, cut paper or tissue paper, and pipe cleaners (for the stems). Use the homemade flowers to design arrangements.

Put Styrofoam craft foam, clay, or playdough in the bottom of small tin cans to hold the pipe cleaners in place for their arrangements. Decorate the cans with construction paper. Have the children arrange their flowers in their vase. Use the arrangement for table decorations or send them home as gifts. For inspiration, look at the beautiful pictures of all different kinds of flowers in *The World Book Encyclopedia* or other books.

### FLANNELBOARD FLOWERS AND VEGETABLES

Make felt cutouts of a variety of flowers or vegetables. Use them for counting activities.

Give directions such as: Plant three tulips in a row and add two yellow daffodils. Pick three potatoes from the vegetable garden . . . and so on.

### VEGETABLE MURAL

Cut construction paper shapes of vegetables for several common vegetables: carrots, beets, potatoes, squash, cucumbers, tomatoes, peas in pods, broccoli, and so on. On a large sheet of paper, draw a line to represent the ground. Paste the vegetables above or below the ground as they would be found when ripe.

Add drawings to show what would appear above or below the ground for each plant, such as roots, stems, flowering tops, stalks, and vines. Talk about which part of each plant people eat.

### MUSIC AND CREATIVE DRAMATICS

Act out the story of *The Carrot Seed,* by Ruth Krauss.

Have children pretend to be plants growing from tiny seedlings to tall plants. Act out planting a garden.

### FRUIT AND VEGETABLE LOTTO

Make lotto games using fruit and vegetable seals or pictures from seed catalogs.

### SCARECROWS

Make a corncob scarecrow. Use the cob for the head and body, and husks for the arms and legs. Dress the scarecrow in old doll clothes, and put it on your garden display table.

Talk about why farmers and gardeners use scarecrows. Do scarecrows really keep birds and animals away?

## Related Trip Ideas to Explore

nursery or greenhouse ● flower shop ● flower section of a grocery store ● vegetable stand or farmer's market ● botanical garden ● conservatory ● arboretum ● specialty gardens such as a Japanese garden

# Songs, Poems, and Finger Plays

**IN THE GARDEN**

*(to the tune of "Oh, My Darling Clementine")*

In the garden, in the garden,
In the garden down the street,
There are flowers, pretty flowers;
And they look so nice and neat.

There are roses and petunias
And some lovely daffodils.
There are tulips and begonias
And some lilacs on the hills.

In the garden, in the garden
That we visit on our street,
Are the flowers, pretty flowers
And their blossoms smell so sweet.

In the garden, in the garden,
In the garden down the street,
We see carrots and some peppers
All in rows that look so neat.

There are green beans and potatoes
And some lovely pumpkin vines.
See the sweet corn and tomatoes,
Vegetables of many kinds.

In the garden, in the garden
That we visit on our street,
See the veggies that will help us
Get the right things when we eat.
(Vary the names of flowers and vegetables, if you wish.)

**DO YOU SEE MY GARDEN GROW?**

*(to the tune of "The Muffin Man")*

Oh, do you see my garden grow,
My garden grow, my garden grow? (move hands up
    to imitate growing)
Oh, do you see my garden grow,
I water it just so. (pretend to sprinkle garden)

Oh, do you see my garden grow,
My garden grow, my garden grow?
Oh, do you see my garden grow,
I rake it nice and slow. (pretend to rake)

Oh, do you see my garden grow,
My garden grow, my garden grow?
Oh, do you see my garden grow,
I weed it, don't you know. (pretend to pull weeds)

**TULIPS**

One red tulip in the garden grew (hold up one finger)
Soon a yellow one opened, (add second finger)
Then there were two.
Two pretty tulips that we could see,
Now there is a pink one, (add third finger)
And that makes three.
The next morning when I looked
out the door I saw another red one, (hold up four fingers)
And now there are four.

## Resources

Aliki. (1988) *A Weed is a Flower—The Life of George Washington Carver*. New York: Simon & Schuster.

Brown, Marc. (1981) *Your First Garden Book*. Boston: Little, Brown.

Brown, Marcia. (1947) *Stone Soup*. New York: Charles Scribner's Sons.

Bunting, Eve. (1994) *Flower Garden*. New York: Harcourt Brace.

Carle, Eric. (1990) *The Tiny Seed*. New York: Simon & Schuster.

Carlson, Nancy. (1982) *Harriet and the Garden*. Minneapolis: Carolrhoda Books.

Carlstrom, Nancy White. (1990) *Moose in the Garden*. New York: Harper & Row.

de Bourgoing, Pascale. (1994) *Vegetables in the Garden*. New York: Scholastic.

Ehlert, Lois. (1987) *Growing Vegetable Soup*. New York: Harcourt Brace.
———. (1988) *Planting a Rainbow*. New York: Harcourt Brace Jovanovich.

Florian, Douglas. (1991) *Vegetable Garden*. New York: Harcourt.

Hudlow, Jean. (1974) *Eric Plants a Garden*. Chicago: Whitman.

Jordan, Helene. (1992) *How a Seed Grows*. New York: HarperCollins.

Kirkpatrick, Rena. (1978) *Look at Flowers*. Milwaukee, WI: Raintree Press.

Krauss, Ruth. (1982) *The Carrot Seed*. New York: Harper & Row.

Lobel, Anita. (1990) *Alison's Zinnia*. New York: Greenwillow.

Muller, Gerda. (1992) *The Garden in the City*. New York: Dutton.

Rockwell, Anne and Harlow. (1982) *How My Garden Grew*. New York: Macmillan.

Ryder, Joanne. (1992) *Dancers in the Garden*. San Francisco: Sierra Club.

Selsam, Millicent. (1971) *The Carrot and Other Root Vegetables*. New York: William Morrow.
———. (1959) *The Plants We Eat*. New York: William Morrow.
———. (1959) *Seeds and More Seeds*. New York: Harper & Row.

Steele, Mary. (1989) *Anna's Garden Songs*. New York: Greenwillow.

Wexler, Jerome. (1987) *Flowers, Fruits, Seeds*. New York: Prentice Hall.

### OTHER GOOD RESOURCES

Podendorf, Illa. (1981) *Weeds and Wild Flowers*. Chicago: Childrens Press.

Selsam, Millicent. (1972) *Vegetables from Stems and Leaves*. New York: William Morrow.

# Home Walk •••••••••••••••••••

Young children are learning all the time—and our own neighborhoods provide excellent opportunities for extending that learning. During a home walk, you can observe many types of homes and learn

- about material used in construction;
- something about architecture and housing design;
- about the parts of homes and all the words used in describing them;
- about different types of dwellings (such as apartments, duplexes, and townhouses); and
- what things attached to or connected to the home are for (such as power lines, telephone lines, TV antennas, oil tanks, and solar panels).

During your home walk, ask the children lots of questions to stimulate their thinking and encourage conversation. Help children focus their attention by pointing out interesting house colors, decorations, and apartment front doors. Look for a particularly interesting home in your area, and ask the owners if your group might explore it up close.

## Before the Walk

### WORDS TO LEARN AND USE

apartment building ● single-family home ● duplex ● condominium ● townhouse ● ranch house ● two-story house ● foundation ● blueprint ● wall ● roof ● window ● door ● awnings ● shutters ● chimney ● porch ● yard ● fence ● gate ● shingle ● brick ● stucco ● stone ● wrought iron ● concrete blocks ● wood ● corbeling ● doorbell ● light ● gutter ● soffit ● TV antenna ● wires ● clothesline ● hose ● sprinkler ● garden ● shrub ● sidewalk ● blacktop ● garage ● mailbox ● driveway ● patio ● hedge

### TALK ABOUT IT

Have each child tell you about his or her home; ask them to bring photographs of where they live.

Talk about what houses and other dwellings are made of. Ask the children if animals live in houses, and why houses are necessary.

### MAKE A BOOKLET

Make a booklet telling something about each child's home. There will be many things they haven't noticed about their own homes. You might suggest going on a walk to see how the nearby homes are similar to or different from their homes.

### THINGS TO BRING

paper and a pen or pencil to record observations ● plastic or paper bag for collecting things ● a camera

## On the Walk

### IDENTIFY

Stop in front of several homes and talk about the type of building it is (house, apartment, townhouse), the materials it is made of, and other distinguishing features. Call attention to several of the words listed above by pointing to examples.

Have the children tell you the things they notice about each home.

Sing "Do You See the House?" as you walk (see the Songs, Poems, and Finger Plays section on page 62). Let the children fill in new verses.

If possible, walk around some homes and see what the back looks like.

### COMPARE

Look for homes made of the same materials or combinations of materials and compare them. Notice similarities and differences. For example: some homes may be made of wood but different colors; some may be made of stucco and brick; some may have yellow or red brick.

### TALK ABOUT IT

Notice and discuss the placement of chimneys, garages, porches, windows (stained glass, various shapes, solar panels, skylights), and any kind of trim (shutters, awnings, "gingerbread," and so on).

Talk about whether the homes look like anything special to the children. Is there one that looks like a castle, a witch's house, a barn? Think about what makes them look that way.

Notice the different shapes of roofs and the materials used to make them. Notice how shingles or tiles overlap and talk about why roofs are made the way they are. Notice if there are gutters and downspouts around the home, and talk about their uses. Where does the water go when it comes out the downspout?

### SPECULATE

Guess who lives in the home. What clues do you see around the yard or garage to help you guess if there are young children, teenagers, pets, or someone who uses a wheelchair living in a particular home? Can you decide if it's a large or small family? Make up pretend stories about some of the homes in the neighborhood.

Count things related to the home—the number of its windows, chimneys, doors, and trees.

Guess how many floors are in the home. How can you tell? Help the children figure out how to tell the number of floors.

Do you see power lines or telephone lines going into the home? If you don't see them, where could they be?

In which homes can the people watch TV or cable TV? How can you tell?

## After the Walk: Follow-up Activities

### TALK ABOUT IT

Talk about the walk and write down the children's comments.

Talk about each child's home again in more detail. Ask the children what they like best about their home. Notice any differences from previous discussions. Make additions to the booklet you started before the walk.

Talk about people who create and build homes.

Invite parents or friends who work in construction, architecture, or decorating to tell about their work.

### CARDBOARD HOMES

Make homes out of large milk cartons. Cut windows and doors into the cartons, then decorate. Make cardboard roofs for the homes. Use a small box to add a chimney. Use small paper or wallpaper squares to cover the roof, overlapping them like the shingles you observed. Put two or more boxes together to make a duplex or large apartment building.

### MURAL

Make a class or group mural of children and their homes. Have children draw pictures of the type of home they live in, and write their names over their home.

### MATCHING GAME

Create a real-life matching game using the photos the children brought of their homes. Spread out the pictures on a table or in the middle of a circle. Let a child pick a home photo and try to guess whose home it is.

You can play this game after the children have told about their own home and have used the photos for a while.

### SHELTERS IN OTHER LANDS

Look up information about shelters in other parts of the world in a picture encyclopedia or in the books *Houses and Homes around the World*, by Josephine Karavasil, or *This Is My House*, by Arthur Dorros. Make a booklet describing homes in other lands.

Use cut-paper shapes, natural materials, and children's drawings to illustrate some of the homes. Use bits of grass and glue to make thatched roofs; sprinkle sand or dirt on glue for mud houses; glue white squares of construction paper or use whipped soap suds for an igloo. Glue on toothpicks for house stilts and paint them brown. Use grass cloth, bamboo, brick, or other samples from wallpaper books that resemble building materials.

Set up a display featuring your booklet, other books on the subject, and the models.

### BULLETIN BOARD MATCH-UPS

Set up a bulletin board display matching people, including those from other countries, and types of homes. Use string, yarn, or wire as tie lines to connect those that go together. Make another display matching animals with their habitats.

## ROOMS IN THE HOME

Make a sorting game. Use shoe boxes or large envelopes and put a picture of a household room on each one. Give children old magazines or catalogs and let them cut out furniture or other items that go in various rooms. Have them sort the pictures into the appropriate boxes or envelopes.

## FLANNELBOARDS

Use felt shapes to make homes on a flannelboard. Discuss the parts of a home.

## DECORATING

Redecorate the housekeeping area. Make pretend wallpaper out of brown packaging paper by printing designs or patterns on the paper. You can also paste wallpaper samples to a screen or large cardboard to use in the area. Add curtains or other suitable touches.

## HOUSEHOLD PICTURE OR MURAL

Have children take the assorted pictures from the "Rooms in the Home" activity and use them for an activity picture or mural. Paste the pictures from one room onto a piece of paper, and then draw people doing whatever activity gets done in that room (for example, cooking/kitchen; cleaning car/garage; sleeping/bedroom; taking a bath/bathroom).

## BUILDING

Build homes and garages with unit blocks. Add props to blocks based on the things seen on the walk. Stuffed animals can be pets, trucks or cars can be parked in driveways, plastic basins can be used for swimming pools.

Cover a small table with oilcloth. Make roads with masking tape. Provide a village set or small blocks and cars to set up a neighborhood scene. Let the children create yards around the homes using scrap materials or drawings for fences, bushes, trees, gardens, pools, toys, or whatever they wish.

## DRAMATIZE

Read a version of *The Three Little Pigs*, and have the children dramatize it.

## BUILDING MATERIALS DISPLAY

Display samples of wood, brick, stucco, shingles, and other materials used in building. Talk about the weight and texture of the materials.

## BLUEPRINTS

Show the children a blueprint. Find the doors, windows, and stairs. Count the number of bathrooms and bedrooms.

Help the children make a blueprint of a dollhouse.

## Related Trip Ideas to Explore

teacher's home ● homes decorated in special ways (for Halloween or other holidays) ● home or museum from a different era or culture ● take a trip to see the homes of the children ● look at dollhouse displays in toy stores or malls

## Songs, Poems, and Finger Plays

### OUR HOUSE HAS MANY ROOMS
*(to the tune of "The Farmer in the Dell")*
Our house has many rooms, our house has many rooms,
Hi-ho the merry-o, our house has many rooms.

Our house has a living room,
Our house has a living room,
Hi-ho the merry-o, we sit there you know.
(Add additional rooms and function: bedroom/sleep, kitchen/cook, dining room/eat.)

### DO YOU SEE THE HOUSE?
*(to the tune of "The Muffin Man")*
Oh, do you see the apartment house,
The apartment house, the apartment house?
Oh, do you see the apartment house,
On the corner of our block?

Oh yes, we see the apartment house,
The apartment house, the apartment house.
Oh yes, we see the apartment house,
At the corner of our block (or "It's built of wood and rock").
(Sing as you walk; make up verses to describe what you are seeing.)

Additional verses:
Oh, do you see the yellow house...
As we walk down the street?

Oh yes, we see the yellow house...
Its shutters (mailbox, windows) look so neat.

Oh, do you see the stucco house...
As we walk down the street?

Oh yes, we see the stucco house...
Its flowers look so neat.

**THREE HOUSES**
A little house, a medium-size house,
And a great big house, I see.
Shall we count them?
Are you ready? 1, 2, 3.

(Make a small house shape using two hands: join thumbs to form floor,
hands form walls, touch fingertips for roof shape; move hands apart for
medium-sized house, and way apart for great big house; repeat motions
as you say "1, 2, 3.")

**A GOOD HOUSE**
This is the roof of the house so good, (put fingertips together to form roof)
These are the walls that are made of wood. (hands straight, with palms
    facing each other)
These are the windows that let in the light, (join thumbs and forefingers
    to form a square)
This is the door that shuts so tight. (clap one hand to other)
This is the chimney so straight and tall, (put arms up above head)
Oh! What a good house for one and all. (put fingertips together and
    form roof)


# Resources

Buchanan, Ken. (1994) *This House Is Made of Mud*. Flagstaff, AZ: Northland Publishing.

Burton, Virginia. (1978) *The Little House*. Boston: Houghton Mifflin.

Carter, Katherine. (1982) *House*. Chicago: Childrens Press.

Carter, Penny. (1993) *A New House for the Morrisons*. New York: Viking Press.

Crews, Donald. (1991) *Big Mama's*. New York: Greenwillow.

De Regniers, Beatrice. (1987) *A Little House of Your Own*. San Diego: Harcourt Brace.

Desimin, Lisa. (1994) *My House*. New York: Henry Holt.

Dorros, Arthur. (1992) *This Is My House*. New York: Scholastic.

Emberley, Rebecca. (1990) *My House—Mi Casa*. Boston: Little Brown.

Flanagan, Terry. (1979) *Snoopy's Facts and Fun Book about Houses*. New York: Random
    House.

Gray, Nigel. (1989) *A Country Far Away*. New York: Orchard Books.

Grifalconi, Ann. (1986) *The Village of Round and Square Houses*. Boston: Little Brown.

Harper, Anita. (1977) *How We Live*. New York: Harper & Row.

Jenson, Patricia. (1990) *My House*. Chicago: Childrens Press.

Krauss, Ruth. (1953) *Very Special House*. New York: Harper & Row.

Le Sieg, Theodore. (1972) *In a People House*. New York: Random House.

Marshall, James. (1989) *The Three Little Pigs*. New York: Dial Books.

Minarik, Elsa Holmelund. (1989) *Percy and the Five Houses*. New York: Greenwillow.

Morris, Ann. (1992) *Houses and Homes*. New York: Lothrop.

Oppenheim, Joanne. (1973) *Have You Seen Houses?* Reading, MA: Addison-Wesley.

Schaaf, Peter. (1980) *An Apartment House Close-up*. New York: Four Winds.

Schembrucker, Reviva. (1991) *Charlie's House*. New York: Viking.

## ANOTHER GOOD RESOURCE

Karavasil, Josephine. (1986) *Houses and Homes Around the World* (International Picture Library). Minneapolis: Dillon.

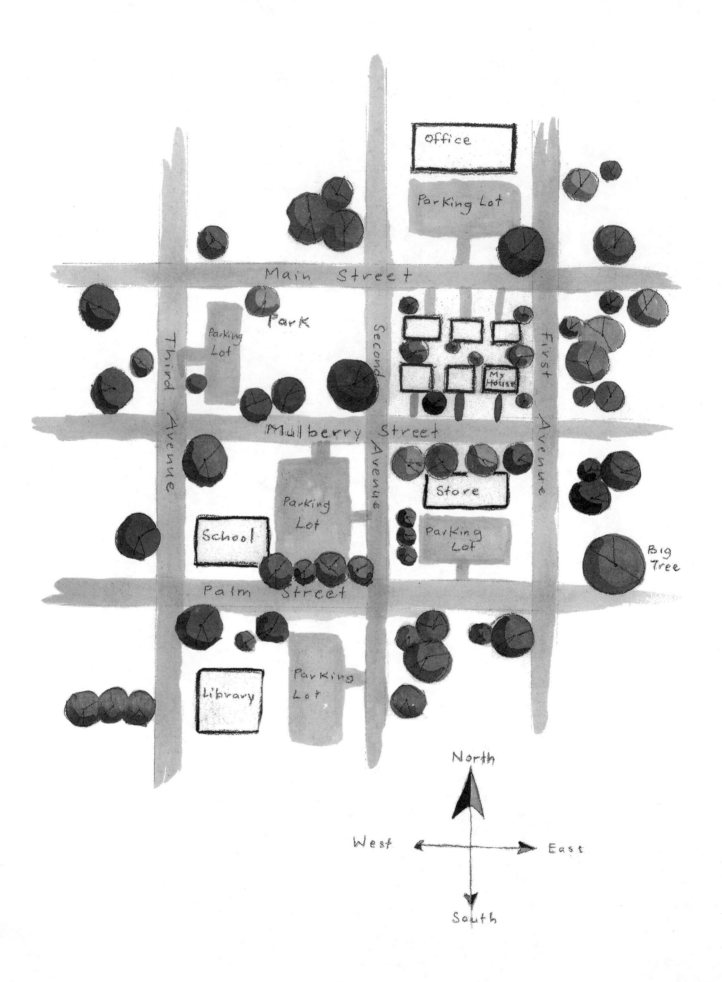

# Map Walk ·················

Many young children can read or recognize picture symbols such as stop signs, ads, or familiar logos (such as those famous arches). They also may know the way to places they go often, such as school or child care, a friend's house, or the park, if these places are not too far away or too complicated to get to. They recognize clues along the way that tell them which way to go and use cognitive skills without knowing it.

Some children develop this interest and skill completely on their own. Others, who may have older siblings that lead them places or do not notice or pay attention to where they are going, may develop this interest or skill with a little encouragement from you.

Understanding the idea of picture symbols, doing things in a set order (sequencing), following a path, and using clues to figure something out (guessing) are all prereading skills. Developing a good memory and recognizing and remembering details are also valuable tools in this process. Mapping walks are a fun way to help children learn and use these tools. They also can help children

- pay attention to the things they see en route from here to there;
- learn to use picture symbols to stand for something, and learn how to read these clues;
- learn how people use maps to find places they need to go, and discover all the different things maps can tell them;
- have the fun of exploring and charting a new course and then be able to repeat it and find the spot again;
- learn how things seemed to be planned and organized in their neighborhood;
- use and play with these ideas to design their own play mats, obstacle courses, treasure hunts, and games or imaginary trips; and
- begin to learn geography and become curious about other people and places in the world.

Your walking trips can serve as an introduction to many of the above concepts. In addition, other chapters in this book suggest using maps. For example, an activity in the next chapter, Park/Playground Walk, suggests creating a map. Other field trips suggest using maps or floor plans as aids in getting around. You and the group could make maps for any of the trips you take and use them on a follow-up activity and as a record or souvenir of the trip.

## Before the Walk

### WORDS TO LEARN AND USE

key or legend ● direction ● sign ● symbol ● measure ● scale ● inch ● equal ● north ● south ● east ● west ● road ● treasure ● neighborhood ● town ● city ● village ● state ● country ● world ● space ● blocks ● distance ● miles ● geography ● globe ● North Pole ● South Pole ● equator ● flat ● round ● continent ● land ● ocean ● chart ● compass ● code ● high ● low ● elevation ● address ● atlas ● weather map ● product map ● physical map ● up ● down ● side to side ● arrows ● route

### READ AND TALK ABOUT

Read the story *The Way to Captain Yankee's,* by Anne Rockwell. Show the children the map of the route and the legend of the roads, the directions, and all the picture symbols on the map. Can they guess what those pictures stand for? Point out where Miss Calico is starting from and where she is going, and then read the story to see what happens, pointing out some of the landmarks along her way and what difficulty she had. Talk about how people use maps, and let the children tell you some things they know about maps.

### MAP THE ROOM

Ask the children to help you make a picture or map of the things in your room. You'll need a large sheet of stiff paper and a marker. Start at the room's main entrance and walk around the entire space. As you walk, draw in all the features of the room, such as doors, windows, cupboards, shelves, and closets.

Decide with the children what symbols to use for furniture or other things, such as C's for chairs, T's for tables, or picture symbols. What things are in the middle of the room; are there some things coming out from the wall? Add those to your map as well. Use picture symbols for the areas in the room, such as stick figures for the doll corner, blocks for blocks, and books for the library.

Look at your map when you have finished and see if it looks like your room. Can the children read the map? Ask them what other places you should map. Plan to map places inside your house or building and outside in the yard, play area, or around the block. If someone lives nearby, plan to map the way to that house. Read and look at *The Whole World in Your Hands*, by Melvin and Gilda Berger, for ideas.

large sketch pad ● marker ● ruler or tape measure ● small coding dots or stickers ● *North, South, East, and West,* by Allan Fowler ● a camera

## On the Walk

### OBSERVE

Use the large sketch pad and the marker to plan your route, such as from the kitchen to the laundry room or from your classroom to the large muscle room. Along the way, have the children tell you all the things you should write down. Draw a simple line for your route and add the names of things as they tell you. You can use the information to make a detailed map later. Use arrows to mark the turns you make, and have the children point in the direction you need to turn.

Notice everything along your route, including doors or hallway openings, large light fixtures, windows, and fireplaces. Indicate light switches, pictures on the wall, furniture or equipment you walked around. Have the children tell you about any large plants or decorations you pass. Notice any hazards (such as toys on the floor, trikes in the middle of the hall, or slippery surfaces). Also notice any change in levels, and put in all stairways and ramps. Notice heat registers, radiators, or air conditioners as well as banners, wall hangings, and draperies. Use the small coding dots or stickers to mark special features.

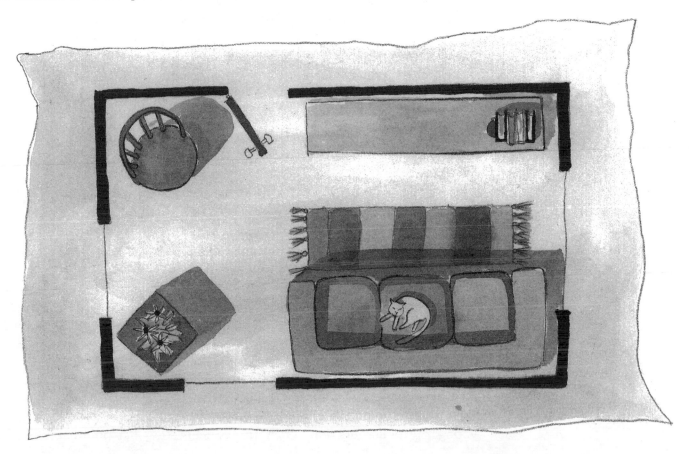

In mapping outdoors, follow the same procedures of picking a destination and charting your route. Outdoors, notice and write down landmarks such as particular trees or bushes, fences, traffic signs, fire hydrants, trash cans, mailboxes, and newspaper containers. Write down the different sizes or shapes of buildings and garages that you pass. Look at all the physical features, such as hills, bumpy or cracked sidewalks, crosswalks, rocks, streetlights, telephone or electric poles and wires, and road intersections. Are there cul-de-sacs or several streets at angles, or is your area a straight grid pattern?

On your return route, if you repeat the same route, see how many things the children remember. Point out the things you wrote down.

### COUNT AND MEASURE

Count inside things, such as doors, windows, shelves, chairs, stairs, and pictures. Notice that some rooms, such as living rooms or kitchens, may have many doors or entrances—while others, such as bedrooms, may have only one entrance. Hallways probably have many things to count. Think about why that is.

Outside, count the number of homes, fences, poles, and real estate signs. Compare the number of mailboxes to the number of homes. Is it the same or more? If it is more, why might that be?

Measure some inside distances, such as from each room to the bathroom or from table areas to the doors, and compare the distances. Are there short and long ways to go to the same places?

What distances can you measure outdoors? Show the children how to measure by counting paces, and compare the distances by how many paces it takes to get to specific points. How many paces to the sandbox or from the sandbox to the climber? A map can be made of the play area, putting in the number of paces to each part. Think about the difference in size between your paces and the children's and what problems that might cause.

### TALK ABOUT IT

Discuss all the things you observe as you walk. Name all the items, types of buildings, or physical features you see. Talk about what they look like and what they are used for. Think about symbols to use for each thing. How can you show a hill, stairs, or light poles? If you cannot decide, plan to look in books or maps or travel guides later to see what symbols or codes other mapmakers have used.

Discuss that only things that are always there are put on maps. Parked cars or trucks might not be there long, so they would not be good to put on a map. Outside, notice where the sun is and talk a little bit about the idea of direction. Explain that the sun always comes up or rises in the east and goes down or sets in the west; that helps people figure out direction. Show them the pictures in Allan Fowler's *North, South, East, and West*. Face where the sun is and point in the different directions. Even if younger preschoolers don't grasp this concept, they like pointing.

# After the Walk: Follow-up Activities

## TALK ABOUT

Collect all your notes and diagrams and use them to construct a larger and more readable map with the group, using newsprint or construction paper. Decide on the symbols to use. How will everyone know what the symbols mean? Make up a list of the items and their symbols, explaining that this legend or key to the maps tells what the pictures mean.

See how much the children remember to tell you to put on the map as you are drawing it. Describe things as you draw them by saying things like "There were three windows on one wall and two windows on the other—this hallway was long and narrow. The playroom was a rectangle and had a clock over the door." Encourage the children to describe the location and appearance of things they remember. Could they tell someone where the light switch is without pointing to it?

Put your finished map on the floor, and use poker chips or something similar to mark the path you walked. You can also move the chips around to show different paths. Say "Let's pretend we walked around the table," and make a path of chips around the table. Let the map and poker chips sit out on a table so the children can play with it and make up different routes to follow.

Take your map and repeat the walk, following the map to check its accuracy. Did you remember everything correctly? Do the children spot any errors? Do they remember things from your first walk? Ask them what is coming next in some places to see if they remember or can guess. Again, encourage them to describe each thing so others can tell what it is.

## ALL ABOUT MAPS

Set up a table display with several books about maps and globes. Look at them with the children, and try some of the experiments they suggest. *Maps and Globes*, by Caroline Arnold, has some ideas to try, such as making a globe out of a balloon and cutting an orange peel to show how something round (like a globe) can be cut up in parts and laid out flat as is done in making maps. There are similar demonstrations or maps to look at and follow in other books, including *The Whole World in Your Hands*, by Melvin and Gilda Berger (particularly good for schoolagers). The book *How We Learned the Earth Is Round*, by Patricia Lauber, has wonderful information in an understandable presentation that preschoolers can follow. It also includes some ways to demonstrate how we learned this.

Some things to add to your display: copies of real maps, map puzzles, a beach ball or plastic blowup globe (cheaper than a real one, although a real one is nice to have), and map place mats or table covers. In some toy stores, you can find wipe-off plastic coloring maps that are useful and fun. Show the children a compass and talk about how it works and who uses it.

## MAP SOME STORIES

Read familiar stories such as "Little Red Riding Hood" or "The Three Little Pigs," and map the stories. Show Little Red Riding Hood's route to her grandmother's house, marking any stops or encounters along the way. Do the same type of mapping for each little pig.

Some contemporary stories to read and map are *Tuesday* (an almost wordless adventure of flying frogs), by David Wiesner, and *Taxi* (a wordy book of city words and places), by Betsy and Giulio Maestro.

Make a map of such old favorite activities as "Going on a Bear Hunt," and draw symbols for the sequence of events—going out the door, through the tall grass, all the way until you spot the Bear. For really out-of-this-world amazing fantasy maps, try mapping one of the Magic School Bus stories (for example, *The Magic School Bus Hops Home*, by Joanna Cole). This series is especially popular with young schoolagers.

## OBSTACLE COURSES

Use your mapping skills to design an obstacle course. Draw the plan of the course first, letting the children decide what things to use. Then follow the plan and set up the course as drawn. Try it out to see how it works. Did your plan work well or do you need to make some changes? Let the children decide how they like it or if they want to change anything.

Set up your obstacle courses either inside or out. Use the same technique to plan future obstacle courses. See if the children begin to do some of this on their own—drawing up a plan and then following it to set something up. Encourage them to draw plans for use in the block area.

## TREASURE HUNTS

Read the story *Penelope and the Pirates*, by James Young, to find out about a most unusual map and pirate adventure. Talk about why pirates buried treasures and why they made maps. If the group is interested in pirates and maps, you can find more pirate storybooks for children, including an informational book titled *Pirates*, by Gail Gibbons.

Bury or hide a treasure, such as chocolate coins or a small new toy for the group, like a barrel of monkeys. Give the children a map to help them find the treasure, and let them hunt for it. Explain that the treasure will be for the whole group, not just the one who finds it. Let them work in small groups and give a copy of the map to each group. The children can also look for the treasure in the scavenger hunt system where the first clue the children find leads to the next, and so on. The scavenger hunt is a bit too complicated for preschoolers, however. Encourage the children to do their own treasure burying and map drawing for others to search.

## DESIGN A TOWN

On a table, place a vinyl play mat that has roads and a village pictured on it. Add small cars, building blocks, and other props to encourage play. Call attention to the roads and their design and other features in the play village. Use this idea or the pictures in the map books to plan your own village.

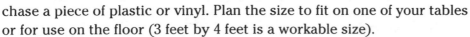

With the children, plan all the things to put into the village. Do they want a park, a school, a fire station, a lake or river, stores, an airport, a railroad? Draw a tentative plan on a large sheet of paper and decide where to put the streets, homes, and all the things you decided on. Next, make a larger copy of that plan. Use the back of an old plastic tablecloth or purchase a piece of plastic or vinyl. Plan the size to fit on one of your tables or for use on the floor (3 feet by 4 feet is a workable size).

Use wide black tape for roads (Mystic colored tape or electrical tape will work). If you want to divide the roads, paint white lines on the tape with Q-tip cotton swabs.

Use contact paper or wallpaper samples to decorate the things in your village. You can probably find a pattern with houses to cut out and stick or tape to your map. Use blue tape for rivers and blue wallpaper for lakes.

Cut other things for your town from the wallpaper sample book or magazines, or make small cut-paper patterns. Cover things that might need protection with clear contact paper. Make trees and parks with green paper. You could use small pieces of real trees and place them in bits of clay. Clip clothespins can hold some things upright.

Add play people, small cars, trucks, and traffic signs. You might be able to find some wallpaper with train tracks, or draw some tracks on the mat and add a small train set. Let the children think of things they want to add to their village.

Encourage dramatic play. If the cars have crashes, use trucks to take them to the garage, or an ambulance to take the people to the hospital. A police car or small fire engine can be kept busy doing things in the town.

In a create-your-own village, you have much more flexibility to add things than you would have in the smaller, already designed play mats. Use the mat until the children get tired of it, then put it away and bring it out again later on.

## WHO SAYS GEOGRAPHY IS NOT FOR YOUNG CHILDREN?

Read Loreen Leedy's, *Blast Off to Earth: A Look at Geography*, the most delightful geography book ever produced. Through amazing pictures, attractive and cryptic aliens convey information young preschoolers can enjoy and remember. Point out on the globe all the places mentioned in the book. If this peaks your children's interest, *Let's Go Traveling*, by Robin Rector Krupp, has more information about interesting places in the world.

For a different view of a faraway place, read *Somewhere in Africa*, by Ingrid Mennen and Niki Daly, about a little boy who lives in a big city in Africa. The boy has never seen all the animals that are supposed to live in his country—except in library books. He does things similar to other children who live in a big city and loves the city noises and shops.

## Related Trip Ideas to Explore

map store ● transit authority (and take a bus trip) ● mall (and map out the stores)

## Songs, Poems, and Finger Plays

### THE TREASURE HUNT
Hi Ho, Hi Ho
A hunting we will go
We'll take our map
It's such a snap
To find the treasure so.

Go forward twenty feet
Turn left and cross the street
Then walk around
Until you've found
A place where two boards meet

Start digging in the sand
The treasure's close at hand
What could it be?
We soon will see
It looks like twenty grand.

(Have a pretend Treasure Hunt or bury Ziploc resealable bags containing play money in a park sandbox—someone should bury the bags right before you arrive at the park. Start reciting this chant as you approach. Alter the directions to fit your approach to the park.)

**TO A CHILD'S HOUSE**
*(to the tune of "Over the River and Through the Woods")*
Past next door and across the street
To _____ 's house we go. (fill in child's name)
The map shows the way
We'll walk today
His house is down below.
Past the trees and down the hill
Is where we want to be.
As the map can tell
Turn by the church bell
And soon his house you'll see.

(Make a map of the route to the child's home, using the clues in the song. Let the child tell you what to put on the map.)

**MAPS**
Maps can tell us a lot, you know,
About where we've been and where to go.
They show us North, South, East, and West
And which route is the very best.

On maps, North is up and South is down
East and West go right through town.
Maps help us when we travel far
So we keep a bunch handy in our car.

# Resources

Balian, Lorna. (1972) *Where in the World Is Henry?* Nashville: Abingdon.

Berger, Melvin and Gilda. (1993) *The Whole World in Your Hands—Looking at Maps.* Nashville: Ideals Children's Books.

Brisson, Pat. (1991) *Magic Carpet.* New York: Bradbury Books.

Cartwright, Sally. (1976) *What's in a Map?* New York: Coward, McCann & Geoghegan.

Cole, Joanna. (1995) *The Magic School Bus Hops Home.* New York: Scholastic.

Fowler, Allan. (1993) *North, South, East, and West* (Rookie Read About Series). Chicago: Childrens Press.

Gibbons, Gail. (1994) *Pirates.* New York: Holiday House.

Hoban, Tana. (1983) *I Read Signs.* New York: Greenwillow Books.

Johnson, Crocket. (1990) *Who's Upside Down?* Hamdon, CT: Linnet Books.

Lauber, Patricia. (1990) *How We Learned the Earth Is Round.* New York: Crowell.

Leedy, Loreen. (1992) *Blast Off to Earth: A Look at Geography.* New York: Holiday House.

Maestro, Betsy and Giulio. (1989) *Taxi: A Book of City Words.* New York: Clarion Books.

Mennen, Ingrid, and Niki Daly. (1992) *Somewhere in Africa*. New York: Dutton.

Rockwell, Anne. (1994) *The Way to Captain Yankee's*. New York: Macmillan.

Wiesner, David. (1991) *Tuesday*. New York: Clarion Books.

Young, James. (1990) *Penelope and the Pirates*. New York: Arcade Publishing.

## OTHER GOOD RESOURCES

Arnold, Caroline. (1984) *Maps and Globes*. New York: Franklin Watts.

Fuchs, Erich. (1976) *Looking at Maps*. New York: Abelard-Schuman.

Knowlton, Jack. (1985) *Maps and Globes*. New York: Crowell.

Krupp, Robin Rector. (1992) *Let's Go Traveling*. New York: William Morrow.

Taylor, Barbara. (1994) *Be Your Own Map Expert*. New York: Sterling Publishing.

Weiss, Harvey. (1991) *Maps: Getting from Here to There*. Boston: Houghton Mifflin.

# Park/Playground Walk •••

When you and the children take a trip to a park or playground, you go to play on the available equipment—and that is its expected use. You can also, however, use parks and playgrounds to learn many interesting things, such as

- how the playground got there and any interesting history;
- who takes care of the playground, and what needs to be done to keep it in good condition;
- what other activities are available in the park;
- safety procedures for using the playground equipment and the park;
- how it was built and how new things get added to it or other parks; and
- many word concepts related to play activities.

As you and the children walk to a park, use some of the suggestions found in other walks in this book. Look for shapes, colors, or shadows; notice homes, gardens, and wind; find the effects of rain; use all your senses to turn the walk into an exciting learning experience. As the children play in the park, encourage them to explore concepts on their own. Trips to the park are also a good time to talk about safety. Make up songs about stopping at the corner and staying together as you walk as well as ones that review rules for keeping safe around the playground equipment.

A walk you take regularly—such as one to the park—is ideal for practicing memory games, guessing what comes next, or designing maps of the routes to take. All of these activities sharpen children's awareness of things around them and focus their attention on details.

## Before the Walk

**WORDS TO LEARN AND USE**

swings ● slide ● glide ● climber ● jungle gym ● sandbox ● ramp ●
tunnels ● seesaw ● teeter-totter ● baseball diamond ● soccer field ● play
equipment ● concession stand ● jogging path ● fort ● basketball court ●

trash cans ● wading pool ● basketball hoop ● bench ● picnic table ●
grill ● monkey bars ● fun ● water fountain ● games ● shelter ● hill ● tire
swing ● jump ● pole ● steering wheel ● grass ● gravel ● sidewalk ●
under ● through ● above ● high ● merry-go-round ● nets ● rings ●
ladder ● rung

### TALK ABOUT IT

Ask the children what things they like to do when the group goes to the
park, and write down their responses. Ask them what other things they
have noticed in the park, and list their answers. They may not have
noticed objects other than the ones they use regularly. Ask them if they
know if the park has a name, or if they can think of a good name for their
park. Talk about some of the things people do in parks, such as play
games, picnic, jog, walk babies, and play with dogs. Are there any playing
fields, picnic tables, benches, trash cans, parking areas, or buildings?

Ask the children to tell you about things they remember from other
parks they have visited. Make plans to explore your park to see if it has
an official name written some place at the park, and to find out what
other activities or people there may be in the park that the children
haven't noticed before.

### READ AND COMPARE

Read the book *Playgrounds*, by Gail Gibbons. Talk about the things in her
book that are the same as those in the group's playground and those that
are different. Are there as many different kinds of swings and climbers in
your park? Do you see people doing some of the things she illustrates,
such as playing hopscotch or skateboarding? Do her pictures give the
group any ideas of things they might take to the park next time? Plan to
look carefully at your own park and write down all the details about the
things there.

### THINGS TO BRING

paper, markers, and a pen or pencil to draw a map and record measurements or other observations ● chalk ● large tape measure (at least 6 feet)
● *Over Under Through and All About Where,* by Tana Hoban ● plastic or
paper bag for collecting things ● a camera

## On the Walk

### OBSERVE

Notice some of the landmarks along the route to the park, such as particular houses and buildings, fire hydrants, or a large tree. Write them down
on the paper. Notice the names of the streets and any turns you take. Call
all these things to the children's attention; these landmarks are useful for
drawing maps to your park. On future trips, use maps or landmarks to
play guessing or memory games such as "What comes next after the fire
hydrant?" or "What color is the house on the corner?"

As you approach the park, notice the name of the street (or streets) it is on and tell the children. Look around for a sign that tells the name or other information about the park. Can you figure out the origin of the park's name from the sign, or do you need to do more research? Look for other signs in the park that tell things people can and cannot do, and read the signs aloud to the children. Can they figure out what the signs mean by any picture symbols?

Walk around your park. Look for playing fields for sports. What sports are they for? Let the children play on those fields. Decide what equipment you need to play on the field (even some plain balls may work).

Are there paths in the park? If so, notice the materials in the paths. Are they dirt or cement? Do they have special signs on them telling if they are for bikes or joggers? Do you see anyone using the paths? Are there benches along the way?

Notice any places to eat in the park. How can you tell they are for eating? Is there a shelter area, and what does it provide? Are there notices or signs there to read or other information about the park? Notice if there are any areas in the park that are particularly attractive. What makes them look so nice? Talk about the landscaping or hills, ponds, or decorations that make this section look different from the rest of the park. Talk about how this section came to look that way. Did it happen naturally as hills or woods might, or did someone design something there?

Notice people using the park. What are they doing? Are more people sitting or being active in the park? Are people visiting the park with children or dogs?

## COUNT AND MEASURE

Count different things you see in the park. How many benches along a path? How many picnic tables, grills, or trash cans can you find? Count the playground equipment itself: How many swings, slides, or teeter-totters are there? Count how many rungs to the top of the ladder or across the climber. Do some simple math problems: If there are four swings, how many children can swing at one time? Do any swings hold more than one child at a time? Talk about the number of sides on each climber. If one child is on each side, how many children would that be?

Write down the numbers of things you count in the park. Count some of the same things on future visits and see if you get the same numbers. Talk about any differences in numbers you get and why that might happen.

Use the large tape measure to measure objects and distances in the park. Measure how tall the climbers and slides are, how far off the ground the swings or teeter-totters are, and how far it is from one piece of equipment to another. Write down your findings. Measure the children in relation to the equipment. Do some comparing: a child is half as tall as the slide or climber, or a child is the same size as the middle bar on the swing set. Measure how far in front and back of the swing set is safe from moving swings and, if possible, use the chalk to draw a line to remind the children. Measure the sides of the sandbox or how long a ramp or tunnel might be. Write down the measurements.

## SENSE

Close your eyes and listen for sounds in the park. Talk about what sounds you hear. Do you hear people sounds, equipment sounds, animal sounds, or water splashing sounds? Let the children tell you what sounds they hear. Stop and listen in different areas of the park. Are some areas noisier than others?

Feel the textures in the park. How do the grassy areas feel, compared to the sidewalks? Are there areas with wood chips, astro turf, or other types of materials? What do they feel like? What materials are used in the shelter area and near benches? Notice the textures in the materials in the playground equipment. Which ones are softer (the rubbery wing seats or soft plastics in some equipment) or harder (the metal in slide frames)?

If there's a grassy hill, roll down it. Talk about how that feels, compared to sliding down a slide. Talk about how it feels to be swinging fast and going up high.

## PLAY GAMES

Bring some balls for throwing or kicking, and ropes to play games such as jump rope, high water, or cross over the river (the rope can be the river). Use chalk to make simple versions of hopscotch games with the children walking the course.

Play tag or racing games where all the children run from one place to another with specific instructions, such as "Run around the swings, then to the climber, over to the tree, and back." (It is important to take safety precautions when children are playing in a park. If other children are playing on the equipment, move your children to an open area.)

### EXPLORE WORD CONCEPTS

Playgrounds and all their equipment offer ideal opportunities for clarifying and playing with word concepts. Here are some examples of the spaces and words to explore:

- climbers (above, below): Tom is above Shawn. Both are below John. All are above me. Climb above this platform.
- climbers/tunnels (over, under): Climb over the top. Three children are under the climber.
- covered slides (through): Crawl through the tunnel.
- fort combinations (high, low): Jamal climbed higher than Gwen.

Teeter-totters are great for illustrating concepts related to balance (however, practice great caution around teeter-totters). Use them to practice words such as *heavier, lighter, high, low, in the middle,* and *equal.* Use the words *up, down, fast,* and *slow* around swings, slides, and merry-go-rounds. Use *inside, outside, around, on top of, underneath, next to, beside,* and *behind* to play a variety of the following direction games: Let's make a circle around the tree; everyone crouch down under the climber; find a place to crawl through the bars and get to the outside; stand next to the thing that you like best. Have the children make up directions to follow. Use Tana Hoban's book *Over Under Through and All About Where* for a list of words to use in the park.

### SPECULATE

Wonder how the grass in the park gets cut. If people are working in the park, ask them about who takes care of the park. Who fixes the equipment if something doesn't work? Who uses the playing fields you saw? Can they be used at night? How can you tell?

Who uses the park the most (children in preschool groups, sports teams, families, older people)? Does anyone ever try to figure that out? What would happen to all those people if the park wasn't there? Do people ever say that your town is "a good place to live and play?" Talk about what that saying means.

## After the Walk: Follow-up Activities

### TALK ABOUT IT

Talk about the walk and think of any questions the children have about your playground. Put the questions on a list. Talk about where you can get the answers to your questions. Is this playground part of a city parks and playgrounds department or a local community? In either case, show the children the phone book that lists phone numbers for parks. Plan to call them to get some answers. Ask for information about the parks in your area.

Show the children a map of your town and how parks are marked on the map. Do the parks have names on the maps? Explain that there are many different kinds of parks: local, county, state, and even national. In a AAA directory or park brochure, show the children the symbols that tell what things are in each type of park. Show them the symbols for playgrounds, swimming, tennis, and picnics. Make a symbol list that tells about your park.

### MAKE A MAP

On a sheet of newsprint, draw a map to your park. Start at your front door and follow the route you took. Add street names and the landmarks you wrote down on the way. Add anything else the children remember. Take the map with you the next time you go. See if the map is correct and make any additions or corrections. If there are other ways to get to your park, add those to the map for future trips.

### ALL ABOUT OUR PARK

Use your notes and the things the children remember to start a book about your park. Staple together several sheets of construction paper; use different colors for the different aspects of your park. Write about the playground and the things the children like best. Describe the park facilities and the attractive parts you explored. Include a section on people you saw in the park and what they were doing. If there were dogs in the park, write what they were doing. Did any of them cause problems like Hugo in Anne Rockwell's delightful book *Hugo at the Park?* Put in information you have about who takes care of your park, what things you can and cannot do in the park, and other things you found out on or after your trip. Let the children add illustrations or photos.

### DESIGN A PARK

Start a large mural depicting the best or ideal playground. Talk over what to have in the best possible playground. Collect playground equipment catalogs and other pictures about playgrounds, and let the children decide what things they want. Do they come up with any unusual ideas like a pirate ship or an enchanted castle? Let them use the catalogs to cut out equipment to put in the playground. Remind them to leave enough space between equipment to be safe. Let them draw pictures or signs for their playground to show people all the things you can do in their park. Give the park a name and create a big decorated sign for it.

After you have finished designing and adding to it and have looked at it for a while, send it to the Department of Parks in your community to let them know what some children would like to see added to their parks.

### PLAYING SAFE

With the children, make up a list of good safety procedures for the park. Write down all the things they tell you, and add others. Include rules for safely using the equipment, walking near equipment, asking adults to pick up glass or dangerous materials, keeping sand in the sandbox, and staying in the same area with the group. Review and discuss the rules frequently, adding to the list as you think of new ones. If you think it might help, make some symbol signs (like puppets) that can remind you of rules. For example, use a picture to illustrate keeping sand in the sandbox and walking by the swings. Take these with you to the park as reminders.

### BUILD IT

Have the children design a playground in their block area, using other construction toys to make things like swing sets. The ramp pieces of blocks can make slides; use other blocks to build fort-type climbers. A small plastic container can be a wading pool. Toy people can play in the playground. Put some pictures of interesting playgrounds in the block area to see if they give the children any ideas. Put labels on the structures the children build.

## Related Trip Ideas to Explore

other parks, such as local, county and state parks (especially those with special attractions) ● rock formations (if suitable for climbing) caves ● waterfalls ● hikes by riverbeds, bridges, dams, locks ● amusement centers

# Songs, Poems, and Finger Plays

### TAKE CARE

Playing safe in the park
Is what we must do.
You remind me,
And I'll remind you!

Keep away from all things that move fast,
'Cuz they can bump you as you run past.
That means stay far from swings and the merry-go-round,
Or they might knock you down to the ground.

### THIS IS THE WAY WE GO TO THE PARK

*(to the tune of "Here We Go Round the Mulberry Bush")*

This is the way we go to the park, (pretend
    to march)
Go to the park, go to the park.
This is the way we go to the park,
So early every morning.

This is the way we pump our swings, (imitate
    pumping motions with arms and legs)
Pump our swings, pump our swings.
This is the way we pump our swings,
So early every morning.

This is the way we climb up high, (pretend to use
    arms and legs to climb)
Climb up high, climb up high.
This is the way we climb up high,
So early every morning.

This is the way we whirl around, (in a sitting
    position, spin around like tops)
Whirl around, whirl around.
This is the way we whirl around,
So early every morning.
(Add other park activities.)

### FUN THINGS TO DO

Sliding, gliding, riding, hiding, (imitate all actions)
Climb up high and jump down low,
Tossing, turning, hurling, whirling—
We're having fun in the park, you know.

**THE PLAYGROUND**

There's a playground where we often go,
With swings, slides, and climbers, high and low,
And something you push to make it go round,
And teeter totters that can go up and down.

There's a house like a fort and a sandbox too.
And funny climbing spaces that are red, yellow, and blue.
These are some bouncing horses to ride,
But my favorite is the curving slide.

## Resources

Aska, Warae. (1984) *Who Goes to the Park?* Plattsburgh, NY: Tundra Books.

Bruna, Dick. (1988) *Miffy at the Playground.* New York: Barrons.

Bunnett, Rochelle. (1992) *Friends in the Park.* New York: Checkerboard Press.

Duke, Kate. (1986) *The Playground.* New York: Dutton.

Gibbons, Gail. (1985) *Playgrounds.* New York: Holiday House.

Hill, Eric. (1991) *Spot Goes to the Park.* New York: Putnam (also available in Spanish).

Hoban, Tana. (1973) *Over Under Through and All About Where.* New York: Greenwillow Books.

Hughes, Shirley. (1985) *When We Went to the Park.* New York: Lothrop.

Matthias, Catherine. (1984) *Over Under.* Chicago: Childrens Press.

Miranda, Anne. (1988) *Baby Walk.* New York: Dutton.

Pocock, Rita. (1989) *Annabelle and the Big Slide.* San Diego: Harcourt Brace.

Reiser, Lynn. (1993) *Margaret and Margarita.* New York: Greenwillow (bilingual in Spanish and English).

Rockwell, Anne. (1990) *Hugo at the Park.* New York: Macmillan.

Takeshito, Fumiko. (1988) *The Park Bench.* New York: Kane/Miller.

Wolff, Ashley. (1995) *Stella and Roy.* New York: Dutton.

# Pond Life Walk・・・・・・・・・・・

Water is not only fascinating to children, but is a magnet for all forms of living things—which makes ponds wonderful places to observe nature. Because so many ponds exist, they are more accessible than other bodies of water. Throughout the year, your group can study these rich areas to

- observe the comings and goings of living creatures that frequent the pond;
- feed the ducks and frogs;
- observe and learn about the plants that grow in the pond;
- learn why so many things grow in ponds;
- observe ripples from tossing things into the pond; and
- collect water and small creatures from the pond to examine more closely.

Be extremely cautious with children around water, and practice water safety at all times. Show the children exactly how far to stand from the water—use markers if necessary. Only adults should collect samples taken from the pond; the group can inspect the collected samples away from the water's edge. Toss food into the pond or leave it on the shore for ducks and birds. Walking around a pond can reveal interesting ecology-related topics to look up and discuss later.

## Before the Walk

### WORDS TO LEARN AND USE

pondweed ● pond grass ● lily pad ● bullfrog ● muskrat ● snails ● ducks ● beaver ● dam ● stream ● bottom feeders ● sucker ● amoebae ● algae ● water mites ● flatworms and roundworms ● dragonfly ● nymphs ● salamander ● frogs ● tadpoles ● fish ● heron ● wren ● cattail ● water ● weeds ● logs ● ripples ● reeds ● habitat

### READ AND DISCUSS

Read Alvin Tresselt's *The Beaver Pond*, a lovely story about a pond the beavers make and all the creatures who come to live in it. This book can serve as a beautiful introduction to a study of pond life. Ask the children if there are other kinds of ponds besides those made by beavers (for example, ponds made by humans). Think about how these might be different from the one in the book. Plan to explore ponds in your area.

### Look at Pictures

Look at *In the Pond,* a beautiful, wordless picture guide to ponds, by Ermanno Crisitini and Luigi Puricelli—or look at any other book with pictures of a pond. Ask the children what they like in the pictures and what they would like to look for at the pond. Write down some of the things your group hopes to see.

### Things to Bring

paper and a pen or pencil to record observations ● plastic or paper bag for collecting things ● *In the Pond,* by Ermanno Crisitini and Luigi Puricelli, or other reference guide ● gallon ice-cream bucket ● magnifying glass ● a camera

## On the Walk

### Observe

Stand and watch the pond. Are there any ducks, birds, or turtles on or by the pond? Do you see bugs or any other signs of animal life? Does the water move or is it still?

Notice any plant life on or by the pond, such as cattails, lily pads, or weeds. Are there any trees, roots, or fallen branches by the pond? Are things growing on them? Are there signs of any animal life around the plants, such as frogs or tadpoles?

What colors do you see in the pond? Is the water all the same color or does it change? Wonder what causes any green color in the pond. Walk along and see what other things you notice about the pond.

Bring along bread crumbs to feed the ducks. Throw some on the water and along the shore and watch how the ducks go after them. Do some ducks get more than others?

### IDENTIFY

Use *In the Pond* or other guides to help you name some of the things you see in the pond. Let the children name some of the plants they know and look up some of the others. Write the names down to talk about later.

Call attention to characteristics that can help you identify things later when you return (for example, flat round leaves in the water, feathery shoots from clumps of grass, droopy branches hanging over the pond).

### SENSE

Take a deep breath. What do you smell? What might cause the smells? Are there many different smells—some good, others bad?

What words describe how it feels to be by the pond? Write down the words the children use to express their feelings.

Listen to sounds you hear around the pond. Find a spot to sit and close your eyes and listen. Do you hear sounds in the water or from small creatures near the pond?

### COLLECT

Use the gallon ice-cream bucket to collect some water from the pond, and a magnifying glass to study the water for anything you can't see with your eyes alone. Are there things you can see, such as snails or water beetles?

Bring back the water samples if they look interesting, and observe them over the next few days for signs of life. If possible, bring back samples of different plants, tree bark, or small branches growing around the pond to use in follow-up projects. Let the children help carry the small, non-spillable samples.

## After the Walk: Follow-up Activities

### TALK ABOUT AND DISPLAY

Talk about all the things seen around the pond. Read *Wonders of the Pond,* by Francene Sabin, and compare the pond in the book to the pond you visited. Also look at *Pond: One Small Square,* by Donald Silver, or some other books for comparisons. Many books about ponds have beautiful pictures in them. Set up a book display with some of these books and use them to plan other displays about pond life. Write down questions the children have about the pond and look in several books for answers.

## POND LIFE MURAL

Make a large mural of a pond using the picture books and your trip for inspiration. Supplies to use may include: brown craft paper or white table cover paper; scrap materials such as construction paper, tissue paper, plastic bubble wrap, and pieces of brown and green plastic (such as garbage bags). Add colored tape or yarn and small paste sticks to use for streams, fencing, or bridges. Provide magazine pictures; wallpaper samples; stickers of butterflies, animals, and plants; tempera paints, brushes, markers, and crayons. Keep a collection of dried weeds, cattails, twigs, bark, and things brought back, as well as glue.

Let the children work on the mural for several days, and let them think of the materials to use to show the pond and surrounding area.

Some suggestions: Use the twigs and bark to make beaver dams or homes. Make colorful butterflies by cutting 6-inch squares of tissue paper, decorating them with paint, and pinching the squares together in the middle. Wrap a twist tie around the center to hold it together and to form antennae. Attach the butterflies to some twigs with clothespins, or stick twigs through the twist tie.

When the children have finished, hang the mural up on a wall and put a table in front of it. Add books and other items for a table display about pond life.

## POND ANIMALS TO MAKE

Use plasticene clay, clay, or playdough to make snails or other small animals. Let the figures harden and then paint them. (Be warned: they may break.)

Create frogs or ducks out of papier-mâché. Using small boxes as a base, wrap pieces of newspaper around them to form a basic body shape. Bunch up newspaper to form head shapes and attach to the body with masking tape. Once you have frog- and duck-shaped animals, cover with strips of newspaper dipped in wallpaper paste. Let the animals dry and paint them. Add painted dots or other features. Make a few of each animal in varying sizes to use on your display table.

Make turtles by decorating paper plates or covering empty masking tape rolls with paper lined and colored to resemble a shell. Add paper cutouts for arms, legs, heads, and tails.

Create crabs or other fanciful creatures by using small tin cans or plastic tubs with plastic lids. Cover the base with construction paper. For the legs, cut or tear strips of construction paper 6 to 8 inches long. Wrap each strip around a pencil to curl it. Fold one end of the curly strips and hook over the can or tub base. Cover with the lid to hold the strips in place. You can glue the strips in place, but they are more rearrangeable if the lid holds them in place.

Place all of these animals on the display table. Add or rearrange animals, just as in a real pond. You can also add artificial birds or other small animals, tree branches, twigs, rocks, and anything else that might fall into a pond. Encourage the children to bring in things for the pond display and use it as a play area.

### POND LIFE DIORAMAS

Small shoe boxes work well to make dioramas. Let the children paint the shoe boxes as backgrounds (green or brown works well). Use blue tissue or construction paper for ponds of different size and shape. Encourage the children to make things found in ponds for their dioramas, such as small animals, cut grasses, plants, lily pads, and shells. Let each child design and make his or her own diorama, encouraging them to look in the books for ideas. Collect natural weeds and plants as needed to decorate these display items.

### CREATE A POND (OR OTHER HABITAT)

Pour the water you brought back from the pond into an aquarium or large clear bowl container. Add some weeds and ferns to float in the water. Put magnifying glasses near the container so you can watch any life developing. The book *Habitats,* by Pamela Hickman, has easy directions for setting up a pond habitat. Add snails or small crabs if you can find some.

### MAKE BOTTLE GARDENS

Cut the upper part off of a clear plastic bottle. Put a layer of small stones in the bottom for drainage.

Have children dig up a patch of small weeds and moss from the edge of the pond (make sure this is permissible). Keep as much of the dirt together as possible. Place the weed patch on top of the stones, moisten it, but don't soak it. Cover the top of the terrarium with cardboard. This terrarium needs very little water. In fact, if it gets steamy or moldy, allow it to dry out by removing the cardboard for a while. Watch how things grow in your moss garden. Keep it on your pond table display.

### INVITE OTHERS TO VISIT

Invite parents and friends to see your informative and attractive pond displays.

## Related Trip Ideas to Explore

pet store that has aquarium displays ● stores or restaurants that have lobster or large fish tanks ● trout farm ● fish hatchery ● aquarium ● museum ● marsh or swamp ● nature centers

## Songs, Poems, and Finger Plays

### IN THE POND

We walked to the pond the other day (walk in place)
And saw some ducks, but they flew away. (imitate flying)
We tossed in some crumbs so they came right back (tossing motions)
And gobbled them all with a quack, quack, quack. (clap hands like quacking)

In the same pond sitting on a log, (put right fist on left arm)
Croaking away was an old bullfrog.
He seemed to be waiting in his old log seat,
For some juicy bugs that he could eat! (pretend to eat)

### FIVE LITTLE DUCKS

Five little ducks close to shore (hold up five fingers)
One flew away and then there were four. (flap arms like wings)
Four little ducks in the pond I see (hold up four fingers)
One flew away and then there were three. (flap wings)
Three little ducks watched as he flew (hold up three fingers)
One dove in the water and now there are two. (make diving motions;
    hold up two fingers)
Two little ducks splashing for fun (flap and splash)
Another dove under and now there is one. (hold up one finger)
One little duck looked up at the sun, (look up)
And dove in the water, so now there are none. (diving motions)

### A FAMILY AFFAIR

A little white duck and a big green frog
Sat together by an old brown log.
Three little ducklings swam nearby
While the frog tried to catch a big black fly—
To feed her tadpoles by and by.

The frog and tadpoles swam away
And went to the lily pads to play
The ducklings walked along the shore
Till mother said, "Let's dive some more"
And off they went 1, 2, 3, 4. (hold up fingers 1, 2, 3, 4)

### TEN LITTLE DUCKS

Ten little ducks went swimming in the pool (hands together
    make swimming motions)
Dove down in the water to keep themselves cool (dive hands
    downward)
Flapped their wings and made a big splash (flap arms)
Swam in circles and then in a flash (hands together again)
Up, up, up and away they all flew (make hands fly away)
And they were all gone in a second or two.

### LITTLE TURTLE (TRADITIONAL)

There was a little turtle (form circle with hands)
Who lived in a box (form box with hands)
He swam in a puddle (swimming motion)
He climbed on the rocks (climbing motion)
He snapped at a mosquito (grabbing motion)
He snapped at a flea (grabbing motion)
He snapped at a minnow (grabbing motion)
And he snapped at me!

He caught the mosquito (catch and eat)
He caught the flea (catch and eat)
He caught the minnow (catch and eat)
But he didn't catch me! (shake head no)

## Resources

Back, Christine, and Barrie Watts. (1984) *Tadpole and Frog.* Morristown, NJ: Silver Burdett.

Clarke, Barry. (1990) *Amazing Frogs and Toads.* New York: Knopf.

Coatsworth, Elizabeth. (1984) *Under the Green Willow.* New York: Greenwillow Books.

Cole, Joanna. (1995) *The Magic School Bus Hops Home.* New York: Scholastic.

Crisitini, Ermanno, and Luigi Puricelli. (1984) *In the Pond.* Old Tappan, NJ: Picture Book Studio.

Curran, Eileen. (1985) *Life in the Pond.* Mahwah, NJ: Troll Associates.

Ets, Marie Hall. (1983) *Play With Me.* New York: Puffin Books.

Fleming, Denise. (1993) *In the Small, Small Pond.* New York: Henry Holt.

George, William T. (1988) *Beaver at Long Pond.* New York: Greenwillow Books.
———. (1989) *Box Turtle at Long Pond.* New York: Greenwillow Books.

Gibbons, Gail. (1993) *Frogs.* New York: Holiday House.

Kent, Jack. (1982) *The Caterpillar and the Polliwog.* New York: Simon & Schuster.

Parker, Steve. (1988) *Pond and River.* New York: Knopf.

Rockwell, Anne. (1994) *Ducklings and Pollywogs.* New York: Macmillan.

Rosen, Michael J. (1994) *All Eyes on the Pond.* New York: Hyperion Books.

Sabin, Francene. (1982) *Wonders of the Pond.* Mahwah, NJ: Troll Associates.

Stone, Lynn. (1983) *Pond Life* (a New True Book). Chicago: Childrens Press.

Tempest, Terry. (1985) *Between Cattails.* New York: Charles Scribner's Sons.

Tresselt, Alvin. (1970) *The Beaver Pond.* New York: Lothrop.

Wyler, Rose. (1990) *Puddles and Ponds.* Englewood Cliffs, NJ: J. Messner.

Zoehfeld, Kathleen Weidner. (1994) *What Lives in a Shell?* New York: HarperCollins.

### OTHER GOOD RESOURCES

Hickman, Pamela. (1993) *Habitats.* Reading, MA: Addison-Wesley.

Mason, Helen. (1992) *Life in a Pond.* Burlington, Ontario: Durkin Hayes.

Milkens, Colin S. (1990) *Discovering Pond Life.* New York: Bookwright Press.

Silver, Donald M. (1994) *Pond: One Small Square.* New York: W. H. Freeman & Company.

*Pond Animals* (See How They Grow Videos). (1994) Sony Kids' Video.

# Senses Exploration Walk

Children constantly use their senses to learn—in fact, for young children, all learning is sensory based: a baby puts everything into her mouth; a toddler touches and moves everything; and a preschooler asks a million questions. All are learning through their senses. As children develop the cognitive processes to sort through this learning and the language to talk about it, they organize the learning into knowledge and useful groupings. A major portion of this sorting process takes place during the preschool years. Sensory walks can play an important role in sharpening those skills by

- encouraging children to be aware of and use all their senses to gather information;
- focusing attention on using particular senses as appropriate and thinking about how many senses we use at times;
- providing practice in using sensory information to describe and learn about things in the world;
- helping children learn about their senses and how they work; and
- allowing children to have fun as they explore their world in their most natural way.

The activities below begin with tasting, which requires advance setup and most likely happens indoors (remind children not to put unknown things into their mouth). Although all the senses are covered in this walk, consider planning separate walks for each sense (which would be especially helpful to younger children). You could also organize the follow-up activities to emphasize one sense at a time. You'll find many books on each of the senses in the Resources section—and enough ideas to pursue for a month of exploring. Regard this walk as an introduction to the topic and a kickoff to more in-depth exploration of the five senses.

# Before the Walk

## WORDS TO LEARN AND USE

see ● hear ● touch ● taste ● smell ● eyes ● ears ● hands ● fingers ●
mouth ● nose ● signal ● brain ● nerves ● receptor ● taste buds ● tongue ●
skin ● feel ● touch sensor ● scent ● odor ● vibration ● listen ● sound

## READ AND TALK ABOUT IT

Read the books titled *My Five Senses* (one is by Margaret Miller, the other
by Aliki). Both offer lovely pictures and descriptions of using the senses.
Aliki's book also talks about times when people use more than one sense
in their activities. Discuss with the children some things they like to
touch, taste, or smell; some sounds they like and do not like; and tastes
they like and do not like. Write down the things they tell you. Talk about
the idea of using more than one sense: How many senses do they use to
watch TV, play with a pet, eat food? Plan to go on a walk around your
building and outdoors to see how many senses you use.

## A TOUCHING TABLE

On a table, put out items that provide a variety of sensory experiences,
and let the children use them. Include things such as a feather, rabbit's
foot, piece of flocked wallpaper, textured paper pieces, sandpaper, a bell,
a small brush, and a key chain with several keys on it. Talk about the
items and write some sensory descriptions of them. Plan to go on a walk
to collect other things to add to the sensory table. These items can later
be used in other activities.

## PREPARE THE KITCHEN

In a kitchen area, put out a number of items to taste. Choose foods that offer a wide range of tastes. Include pretzels, small slices of lemon, marshmallows, M&M candies, pieces of fruit snacks, and slices of cucumbers and pickles. Also have available items that have distinctive aromas, such as spices and flavorings.

## THINGS TO BRING

paper and a pen or pencil to record observations ● large and small plastic or paper bag for collecting things ● a tape recorder for recording sounds ● scrap paper and crayons for making rubbings ● a camera

# On the Walk

## TASTE

Start in the kitchen area where you assembled the food. Encourage the children to taste many different things and tell you what they taste like. Write down all the different words they use to describe things. Talk about which foods they liked and which they did not. Try to get lots of different descriptive words such as *crunchy, chewy, gooey, gummy, soft,* and *fluffy,* in addition to *sweet* and *sour.*

Talk about other foods that have similar tastes, or other foods the children associate with the foods they are tasting. Notice how much taste memory the children have. Can they tell you anything about these foods or things the foods make them think about—such as "I always say 'no pickles on my hamburger" or "My cat's name is Marshmallow." Taste is a very strong sense for young children, and the discussion may produce some interesting reactions—even more so than to things they hear or smell. Make some notes during your conversation with the children to use in follow-up activities.

## USE OTHER SENSES INDOORS

In thinking about foods, talk about how many senses the children are using besides taste. Are they touching the foods, seeing and smelling them, and making some comments based on those senses as well? It is hard to separate our senses.

Use senses to find indoor smells, textures, sounds, and sights. Write down the descriptive words the children use as they explore the kitchen.

Can they smell flowers, garbage, spices, flavorings, things baking or cooking? Try a smelling activity when walking in the food court of a mall. Your group will smell many different aromas—from cinnamon buns to coffee to pizza—all with strong and characteristic smells.

What textures are there to feel in this area? How do the counters or table feel, the floor covering and walls? Are there other textures to explore, such as sponges, Brillo scouring pads, towels, plastic or steel cooking utensils, strainers or graters? Feel some of the glass, china, or aluminum pots. Are there any rough or irregular surfaces you might want to try to take rubbings of such as the grater, a vegetable brush, a pattern on a trivet , the floor tile, or any other raised surface?

What sounds do you hear? Turn on your tape recorder for a few minutes as you continue walking into the next area. Listen there as well for a while before turning it off.

Look around the hallways or play areas for any other things to touch, smell, or hear. Do you hear sounds from the playroom, smell soap in the bathroom, feel bumpy fabrics on the furniture, notice cool hard slate in the entryway? Write down observations and comments the children make.

## USE SENSES OUTDOORS

Go outdoors and listen. Do you hear car and traffic sounds, animal sounds (such as moving around and barking), bird sounds (such as flying, chirping, pecking, or insect noises), people working sounds (such as lawnmowers), construction sounds, people sounds (such as walking and talking), or playing sounds (such as music from a radio)? Talk about all the sounds you hear; write down the sound and a description. Turn on your tape recorder to record sounds outdoors. Plan to listen later to see if you can identify the sounds. Remind the children to listen carefully so they will remember.

Lie down on the grass and put your ear next to the ground. Listen. Do you hear any sounds under the ground? Talk about what they might be. Cup your hand around you ear. Does that make the sound seem louder? Try cupping your hand over your ear when you are listening at other times, to see how it affects hearing. Do you hear very quiet sounds, such as the wind rustling leaves?

Now explore with you nose. What kinds of things can you smell outdoors? Start with general aromas. Do you smell smoke from chimneys or burning leaves or fires? What do you smell if you walk near a store or restaurant? Can you recognize what is cooking by the smell? Do you smell grass being cut, lilacs or other fragrant shrubs in bloom,  or the streets being tarred or cleaned? Smell items up close, such as flowers, pine trees, pinecones, and leaves. Write down your findings and the words the children use to describe the scents. Bring back samples of pine needles, pinecones, and any herbs or plants to add to your sensory table.

Notice textures in your outdoor explorations. Touch house or building materials and talk about their different textures. Wood may not feel as smooth as it looks, and some woods can be rough; aluminum siding may be the smoothest feeling of all the materials. Feel textures of different leaves and plants, barks, different types of rocks, and sand. Write down the items and their textures using many different descriptive words. Make rubbings of a variety of textures, label them and bring them back to add to the sensory table. Collect samples of other items such as stones, leaves, wood chips, and various evergreen clusters, that you have not already collected to add to the table display.

## After the Walk: Follow-up Activities

### TALK ABOUT IT

Talk about the walk and go through all the materials you collected. Do the children remember what the rubbings are from? Which part of the walk did they find most interesting? Summarize some of the information by starting lists that discuss things the group liked to hear, touch, taste, see, and smell on one list, and things the group did not like on the other list. Some things might be pleasant for one sense and unpleasant for another. For example, vanilla extract smells wonderful but tastes terrible to most people.

Listen to your tape recording, and see if the sounds are recognizable. If they are, talk about the various sounds and write up a summary organizing the sounds into categories, such as nature sounds, people sounds, and machine sounds. Put the tape and tape player and the list of sound categories on your sensory display table. Label all the other items you brought back and add them to the table.

By now this table may have many things on it and may need some organizing itself. Use shoe box lids or small plastic trays as containers, and let the children decide how to group various items. Talk about different ways to group the items. For example, you can group them by the sense most involved, how the item feels, the type of item (such as things found in nature), and things that are made. Let the children manipulate the items and rearrange the categories as they wish.

### READ AND EXPERIMENT

Read parts of *Find Out by Touching* and *Ears Are for Hearing*, both by Paul Showers, and *You Can't Smell a Flower with Your Ear*, by Joanna Cole. Try out some of the simple experiments suggested. Also check out the Think About series (*Hearing, Seeing, Smelling, Tasting, Touching*) by Henry Pluckrose. Through gorgeous pictures and simple text, the books in this series provide much to think about and discuss.

## SOUND IDEAS

Make a simple guitar by stretching different-sized rubber bands over empty tissue boxes. Pluck the strings to hear the various sounds. Many books about hearing discuss vibrations and the role vibration plays in producing sound. You can illustrate vibration and sound with the simple guitar by varying the way you pluck the strings (fast, slow, in different positions) and observing the effect on the sound. Use different-sized boxes to see how that effects the sounds too.

Read books that focus on sounds, such as *City Sounds*, by Craig Brown, *The Maestro Plays*, by Bill Martin Jr., and *What Noise?*, by Debbie Mackinnon. Have the children fill in the sounds, imitate them or answer the questions the books ask. Watch the *Sounds Around* videotape, and do some of the same type of activities with it.

Make sounds using objects the children cannot see. Can they guess what's making the sound? Use objects such as a bell, triangle, drum, and alarm clock.

Fill jars with different amounts of water and tap them with a spoon to hear the different sounds. Try other experiments in *Talk about Sound*, by Angela Webb.

Play hide-and-seek type games using sound clues. One example: choose a mother and father cat and several baby kittens. The mother and father cat fall asleep and the baby kittens run away and hide. When the parent cats wake up, they cannot find their kittens so they call to them, "Meow." The kittens meow and the parents try to find them. The parents can meow as much as they like until all the kittens are found. Encourage the kittens to hide in separate places and remember they must meow in answer to a call so the searchers can follow the sound.

## TOUCH ACTIVITIES

Make texture-matching games. Mount two pieces of matching textures (such as fabrics, wallpaper samples, sandpaper, wire mesh, steel wool, or furry pieces) on metal juice can lids. Put them inside a box and have children find the matching pairs by touch. This can also be done without the box, allowing children to use two senses (sight and touch) to make the matches.

Another variation is to make a touchy-feely shoe box. Mount one sample of each texture on the shoe box lid. Put the second sample inside the box. Cut a hole in one end of the box for the children to use to reach inside. To use, have the child touch one texture on the lid with one hand and reach inside with the other hand to find the matching texture.

Make texture sorting games. Label small boxes with words (such as *smooth*, *rough*, and *hard*) and glue one sample to illustrate the label in each box. Children can sort a variety of objects (from the display table or added collections) into the boxes by like texture.

Make a Touch and Tell scrapbook using samples from your sensory display table (when the children are not using the table anymore). If you do not have a store-bought scrapbook, you can make one using construction paper and yarn. Cut the construction paper to the size you want. Punch holes in one side of the paper and string together loosely with yarn (allow the pages to turn easily). Paste each sample into the scrapbook, and add some words that describe how it feels. Have the children use the scrapbook with their eyes closed to see if they can tell what the items are by touch alone. To turn the scrapbook into a matching game, make a set of labels on small cards that match each texture. Put a small piece of the texture on the label. Put all the labels in an envelope. Children then match the label to the item in the scrapbook.

Play games. Have children find things in the room by your description using texture clues. Describe things such as stuffed animals, small metal cars, smooth plastic, and rubbery items (animals or tires). Children search around and point to the objects they think you are describing. They will use more than one sense since they are looking and touching.

Read books that emphasize touch, and try any experiments they mention. Talk about how people can feel things with all their skin and not just with their fingers. Feel things with arms, feet, legs, and cheeks. Compare feeling an object, such as a tennis ball, with your fingers and then with your arms or legs. Do they notice any difference?

### TASTING AND SMELLING ACTIVITIES

Read books that focus on these senses, and try out any experiments they suggest as well. Let the children tell you things they use that have special smells, such as shampoo, baby powder, wipes, and lotions. Bring in some small samples of such items to compare smells.

Make sniffy jars: two of each kind, using various smells. Place a few drops of a liquid on cotton balls, and put the cotton balls in small jars or containers with a lid, such as baby food jars or film canisters. Let the children find the matching pairs by opening the lids and smelling inside. Use items with strong smells, such as peppermint, vanilla, or other extracts; coffee; alcohol; vinegar; and onion juice. The children can also decide which ones smell good and which ones they do not like. Can they guess what things the smells signal?

Play "What Is It?" games that involve smelling and tasting. Put out items in small dishes that look very much alike (such as sugar and salt, flour and cornstarch, and powdered cinnamon and cloves). Ask the children if they know what the items are by looking at them. Can they tell by smelling them? When they still have not decided for sure, have them taste a tiny speck of each. They should be able to tell the difference very quickly and know most of the items. This same activity will work with different types of juices or other beverages that, once poured into small cups, can only be identified by tasting.

Compare tastes of things that look and are alike but may taste different, such as various flavored potato chips and crackers.

Talk about and compare tastes of foods that have similar looks and textures but different tastes, such as lemons, oranges, and grapefruit; mashed potatoes, mashed squash, and sweet potatoes, and yogurt, pudding, and sour cream.

Talk about and compare foods with similar taste but different textures, such as strawberry gelatin and strawberry drink; chocolate ice cream and chocolate milk; bananas and banana chips; and applesauce and apples.

## Related Trip Ideas to Explore

Separate walks for each sense ● color-matching walks ● sock walks ● opposites walk

## Songs, Poems, and Finger Plays

### HOW DOES IT TASTE?

Pretzels taste salty, candy tastes sweet
Marshmallows are fluffy and fun to eat.
Lemon tastes sour, fruit rolls are sticky
Cucumbers are crunchy, but _____ are icky.
(substitute foods the children say are icky, such
    as pickles)
Pudding is squishy and caramel is gooey
Bananas are mushy, whole apples are chewy.
Tasting things is lots of fun;
But I'd rather taste cookies or a cinnamon bun.

### SENSES ALL AROUND

Kittens are furry and soft to touch
But prickly things I don't like very much.
Music is something I like to hear
But blasting noises hurt my ear.
I love the sounds and smells of popcorn popping
But not the ones of garbage chopping.
And I love to look at the twinkling lights
That light up the houses on December nights.

### SENSES

With my eyes I can look and look (put hands above eyes and look around)
My ears help me hear the story in a book (cup hands around ears)
My nose tells me which things smell sweet (point to nose and sniff)
My taste buds tell me what I like to eat (point to tongue and smack lips)
My skin and hands I use so much
To feel all the things I have to touch. (pretend to rub something)

# Resources

Aliki. (1989) *My Five Senses*. New York: Crowell.
———. (1990) *My Hands*. New York: Crowell.

Benjamin, Alan. (1987) *Rat-a-Tat, Pitter Pat*. New York: Crowell.

Branley, Franklin M. (1967) *High Sounds, Low Sounds*. New York: Crowell.

Brown, Craig. (1992) *City Sounds*. New York: Greenwillow Books.

Brown, Margaret Wise. (1992) *Indoor Noisy Book*. New York: Harper & Row.
———. (1992) *The Summer Noisy Book*. New York: HarperCollins.

Cole, Joanna. (1994) *You Can't Smell a Flower with Your Ear*. New York: Grosset &
    Dunlap.

Emberly, Rebecca. (1989) *City Sounds*. Boston: Little Brown.

Fowler, Alan. (1991) *Hearing Things* (Rookie Read About Series). Chicago: Childrens
    Press (also in this series: *Feeling Things*, *Seeing Things*, *Smelling Things*, and
    *Tasting Things*).

Hoban, Tana. (1984) *Is It Rough, Is It Smooth, Is It Shiny?* New York: Greenwillow Books.

Mackinnon, Debbie. (1993) *What Noise?* New York: Dial Books.

Martin, Bill Jr. (1994) *The Maestro Plays*. New York: Henry Holt.

McMillan, Bruce. (1994) *Sense Suspense*. New York: Scholastic.

Miller, Margaret. (1994) *My Five Senses*. New York: Simon & Schuster.

Moncure, Jane Belk. (1982) *The Touch Book* (The Five Senses Series). Chicago:
    Childrens Press (also in this series: *The Look Book*, *Sounds All Around*, *The Tasting
    Party*, and *What Your Nose Knows*).

Otto, Carolyn. (1994) *I Can Tell by Touching*. New York: HarperCollins.

Pluckrose, Henry. (1986) *Think about Hearing* (Think About Series). New York:
    Franklin Watts (also in the series: *Seeing*, *Smelling*, *Tasting*, and *Touching*).

Podendorf, Illa. (1970) *Sounds All About*. Chicago: Childrens Press.

Rius, Maria. (1985) *The 5 Senses*. New York: Barrons.

Showers, Paul. (1990) *Ears Are for Hearing*. New York: Crowell.
———. (1961) *Find Out by Touching*. New York: Crowell.
———. (1961) *The Listening Walk*. New York: Crowell.

Webb, Angela. (1988) *Talk About Sound*. New York: Franklin Watts.

Wright, Lillian. (1995) *Touching* (A First Start Book). Austin, TX: Raintree, Steck-
    Vaughn (also in this series: *Hearing*, *Seeing*, *Smelling*, and *Tasting*).

## OTHER GOOD RESOURCES

Billingslea, Kathie, and Victoria Crenson. (1988) *Smelling*. Mahwah, NJ: Troll
    Associates (also in this series: *Tasting*, *Touching*, *Hearing*, and *Seeing*).

Broekel, Ray. (1984) *Your Five Senses* (A New True Book). Chicago: Childrens Press.

Gaskin, John. (1985) *My Senses*. New York: Franklin Watts.

*Sounds Around* (video). (1994) Bo Peep Productions.

# Shadow Walk···············

On summer days, children and their parents or providers often look for shady spots to sit in—and it's not often we stop to explain what makes the shade. In some languages, the word *shadow* describes shade, but the English language uses different words, so many do not automatically make the connection between shadow and shade. Taking a shadow walk offers an ideal opportunity to help children learn that concept. A shadow walk also provides opportunities to

- learn what causes shadows and how they change;
- observe our own shadows and how we can make them do things;
- play games using shadows; and
- learn how sun and shadows relate to telling time.

Take trips to observe shadows at different times during the day and at different times of the year. Late afternoon in the fall has a very shadowy feeling, which is different from the same time of day in the spring or summer. If you want, repeat the activities on subsequent trips. Save the descriptions and measurements from your first trip experiments so you can compare them. It might be a good idea to date everything you write down so you get results for the whole year. You and the children can write up a firsthand report of what happens to shadows over a year's time.

## Before the Walk

### WORDS TO LEARN AND USE

shadow ● light ● dark ● reflection ● angle ● sunshine ● shade ● silhouette ● shadow picture ● shadow play ● sundial ● eclipse ● opaque ● hazy ● diffuse ● direct ● cast ● shape ● size ● oblique ● elongated ● projector

### READ AND TALK ABOUT IT

Read Robert Louis Stevenson's poem "My Shadow" to the children. Ask them if they know what a shadow is, and if they have noticed their own shadows. What do they think causes shadows? Why did the boy in the poem say his shadow was lazy and still in bed?

### DEMONSTRATE

Use a doll, water glass, and flashlight to demonstrate how shadows are produced. Stand the doll on a table placed near a wall. Shine the flashlight at the doll, toward the wall, so the light comes from one side. The light should cast a shadow on the wall. Explain that because the doll is an opaque object and doesn't let the light shine though it, the dark shape of the object is passed on by the light and makes a shadow of the object.

Move the flashlight around so that it shines at different angles on the doll. Move it so it is closer to the doll, and then further away. Does moving the light change the shadow? If you want, measure the shadow as it is cast from different angles, and write down your findings. Plan to go outside at different times of the day to look for and measure shadows.

Shine the light on an empty water glass and see what happens. The light passes right through the glass so it doesn't leave any outline of its shape.

### THINGS TO BRING

paper and a pen or pencil to record measurements and other observations ● chalk ● rulers ● tape measure ● thermometer ● plastic or paper bag for collecting things ● a camera

## On the Walk

### OBSERVE

On a sunny day, look for shadows as you walk. Notice the shadows of cars, trees, houses, street signs, people, animals, and anything else you can find.

Plan to look for shadows in the morning and again in the afternoon to see if they look different.

Let the children observe their own and each other's shadows. Can they make their shadows move or do things? Observe what happens. Sing one of the shadow songs and imitate its actions. Make different shapes of the shadows by moving arms and legs or by sitting down.

Look for shadows from clouds, airplanes, kites, balloons, and clothes hanging on lines. If you see some shaded areas in the yard or street, try to figure out what is producing that shade.

Are the shadows the same on both sides of the street? Are there places where there aren't any shadows?

Do moving things also have shadows? Do you see shadows from moving cars, running animals, or other things? What do you notice about the shadows as they move?

## EXPERIMENT

Trace around the children's shadows in the morning. Mark where their feet were placed so they can stand in the same spot again later in the day to see what happens to their shadows. Measure their shadows each time to see how they change. When are their shadows the longest? When are they the shortest? Test frequently throughout the day to see how it changes. Write down the length after each measurement. Are their shadows in the same places each time, or do they move? Make little lines to show where their shadows are each time.

Take along a thermometer to measure the temperature in the sun and in the shade. Talk about the difference and note why it feels cooler in the shade.

Measure the size of shadows from parked cars, signs, fire hydrants, trees, and other objects.

Measure either with the ruler or tape measure or by pacing. Keep track of the size of those shadows. Measure them at other times of the day to see if they change also.

Take some pictures and try to get the shadows in the pictures.

Go out on a cloudy, hazy day to see if you can find any shadows.

## PLAY GAMES

Play games with the shadows, such as running and standing in someone else's shadow, connecting shadows with rope or chalk, tracing around shadows, and catching shadows in hoops.

Play "Don't Step on My Shadow" tag. The child who is "it" tries to step on the shadow of another child who then becomes "it." For the most fun, play this game in a large open area or designate the large shadows of buildings or trees as safe zones.

## After the Walk: Follow-up Activities

### TALK ABOUT IT

Talk about your observations of shadows. Write a story about those observations, making some generalizations about shadows. For example: shadows are longest late in the afternoon, shortest in the middle of the day, and there are no shadows when it is cloudy. How do these observations compare to those of the doll's shadow done inside before the walk? Think about how the size of the shadow may be related to the position of the light in relation to the object.

Look for magazine pictures that have shadows in them and cut them out to discuss. Wonder where the light would be to make the shadows fall as they do.

Talk about the word *eclipse,* and explain that it occurs when one celestial body comes between another body and the sun, blocking light and producing a shadow. An eclipse of the moon occurs when the earth comes between the moon and the sun, producing a shadow of the earth on the moon.

Demonstrate this concept with a flashlight and two balls in a darkened room.

### MAKE A SUNDIAL

Insert a pencil or dowel into the center of a paper plate. Place the pencil into a small container of clay so that the pencil will stand erect with the plate at its base. Place the sundial in a sunny window. Look at it every hour during the day, and draw a line of the shadow of the pencil on the plate each time. Think about what the finished picture looks like. Discuss how ancient civilizations used the sun to tell time.

### DRAWING SHADOWS

Have the children draw pictures of trees, houses, cars, and other objects on a mural, leaving room between items. Then have the children make shadows of the things in the mural. Will the shadows all go in the same direction?

### HOMEWORK WITH SHADOWS

Read the story *What Makes a Shadow?*, by Clyde Bulla, and try out some of the suggested experiments. Have the children try to make shadows at home at night; the next day, they can tell the group what they noticed. It might be a good idea to let parents know you have suggested this activity, so they can help find a good light source and a wall or counter surface. Also, ask the children to notice shadows in their houses at night. Are there shadows of furniture, plants, railings, doors, and other objects? Perhaps the children can make pictures of the things that made shadows in their houses.

Ask parents to write down their children's observations to help them remember.

### PRETENDING

Divide the children into pairs. Let one child be the leader and the other be the shadow who does whatever the leader does. The leader can try all kinds of actions, with the shadow following the movements exactly. Have the children change positions so they both have turns to be leaders and shadows.

### SHADOW PICTURES

Bring in an overhead projector or any type of projector. Turn it on so light shines on one wall. Let the children make shadow pictures with their hands. Hold objects in front of the light to see what kind of shadow they project.

Mount large sheets of white paper on the wall and let the children trace around the shadows with markers. To make silhouette pictures of the children, have them stand sideways between the light and the paper mounted on the wall. Trace around the profile projected onto the paper. Cut out and mount on a larger piece of paper or tagboard (a very nice gift idea).

### SHADOW PLAYS

Hang up a white sheet and place a projector behind it. Have a few children stand between the light and the sheet. Let the others stay on the opposite side of the sheet to see what happens. Have a child perform an action, such as eating, waving, or pretending to sew, and have the audience guess what the performer is doing. Have the child behind the sheet hold up objects and see if the audience can guess what they are from their shadows.

### MAKE COLORED SHADOWS

Bring in two flashlights and cover them with different colored cellophane such as colored candy wrappers or plastic wrap.

Hold some small objects up in front of the white paper on the wall. Shine the light on the object and see if a colored shadow is made.

## Related Trip Ideas to Explore

shadow puppet show ● shadow displays in children's museums ● art or photography shows that include shadows ● notice shadows on bus trips to other sights

## Songs, Poems, and Finger Plays

### FIVE PEOPLE ALL IN A ROW
See the five people all in a row; (hold up five fingers)
See their shadows facing just so. (hold second hand parallel to first)
The first one bends and says, "How do?" (bend thumb)
And then his shadow does so too. (bend second thumb)
The next one starts to twirl around; (twirl finger on first hand)
And so does her shadow without a sound. (corresponding finger does same)
Whatever the first person tried to do, (fingers on first hand make different
   motions)
The second one says, "I'll do the same as you." (fingers on second hand
   repeat motions)
(This can also be done with pairs of children, one child doing the motions
   and the other following exactly.)

### OH DEAR, WHERE CAN MY SHADOW BE?
*(to the tune of "Oh Dear, What Can the Matter Be?")*

Oh dear, where can my shadow be,
Oh dear, where can my shadow be,
Oh dear, where can my shadow be,
When the sun's high in the sky?

It's lost, lost, lost at the foot of me,
Lost, lost, lost at the foot of me,
Oh dear, lost at the foot of me,
'Cuz the sun's high overhead.

Oh dear, where can my shadow be,
Oh dear, where can my shadow be,
Oh dear, where can my shadow be,
When the sun hides in the clouds?

It's gone, gone, gone far away from me,
Gone, gone, gone far away from me,
Oh dear, gone far away from me,
'Cuz the sun hides in the clouds.

### DO YOU SEE MY SHADOW GO?
*(to the tune of "The Muffin Man.")*

Oh, do you see my shadow go, (children walk along)
My shadow go, my shadow go?
Oh, do you see my shadow go,
It goes along with me.

Oh, do you see my shadow bend, (children bend)
My shadow bend, my shadow bend?
Oh, do you see my shadow bend,
It bends along with me.

Additional verses:
Oh, do you see my shadow wave...
Oh, do you see my shadow jump...
Oh, do you see my shadow stretch...
Oh, do you see my shadow hop...
(Sing this outdoors on a sunny day.)

# Resources

Bartolos, Michael. (1995) *Shadowville*. New York: Viking.

Branley, Franklyn. (1973) *Eclipse: Darkness in Daytime*. New York: Crowell

Brown, Marcia. (1982) *Shadow*. New York: Charles Scribner's Sons.

Bulla, Clyde. (1994) *What Makes a Shadow?* New York: HarperCollins.

DeRegniers, Beatrice, and Isabel Gordon. (1960) *The Shadow Book*. New York: Harcourt Brace.

Dodd, Anne W. (1992) *Footprints and Shadows*. New York: Simon & Schuster.

Dorros, Arthur. (1990) *Me and My Shadow*. New York: Scholastic.

Farber, Norma. (1992) *Return of the Shadows*. New York: HarperCollins.

Goor, Ron and Nancy. (1981) *Shadows Here, There and Everywhere*. New York: Crowell.

Gore, Sheila. (1989) *My Shadow*. New York: Doubleday.

Mahy, Margaret. (1987) *The Boy with Two Shadows*. New York: Lippincott.

Mitsumasa, Anno. (1988) *In Shadowland*. New York: Orchard Books.

Narahashi, Keiko. (1987) *I Have a Friend*. New York: Macmillan.

Paul, Ann. (1992) *Shadows Are About*. New York: Scholastic.

Simon, Seymour. (1985) *Shadow Magic*. New York: Lothrop.

Stevenson, Robert Louis. (1990) *My Shadow*. New York: Putnam.

## ANOTHER GOOD RESOURCE

Taylor, Barbara. (1990) *Fun with Shadows and Reflections*. Easthampton, MA: Warwick.

# Shape Walk •••••••••••••••

During their preschool years, children begin to learn cognitive concepts such as shape, color, size, space, and number, and all the words associated with these concepts. Children learn by doing, and walks focusing on a particular concept offer an ideal way to help them actively learn about a concept. This walk focuses on one specific concept—shapes. (Ideas for other concept walks are listed later in this chapter.) When you take a shape walk, you reinforce learning by

- having children notice the shapes of many things, both indoors and out;
- encouraging children to notice and match shapes;
- helping children to identify the characteristics of common shapes and to learn their names;
- helping children categorize objects by noticing specific characteristics; and
- making some generalizations about objects that are particular shapes.

While the ideas and activities in this walk focus on shape, you can easily adapt them to apply to walks focusing on numerous other concepts, such as color, size, and number walks.

There are a large number of shapes—from the standard geometric ones to the more generic groups such as stars, crescents, and diamonds, where we have assigned a shape name to things resembling a particular form.

Whether something is a true geometric shape or not matters much more to mathematicians than to preschoolers. The concept becomes even more complicated when you consider two-dimensional shapes (circles, squares, triangles) versus three-dimensional ones (spheres, cubes, pyramids). The activities, ideas, and resources in this walk make reference to this broad range of considerations—with more emphasis on the simpler concepts that younger children can grasp. Older children may become interested in the subtle distinctions of more complicated shapes from octagons or ovals (ellipses) to the fascinating puzzles of three- or four-sided pyramids.

This walk is not intended to emphasize right or wrong answers from the children, but to begin to develop greater awareness. How children define shape will be related to which characteristics they notice most (for example, things with corners are squares). Their definition offers a clue to their thinking process, which for each child is obviously right. Looking, measuring, comparing, and discussing are all ways of helping children notice more details in the learning process.

## Before the Walk

### WORDS TO LEARN AND USE

circle ● square ● triangle ● rectangle ● oval ● egg-shaped ● octagon ● diamond ● corner ● side ● heart ● round ● point ● angle ● wide ● long ● short ● equal ● star ● half-moon ● crescent ● curve ● oblong ● cone ● polygon ● cube ● pyramid ● spiral

### LOOK AT PICTURES

Look at the pictures in Tana Hoban's books *Circles, Triangles, and Squares*; *Shapes and Things*; or *Shapes, Shapes, Shapes*. These wordless books capture many shapes in sharp photographs and offer a great starting point for focusing attention on this concept. Some pages emphasize circles, some squares, and some combinations of several shapes.

After looking at the books, ask the children to look around the room and tell you what shapes they see. Ask them if they would like to go exploring for shapes around the house or building, or look around outside. The book *Look Around: A Book about Shapes*, by Leonard Fisher, is also good for noticing basic shapes in common objects.

### MAKE SHAPE PUPPETS

Cut out some common shapes from tagboard and mount them on flat wooden craft sticks. If you wish, make faces on the shapes. Explain that

these are shape puppets, and use some of the verses in the Songs, Poems, and Finger Play section to point out the characteristics of their shapes. Suggest taking the puppets on your walk to see if you find things that have the same shape. As the children master basic shapes, create new shape puppets.

## THINGS TO BRING

paper and a pen or pencil to record measurements and other observations ● a ruler or tape to measure objects ● shape puppets ● shape books ● small paper bags with a different shape outline drawn on each bag, and some counters (such as beans or poker chips) ● garbage bag and plastic or garden gloves ● plastic or paper bag for collecting things ● a camera

## On the Walk

### IDENTIFY

Indoors, look at floors, walls, and all around the rooms of the house or building. Notice shapes of furniture, lamps, pictures, light fixtures, windows, doors, fireplaces, and appliances. Have the children name as many shapes as they can. Write down all the different shapes, you see, and talk about things that use combinations of shapes, such as chairs that may have squares seats and oval tops. Look for designs made by using shapes in floors or wall covering fabrics. Notice patterns made by repeating shapes.

Outdoors, notice the shapes in garages, houses, windows, doors, roofs, mailboxes, traffic signs, cars, trucks, trees, bushes, patios, outdoor furniture, bird feeders, and trash cans. Many buildings, especially apartment buildings, use many shapes for architectural design. Talk about the designs made by using different shapes.

### COMPARE

Match the shapes you see to your shape puppets and talk about the size differences. Triangles, for instance, come in all kinds of variations and different sizes, but if they have three points (or angles) they are all triangles. Point out that all shapes can vary in size without changing their basic characteristics. Notice size differences such as big squares or circles and small ones.

Measure some shapes to help you decide whether something is a square or a rectangle. Measure a diamond shape to see if its sides are all the same size as well. Write down the things you find out.

### COUNT

Each time you see a shape, put a counter in the corresponding small paper bag you brought along. Periodically, count how many counters are in each bag, but keep the counters in the bags and tabulate the results after the walk. Are there more of some shapes than others?

## COLLECT

Collect small stones and other small items you find to use in shape sorting activities. Take along a garbage bag and gloves to use to collect trash you find as you walk along. Define the shape of the items you pick up and talk about the most common shapes.

## After the Walk: Follow-up Activities

### TALK ABOUT IT

Talk about the walk; what generalizations can you make about shapes? Write down the children's observations. You might find such things as: rectangles are the most common shapes; roofs have a triangle shape; things that are round can roll; building materials (bricks, blocks) are usually rectangles; pictures are usually rectangles; floor tiles or patio tiles are usually square; and garbage cans are usually round (actually cylinders). Your generalizations will depend on the things you see and may change from indoors to outdoors.

Count the counters in each of the bags to see how many of each shape you saw. Do the numbers support your generalizations? If you wish, make a graph to show how many of each shape you saw.

If you have older children, talk about the differences in the two-dimensional shapes you saw (such as traffic signs) and the three-dimensional ones (such as evergreen trees or trash cans). Give names to the three-dimensional shapes.

### SHAPE SORTING

Cut out large basic shape patterns from construction paper and put them on a table. Sort the rocks and other small objects to match the shape patterns. Collect all the rocks that are not a regular shape and put them in a separate container. Trace around some of those irregular stones to see what their shapes look like. Are they close to any of the basic ones you see? Some of the books listed in the Resources section include many different shapes; see if you can find any that match the stone shapes. Make shape patterns for those shapes and label them by name (for example, octagon, pentagon, hexagon, parallelogram, heart, and diamond).

Set up shoe box shape sorters. Mount a different-shaped pattern on each shoe box. Encourage the children to find things in the room to sort into the corresponding shape boxes (beads, blocks, buttons, and construction toys all have different shapes).

Look for magazine pictures to add to your shape sorting activities. Have children cut or tear out pictures of things that are different shapes and put them on the matching shape in the table display or shoe boxes. The pictures could also be put into a book or mural about different shapes.

### SHAPE COLLAGES

Read *Color Farm* or *Color Zoo*, both by Lois Ehlert, and talk about all the interesting shape combinations. Provide small construction paper shapes and glue and let the children make picture collages. Did the stories offer any inspiration? Use a large variety of cutout shapes on a flannelboard to create interesting pictures, real or imaginary. Let the children create their own pictures.

### PLAY SHAPE GAMES

Give each child a shape object (for example, a block, bead, or shape puppet) to hold. Make sure they know which shape they have for the game. Call out instructions for each group to follow such as squares all jump, circles march, and rectangles clap hands. Be sure to tell them when to stop each action as well.

Make shapes. Children are used to getting into circles for games. Just for fun try making a square or triangle shape with the group. Can they practice marching in that shape?

Go on shape hunts. Again, give each child a shape object or cue card. Have children find something in the room that is the same shape as the one they are holding. Add small paper bags and turn the game into a scavenger hunt. Have pairs or teams look for five items of that shape; add a few additional cue cards for each team's search.

### I SPY SHAPES

Read *The Shapes Game*, by Paul Rogers, a delightful book that plays I Spy in story form. Make up your own version of I Spy using shapes. Think of an object of a particular shape and tell a use for it. Let the children guess what shape you are thinking of. For example: "I'm thinking of something round that we play with and it bounces (a ball); I'm thinking of something round we sit at the table with and eat our food on (a plate)," and "I'm thinking of something square that we sit on (a chair); and I'm thinking of something square we ate today at snack time (crackers)."

Use objects that are familiar to the children and in your environment so they can look around to find the answers.

### SOCIABLE CRACKER GAME

Make a path game on a file folder or piece of tagboard using the shapes in a box of Sociable brand crackers. Trace each cracker shape to use as a pattern, and then trace all the shapes onto a path running from start to finish on the game board. Start can be a child's picture, finish can be the snack table or a smiley face. Make four playing cards approximately 2 inches square of each of the six shapes (an 8-by-12-inch folder of tagboard should produce the 24 playing cards).

Children play the game by drawing cards and moving their player ahead to that shape. Children take turns and continue until they reach the finish. This can also be played as a snack time game. Children draw a card, move their player to that shape, and take that shape cracker to eat.

You can make similar path games using six basic shapes. Trace shapes in an alternating pattern on the game board. Cut the six shape patterns out of colored tape or solid-colored contact paper to fit on a die. Mount one shape on each side of the die. Children throw the die and move their player to that shape.

### ODDS AND ENDS WITH SHAPES

Label all the shapes around the room and put signs on them. Notice the shapes in children's buildings or the things they make with construction toys, and call attention to them. Notice any patterns of shapes they make with beads or parquetry blocks.

Talk about shapes the children make in painting or in working with clay, and label them. Start a display of clay shapes and encourage the addition of complex shape creations.

Read some of the books in the Resources section or add them to your library corner. Several use building with shapes as a theme. Rebecca Emberley's book *Taking a Walk,* shows many shapes seen in buildings and on walks, and gives the words for objects in both English and Spanish. It is a fun book to take along for language learning ideas.

## Related Concept Ideas to Explore

color walk ● number concepts walk (counting, size) ● word concepts walk (place words, adverbs, adjectives) ● imagination or fantasy walk (make up stories about things seen) ● up-in-the-air walk ● memory or guessing walks (Is it still here?) ● what-makes-it-work walk

## Songs, Poems, and Finger Plays

### SQUARE

Square Puppet is my name (hold up square puppet)
My four sides are all the same. (point to each side)
Count one side, (point to one side)
Then count some more (point to each side in turn)
Count to two, then three, then four.
Turn me around, I don't care (rotate puppet)
I'm always the same 'cuz
I'm a square.

**RECTANGLE**

Rectangle Puppet is my name (hold up rectangle puppet)
My four sides are not the same. (point to sides)
Two are short and two are long. (point to each set of sides)
Now count my sides—come along
1, 2, 3, 4. (point to each side as you count)

**ANGLES**

Some shapes have angles (point to the angles in a shape)
But others do not (hold up a circle)
If there aren't any angles
A circle is what you've got.

Angles have points (point to the corners of the shapes)
As you can see
And they tell what the shape
Is going to be.

Triangles have three (hold up a triangle)
Other shapes have four (hold up square and rectangle)
But there are some shapes
That have a lot more! (hold up pictures or blocks that are
octagons or pentagons and point to the angles)

You can explain to the children that the name of the shape comes from the
number of angles or points, which determines the number of sides; for
example, octagon (8) and pentagon (5).

**TRIANGLE**

Triangle Puppet is the name for me (hold up triangle puppet)
Count my sides
There's 1, 2, 3. (point to each side as you count)

**CIRCLE**

I'm Circle Puppet (hold up circle puppet)
Watch me turn (rotate puppet)
Round and round
And you will learn (make circle around puppet)
I'm not straight,
And I don't bend,
My outside edges never end.

**THE SHAPE OF THINGS**

Look outside and what do I see?
All kinds of shapes looking at me.
Signs and windows look quite square,
Doors are rectangles everywhere.
Bushes and tires look quite round,
Evergreen trees look like triangles sitting on the ground.
What fun it is to look around
And see how many shapes I've found.

**CHANGING SHAPES**

A square can do a funny trick (hold up a square puppet)
And change before your eyes.
Just turn it so a point's on top, (rotate so points are at an angle)
And you will realize,
It's turned into a diamond shape
How's that for a surprise?

## Resources

Allington, Richard L. (1979) *Shapes.* Milwaukee, WI: Raintree Books.

Carle, Eric. (1974) *My Very First Book of Shapes.* New York: HarperCollins.

Dodds, Dayle Ann. (1994) *The Shape of Things.* Cambridge, MA: Candlewick Press.

Ehlert, Lois. (1990) *Color Farm.* New York: Lippincott.
———. (1989) *Color Zoo.* New York: Lippincott.

Emberley, Rebecca. (1990) *Taking a Walk—A Book in Two Languages.* Boston: Little Brown.

Falwell, Cathryn. (1992) *Shape Space.* New York: Clarion Books.

Feldman, Judy. (1991) *Shapes in Nature.* Chicago: Childrens Press.

Fisher, Leonard Everett. (1987) *Look Around: A Book about Shapes.* New York: Viking Kestrel.

Goldblatt, Eli. (1990) *Leo Loves Round.* Tucson, AZ: Harbinger House.

Goor, Ron and Nancy. (1983) *Signs.* New York: Crowell.

Hill, Eric. (1986) *Spot Looks at Shapes*. New York: Putnam.

Hoban, Tana. (1974) *Circles, Triangles, and Squares*. New York: Macmillan.
——. (1983) *I Read Signs*. New York: Greenwillow.
——. (1978) *Is it Red, Is it Yellow, Is it Blue?* New York: Greenwillow.
——. (1989) *Shapes and Things*. New York: Greenwillow.
——. (1989) *Shapes, Shapes, Shapes*. New York: Greenwillow.

Hughes, Shirley. (1986) *All Shapes and Sizes*. New York: Lothrop.

Kightley, Rosalinda. (1986) *Shapes*. Boston: Little Brown.

MacKinnon, Debbie. (1992) *What Shape?* New York: Dial Books.

Margolin, Harriet. (1985) *Busy Bear's Room*. New York: Grosset & Dunlap.

Pluckrose, Henry. (1986) *Think About Shape*. New York: Franklin Watts.

Pragoff, Fiona. (1989) *Shapes*. New York: Doubleday.

Reiss, John. (1987) *Shapes*. New York: Aladdin Books.

Rogers, Paul. (1990) *The Shapes Game*. New York: Henry Holt.

Turner, Gwenda. (1991) *Shapes*. New York: Viking.

# Tree Walk· · · · · · · · · · · · · · · · · · · ·

With so much emphasis today on preserving the ecology, children hear many complicated ideas about trees that they may not understand. The best way for children to learn about trees and why they are important is to observe and study the ones in their own yard or neighborhood. A tree walk can help children learn

- about seasonal changes and the yearly cycle and growth of trees;

- the names of different types of trees, and some specific trees;

- about the various parts of trees, their characteristics, and differences among trees;

- what trees provide for people and animals;

- the many uses people make of tree products; and

- appreciation for the beauty of trees.

You and your group can observe trees throughout the year; think about taking this walk on a regular basis to observe changes. The children can learn about trees a little at a time, and you can extend the discussions and activities over a period of time. Children's interest in nature is ongoing, and trees easily lend themselves to review and revisiting. Add books about trees and nature to library areas on a regular basis, and look at them as these revisits take place, adding new perspective or purpose each time.

## Before the Walk

### WORDS TO LEARN AND USE
leaf ● trunk ● shade ● bark ● branch ● crown ● twig ● bud ● acorn ●
seeds ● nuts ● fruit ● berries ● roots ● deciduous ● coniferous ●
evergreen ● birch ● maple ● oak ● pine ● elm ● poplar ● spruce ●
needles ● pinecones ● wood ● broadleaf ● needle leaf ● log ● timber ●
lumberjack ● forest ● orchard ● sapling

### DISPLAY
Put leaves, nuts, acorns, and berries on a low table along with a magnifying glass and some books about trees. Ask the children questions about some of the items. Let the children look at pictures of trees in the books.

To stimulate discussion, use pictures from books or magazines of different kinds of trees at different seasons of the year. Ask: Do trees look like this where we live? Why or why not? Shall we go look?

### THINGS TO BRING

paper and a pen or pencil to record measurements and other observations ● a book about trees ● tape ● small plastic or paper bags children can use to collect things in ● a larger bag for extra items and supplies ● ruler or measuring tape ● crayons and paper ● small paper plates and Hold-It glue for collages or contact strips for bracelet collages ● small bag for trash ● a camera

## On the Walk

### IDENTIFY

Take a picture book with good, clear pictures of trees, leaves, and bark to help identify the trees you see. The *T* volume of an encyclopedia, a field guide to trees, or catalogs from local nurseries are sources for pictures.

Keep a list of the common trees you are able to identify. If you wish, collect leaves or bark samples from the unknown trees so you and the children can look them up later.

To help you remember the leaves and bark you have identified, tape a leaf next to the name on your list.

### COLLECT

Have the children bring bags to collect nuts, seeds, pinecones, and leaves to use for later projects—either for identification activities or art projects. (You might want to collect and label some master samples so you'll be able to help sort out and identify items in the children's collections later on.)

Another way of collecting items is to create a collage as you go. Give each child a small amount of a gummy glue (such as Hold-It) and a small paper plate. As they collect objects, they can stick the items to the plate. After the walk, let everyone show their collage and see if you can put names on the items before they go home.

For a bracelet variation of this collage: Cut 2-inch-wide strips of clear contact paper to make a bracelet for each child. Use a small piece of self-sticking Velcro so the children can easily remove and put on the bracelet or make the bracelet large enough to slip off. Wrap the contact paper around the child's wrist with the sticky side out and have children stick small items to their bracelet. This project is best done in warm weather, when sweaters and jackets are not necessary and will not stick to the bracelet. You can spray the bracelets with glitter or clear acrylic finish for decoration or they can be worn home as is.

### OBSERVE

Notice the shade around trees. Decide which trees would be good for climbing and which ones would be good for sitting under.

Look for unusual things about the trees: split trunks or branches, strange formations, or trees that bend in one direction. Wonder what caused these things.

Look for signs of animal life around trees. Are there birds, birds' nests, squirrels, or insects using the trees?

Watch quietly for any signs of life in the trees. Listen for sounds of birds singing or pecking at trees, or squirrels running up and down trees.

**SPECULATE**

Look for things that are edible from trees and things that are nonedible (or even poisonous). What things do animals or birds eat from trees?

Notice the trunks of large trees and the heavy root structure going into the ground. Guess how far the roots of the tree may go and make a circle around the tree to show how far the roots may extend. Can you see any roots for the small trees? The root systems go 15 feet or more under the ground and spread out to take up as much room under the ground as the branches and leaves (the crown of the tree) take up above the ground. Measure out 15 feet from the tree and show the children how far that is. Talk about what the roots do for the tree. Do the roots of trees ever cause problems? What kinds? Make some guesses about roots of big and little trees. Why are some very small trees supported by stakes and ropes?

## COMPARE

Stop and carefully examine several different trees. Look at size, shape, color, and texture. Notice the trunk, bark, and leaf structure and name those parts of the tree. Talk about the differences in the trees. Call the children's attention to the difference between evergreen trees and deciduous trees in terms of structure, texture, and color. Pick a favorite example of each tree kind. Plan to visit the trees frequently during the year to watch what happens to them (do they bear fruit, shed leaves, and grow?).

Take a tape measure and measure around the trunks. Children can also measure with their arms; some very large trees will need two or more children to reach around them.

## SENSE

Examine the trees in multi-sensory ways. Huddle up close to the trunk of the tree and look up at the sky through the branches. Feel the textures of the trees.

Close your eyes and listen to the trees. Can you hear them? What can you tell about them? Look at trees from the distance as well, to take in the whole effect.

Take along some crayons and paper and make rubbings of the bark or have the children make simple drawings of the trees.

## TALK ABOUT IT

Encourage the children to describe how the trees look to them and the things about the trees that especially interest them. Which trees look the prettiest to them? As the year goes along, continue that discussion and decide when trees look the prettiest or the most interesting. Talk about what happens to the trees at each season.

Make generalizations about some of the trees you have seen related to size, branch structure, and so on. Some examples might be: Evergreen trees have branches that start right at the ground while other trees branch high up off the ground. New trees have very small trunks; older trees have thick trunks.

# After the Walk: Follow-up Activities

## TALK ABOUT IT

Talk about the walk and write a story about what the children saw on the walk.

Let the children dramatize the growth of a tree from a seedling in the ground to a tall tree. Talk about what trees need to grow. Start a book about some trees, making entries each month or so as you observe these trees. Take pictures of the trees to put in the book.

## SPONGE PAINTING

Have children make sponge painting pictures of trees as many of them look in the fall. Trace around the child's arm and hand to form the trunk and branches. Color the branches with brown crayon or chalk.

Set out small containers of yellow, red, orange, and green paint. Cut sponges into small pieces and use clothespins as handles. Have children dip the sponges into the paint and press lightly on the paper around the trunks and branches to produce the effect of colorful leaves.

## SEASONAL MURAL

Make seasonal murals using trees and the appropriate creatures found in trees each season.

Show how the trees and their foliage look during each season. Add birds' nests and bees to the trees in spring, bugs in summer, and squirrels in the fall. Include the flowers and fruits some trees have in various seasons. Be sure to include evergreen trees in each season. Expand the murals to include diverse sections of the country where trees may look different, such as palm trees in the south and evergreen trees in the north or mountain areas.

## TREES AND LEAVES MATCHING CHART

Make a large mural, bulletin board, or chart on poster board to match trees with their leaves and fruits, nuts, and seeds. Use colorful yarn to connect the trees with the appropriate leaves. You can use items collected on walks or cut out pictures of trees and leaves from magazines and books.

Examples for mural or chart include (use tree types found in your neighborhood):

Oak tree: oak leaves, acorns
Pine tree: pine needles, pinecones
Fruit tree: leaves and blossoms, fruit
Cottonwood tree: leaves, cotton fluff

## READ AND TALK ABOUT IT

Read books, such as Doug Florian's *Nature Walk* and Gail Gibbons' *Nature's Green Umbrella,* and talk about different kinds of forests. Would the children like to go hiking or camping in a forest? Would it be scary? Take an imaginary walk in the woods (like going on a bear hunt), using the ideas and experiences in these books.

## TREE PRODUCTS

Discuss tree products such as timber, paper, chopsticks, and toothpicks. Discover items in the room that are tree products. Look up *trees* in an encyclopedia and look at pictures of trees and their products. Set up a display area featuring trees and their products. Collect different samples of bark, wood scraps, and small items made from wood.

## TORN PAPER TREES

Provide cut-paper trunks and branches to make tree pictures. Let the children tear paper scraps for leaves, and glue them onto a large sheet of paper. If you wish, add roots using scraps of paper and string.

## FOR THE BIRDS

Make a bird-nesting ball to hang on a tree in the spring, and a bird feeder in the fall.

For the nesting ball, put bits and pieces of yarn, ribbon, or string in a piece of netting cut from an onion bag. Tie and hang near a tree. Watch the birds pick at the contents.

For a bird feeder, roll a large pinecone in peanut butter and dip it in birdseed. Hang on a tree where you and the children can watch the birds eat.

## LEAF RUBBINGS

Make leaf rubbings by placing a piece of paper over a leaf. Rub the paper with the side of a crayon. Do the same for pieces of bark, clusters of evergreen needles, pinecones, and seed pods. Display the rubbings on a bulletin board about trees.

## COLLAGES

Make a large group collage of twigs, nuts, leaves, and other treasures found on the walk.

## Related Trip Ideas to Explore

tree nursery ● forest preserve ● observe workers trimming trees or cutting them down ● take a nature walk in a wooded area

# Songs, Poems, and Finger Plays

## OH, MAPLE TREE

*(to the tune of "Oh, Christmas Tree")*

Oh, maple tree, oh, maple tree,
How pretty are your branches.
Your pointed leaves are colored bright;
All red and gold in the sunlight.
Oh, maple tree, oh, maple tree,
How pretty are your branches.

Oh, evergreen tree, oh, evergreen tree.
How lovely are your branches.
Your many needles, soft and fine;
Your special cones and scent of pine.
Oh, evergreen tree, oh, evergreen tree,
How lovely are your branches.

## FALL

The leaves are green, the nuts are brown,
They hang so high, they'll never come down.
But leave them alone 'til the bright fall weather,
And then they will all come down together.

## CHANGING TREES

Have you ever noticed that the trees
Can tell us about the seasons?
I don't know exactly why
But I'm sure they have their reasons.

In fall their leaves change color
And then fall off the tree.
But in spring new buds start growing
And soon green leaves we'll see.

Some trees grow beautiful blossoms
That in summer turn to fruit.
Trees produce different seeds
And some of them look cute.

## FALL

Fall has come again,
And on each flower and weed—
Where little blossoms used to grow—
I found a pod of seed.

### The Big Tree

I see a tree; (point to eye and then
  point outward)
It looks mighty big to me. (make a large
  overhead circular motion with arms)
It's branches are so very high, (extend
  two arms upward overhead)
It almost seems to touch the sky. (jump
  as if to touch ceiling)

## Resources

Aronsky, Jim. (1991) *Crinkleroot's Guide to Knowing about Trees.* New York: Bradbury Press.

Behn, Harry. (1992) *Trees.* New York: Henry Holt.

Brandt, Keith. (1982) *Discovering Trees.* Mahwah, NJ: Troll Associates.

Bulla, Clyde R. (1960) *A Tree Is a Plant.* New York: Crowell.

Cherry, Lynn. (1990) *The Great Kapok Tree.* San Diego: Harcourt Brace.

Ehlert, Lois. (1991) *Red Leaf Yellow Leaf.* San Diego: Harcourt Brace.

Ernst, Kathryn. (1976) *Mr. Tamarin's Trees.* New York: Crown.

Florian, Doug. (1986) *Discovering Trees.* New York: Charles Scribner's Sons.
———. (1989) *Nature Walk.* New York: Greenwillow.

Gackenbach, Dick. (1992) *Mighty Tree.* San Diego: Harcourt Brace.

Gallimard, Jeunesse, and Pascale de Bourgoing. (1992) *The Tree.* New York: Scholastic.

Gibbons, Gail. (1994) *Nature's Green Umbrella.* New York: William Morrow.

Ingoglia, Gina. (1989) *Look Inside a Tree.* New York: Grosset & Dunlop.

Lionni, Leo. (1992) *A Busy Year.* New York: Knopf.

Lyon, George Ella. (1989) *Trees.* New York: Dorling Kindersley.

Maestro, Betsy. (1994) *Why Do Leaves Change Color?* New York: HarperCollins.

Markle, Sandra. (1993) *Outside and Inside Trees.* New York: Bradbury Press.

Nikly, Michelle. (1982) *The Emperor's Plum Tree.* New York: Greenwillow.

Podendorf, Illa. (1982) *Trees* (A New True Book). Chicago: Childrens Press.

Ryder, Joanne. (1991) *Hello, Tree.* New York: Lodestar Books.

Silverstein, Shel. (1964) *The Giving Tree.* New York: Harper & Row.

Tresselt, Alvin. (1992) *The Gift of the Tree.* New York: Lothrop.

### Another Good Resource

Gamlin, Linda. (1993) *Trees.* New York: Dorling Kindersley.

# Truck Walk · · · · · · · · · · · · · · · · ·

Trucks and moving vehicles hold endless fascination for children—the huge number of books and materials on this subject and the large truck and vehicle sections of toy stores confirm this notion. Truck walks capitalize on that interest and help children to become observant learners. On truck walks, you can encourage children to

- observe different kinds of trucks and think about the work they do;
- notice characteristics of trucks and learn about their various parts;
- observe how trucks are driven and learn about safety around trucks; and
- compare buses, cars, and trucks and think about the parts they play in the transportation system.

When looking for trucks to observe, keep the children's safety foremost in your mind. If you are watching for trucks near a busy street, be sure all children are far removed from the street and intersections. When looking at parked trucks, be sure the children stand at a safe distance from the street and a safe distance from any possible moving vehicle, such as one deciding to park or pull out of a parking spot. The safest spots for truck watching are on your own grounds. Watch for trucks driving by or visit one parked on your street or in a nearby parking area. Try to time your looking to take advantage of trucks visiting your more immediate area rather than venturing into busy places that may present safety problems.

## Before the Walk

### WORDS TO LEARN AND USE

tow truck ● dump truck ● cement mixer ● steam shovel ● crane ● derrick ● car carrier ● panel truck ● semitrailer ● refrigerator truck ● caterpillar truck ● tank truck ● livestock truck ● sanitation truck ● pickup truck ● moving van ● fire truck ● delivery truck ● wheels ● chassis ● gasoline ● diesel oil ● engine ● motor ● body ● cab ● truck driver ● bookmobile ● bus

### TALK ABOUT IT

Display picture books about trucks along with model or toy trucks. Ask the children how cars and trucks are different. Ask the children if there are different kinds of trucks. What makes them different? Read the two books titled *Trucks* (one is by Gail Gibbons; the other is by Stephen Oliver) to point out many features about trucks. Suggest going for a walk to see if there are any trucks in the neighborhood and to see what kinds they are.

### LIST

Let the children tell you all they know about trucks. Make a list of the things they mention.

### THINGS TO BRING

paper and a pen or pencil to record observations ● picture books about trucks and their parts ● plastic or paper bag for collecting things ● a camera

## On the Walk

### IDENTIFY

Find a parked truck and examine it, noticing the way the truck is put together. Look at the picture book you brought. Identify the parts and compare the pictures to the real thing.

Make a list of all the different trucks or larger vehicles you see. Point out the names of as many types of trucks as you can. Make notes of the ones with which the children are most familiar and the ones about which they want to learn more.

## COMPARE

Observe the differences between trucks that are in one piece (such as smaller mail trucks, delivery vans, and pickups) as opposed to those that have a cab and trailer.

Count the number of wheels on different trucks. Are the tires the same size on all types of trucks?

Compare cars and trucks. In what ways are they alike and how are they different? Look for specific parts that each might have. Notice their similarities and differences, such as in gas tanks, mirrors, windows, seats, and tires.

Listen to the sounds trucks make as they go by. Compare the sounds of trucks and cars. What can you tell from the sounds?

## OBSERVE

Notice how different trucks are driven. Where does the driver sit? Observe any differences about where the driver sits in a car compared to other vehicles (such as buses, large trucks, vans).

If possible, have a driver show the children the inside parts of a truck's driving area. Ask the driver about the vehicle and how it is driven; inquire about special features of that truck.

## SPECULATE

Wonder what type of loads the trucks are carrying. What clues do you have about what work the truck does? How is the truck suited to the work it does? What parts does it need for its job? Could a mail truck tow a car?

How might it feel to drive a truck? What are some problems the driver could have in your neighborhood?

Can trucks go backward? How can drivers see? What happens with trucks that have trailers when they need to go backward? Do you hear a ringing noise like a bell made by some trucks when they begin to go in reverse (a warning to those around that the truck is backing up)?

Can big trucks get gas nearby?

Think about why some trucks have more wheels than others.

Wonder if just anyone can drive a truck. Would you need to know special things? What about the driver's license?

## GENERALIZE

What general statements about trucks can you make on your return walk? Some samples might be:

> Trailer trucks have many more wheels.
> Trucks that carry heavy loads need more wheels.
> Trucks have very large gas tanks.
> Big trucks are hard to back up and need a lot of room to turn.
> Drivers need to be way up high to see the road well and judge distances.
> Big trucks and buses have big steering wheels.

Questions you ask might help the children think of these and other statements. Try to get the children to tell some general things they have noticed about trucks.

## After the Walk: Follow-up Activities

### TALK ABOUT IT

Talk about the walk and write down the children's observations.

Discuss the ways people use trucks, and set up a transportation bulletin board showing trucks, the products they carry, and the places they take those products (for example, a car carrier taking cars to a car dealership). With older children, discuss the role of trucks as part of the transportation system. Some sample questions might be: How do people transport big items (such as furniture and refrigerators) from stores to home, or from their home to a new house when they move? How does gasoline get into the tanks and pumps at the service station? How do farmers get the things they grow to market? What other things do trucks carry from factory to store?

Invite a truck driver to visit your group, preferably with a truck. One source would be service or delivery trucks in your area. If possible let children, a few at a time, climb up into the truck's cab section. Write a story about the visit and the truck. Be sure to include what it feels like to be way up in the cab. Talk about the work the truck driver does. Ask the child how a tire gets changed.

### DRAMATIC PLAY

Encourage children to use toy trucks to carry blocks or other things. Build roads for different types of trucks. Talk about the work trucks do and encourage the children to make up activities using large vehicles in their play, such as helping to move furniture to the doll house.

Use trucks, tractors, tow trucks, and graders in the sandbox to make roads and use in play. Think of other ways to use large vehicles in outdoor dramatic play such as for deliveries, construction projects, and road repairs.

View a video about trucks and larger vehicles, such as *Moving Machines* (many are available at the library), and talk about the way trucks worked in the videos. What additional dramatic play ideas can you get from the videos?

## MURAL

Have the children find and cut out pictures of trucks in magazines. Paste the pictures on a long sheet of paper for a truck mural. Discuss what each truck does.

## TRUCK LOTTO

Create homemade games about trucks. Make a lotto game using pictures of real or toy trucks from catalogs or magazines, or using truck stickers available in school supply or gift shops. Make three or four master boards with four to six pictures of trucks on each. Mount a duplicate picture of each truck on a small card to use to match those on the master board. A Tonka Toy Company catalog, day care center supply catalog, or large equipment brochures are sources for truck pictures. Remember, you need two identical pictures of each truck.

## OUR BIG BOOK OF TRUCKS

Make a book of trucks using magazine pictures. Be sure to include pictures of different parts of trucks, and write in the names of those various parts. Include other information children tell you about each truck. Notice how much they have learned. Use books in the Resources section for additional information.

## TRANSPORTATION MATCH-UP

Make a transportation matching game. Children match the pictures of products or items to be transported to the picture of the type of truck that would be used.

Select samples from magazines or catalogs. Some suggestions for the game include:

> Boats: truck with boat trailer
> Cars: car carrier
> Fruits, vegetables: pickup truck
> Milk: refrigerated tanker
> Cement: cement mixer
> Parcels: UPS truck
> Furniture: moving van

## WOODWORKING

Let the children make trucks out of scrap wood to use in play. Keep markers nearby so the children can add windows, fenders, and other accessories to their vehicles.

## CUT PAPER TRUCKS

Cut different shapes out of construction paper. Let the children paste them together to make a variety of trucks. Attach circles for wheels using brass fasteners.

### TRUCK REPAIR SHOP
Set up a truck repair shop or a truck service station for all the trucks you have. In warm weather, set up an outdoor truck wash for your plastic trucks.

### CARDBOARD BOX TRUCKS
Make a variety of trucks out of cardboard boxes. Children can pretend to drive them and deliver whatever comes in that truck.

## Related Trip Ideas to Explore

truck wash ● truck dealership ● garage or storage area (such as a city service vehicle storage area) ● site where trucks load or unload

## Songs, Poems, and Finger Plays

### DROVE A TRUCK
*(to the tune of "Mary Wore a Red Dress")*
(Use all the children's names and several different trucks; let the children choose the type of truck they wish to drive)

_____ drove a dump truck, dump truck, dump truck,
_____ drove a dump truck, all day long.
_____ drove a tow truck, tow truck, tow truck,
_____ drove a tow truck, all day long.

### FIVE BIG TRUCKS
Five big trucks outside our door, (hold up five fingers)
The dump truck drove away,
Then there were four. (hold up four fingers)

Four big trucks that I can see,
The garbage truck drove away,
Then there were three. (hold up three fingers)

Three big trucks with work to do,
The moving van drove on,
Then there were two. (hold up two fingers)

Two big trucks shining in the sun,
The milk truck pulled away,
And then there was one. (hold up one finger)

One mail truck whose work was all done,
Pulled away and then there were none. (no fingers)

(You could also have five children hold pictures of trucks
named in the verse; as each truck drives away, that child sits down.)

### TRUCKS WORK

The moving van carries a great big load;
Look at all the furniture it can hold.
The car carrier hurries down the road;
Taking cars to a dealer to be sold.
Trucks keep working all day long;
Carrying loads to the places they belong.

### OLD MACDONALD HAD A TRUCK

*(to the tune of "Old MacDonald Had a Farm")*

Old MacDonald had a truck, E-I-E-I-O;
And on his truck he had a horn, E-I-E-I-O.
With a beep-beep here and a beep-beep there,
Here a beep, there a beep, everywhere a beep-beep,
Old MacDonald drove his truck, E-I-E-I-O.

Additional verses:
Wheels, with a whrr-whrr
Windshield wipers, with a swish-swish
Brakes, with a screech-screech
Radio, with a rock 'n roll

# Resources

Barton, Byron. (1986) *Trucks.* New York: Crowell.

Borden, Louise. (1990) *The Neighborhood Trucker.* New York: Scholastic.

Broekel, Ray. (1983) *Trucks* (A New True Book). Chicago: Childrens Press.

Burton, Virginia. (1943) *Katy and the Big Snow.* New York: Houghton Mifflin.

Coutler, Hope Norman. (1993) *Uncle Chuck's Truck.* New York: Macmillan.

Crews, Donald. (1980) *Truck.* New York: Greenwillow.

Day, Alexandra. (1994) *Frank and Ernest on the Road.* New York: Scholastic.

Gibbons, Gail. (1985) *Trucks.* New York: Crowell.

Herman, Gail. (1990) *Make Way for Trucks.* New York: Random House.

Mathieu, Joseph. (1974) *Big Joe's Trailer Truck.* New York: Random House.

McNaught, Harry. (1978) *The Truck Book.* New York: Random House (also available in Spanish).
———.(1976) *Trucks.* New York: Random House.

Oliver, Stephen. (1991) *Trucks* (Eye Openers). New York: Aladdin.

Petrie, Catherine. (1982) *Joshua James Likes Trucks.* Chicago: Childrens Press (also available in Spanish).

Robbins, Ken. (1993) *Power Machines.* New York: Henry Holt.

Royston, Angela. (1994) *Big Machines.* Boston: Little Brown.
———. (1991) *Diggers and Dump Trucks* (Eye Openers). New York: Aladdin.

Thompson, Graham. (1986) *Cars and Trucks.* Milwaukee, WI: Gareth Stevens.

## OTHER GOOD RESOURCES

Jeffries, David. (1991) *Giants of the Road.* New York: Franklin Watts.

Lines, Cliff. (1984) *Looking at Trucks.* New York: Bookwright Press.

*Awesome Big Rigs* (video). (1994) Greg James Productions.

*Big Rigs: Close Up and Very Personal* (video). (1993) Stage Fright Productions.

*Moving Machines* (video). (1989) Bo Peep Productions.

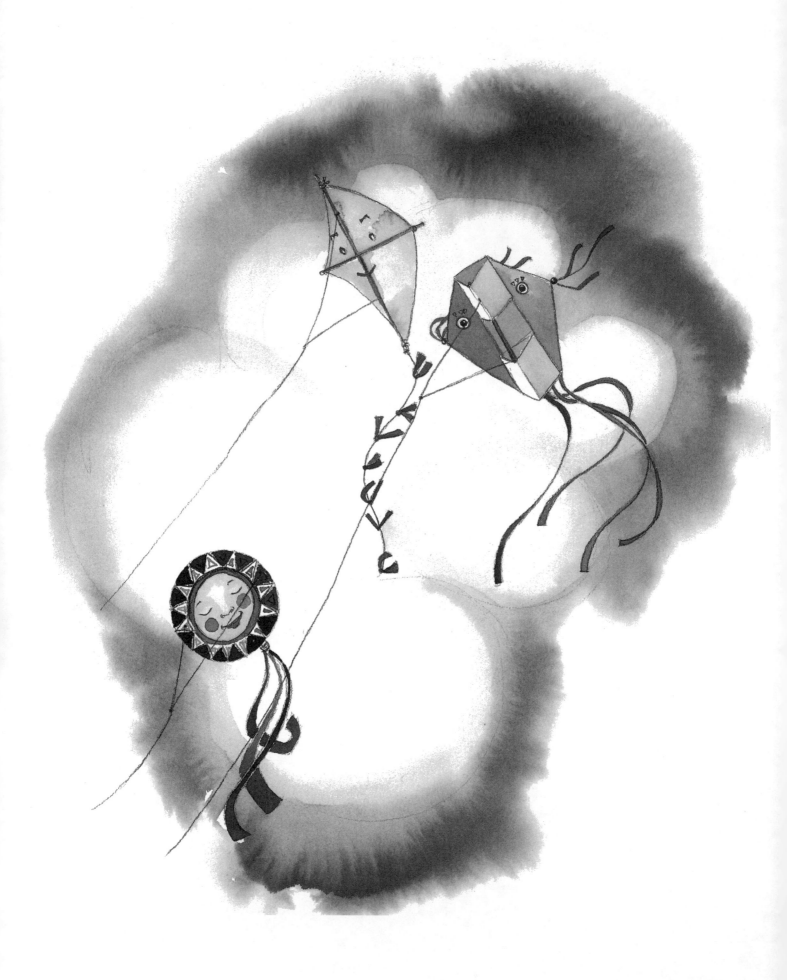

# Windy Day Walk··········

Children have felt the wind blow in their face—but otherwise have little information about the wind. A windy day walk offers many new areas of exploration. Taking a walk on a windy day can be fun, provided it is not too cold and blustery. Viewing the videotape *Winnie the Pooh and the Blustery Day* is a good way to introduce some of the ideas explored in this walk. A windy day walk gives children an opportunity to

- learn about the wind and how we measure it, even when we can't see it;
- notice how the wind transports things;
- see the effect of wind on different objects, from tree to puddles;
- feel the wind in different directions and places; and
- experiment and play with different objects to see what the wind does to the objects.

This walk makes use of many items such as weathervanes, pinwheels, and kites. Use the items on separate walks to see what happens to them in the wind. Try out the pinwheels on one walk and the weathervanes on another. After the first few experiments, repeat them frequently and keep notes to compare findings. You can perform some experiments during an outdoor play time or anytime it happens to be windy.

## Before the Walk

### WORDS TO LEARN AND USE
blowing ● breeze ● gale ● calm ● becalmed ● tornado ● hurricane ● whirl ● whirlwind ● prevailing ● knots ● velocity ● weathervane ● direction anemometer ● wind speed ● wind chill ● meteorologist ● pressure ● high ● low ● gust ● windmill ● blustery

### TALK ABOUT IT
Ask the children if they have watched the weather report on TV. Talk about the things the weather report always mentions, such as storm fronts moving in and high or low pressure areas. Ask the children what

makes the storm fronts move and how the meteorologists can predict some types of weather. Ask the children if they have heard weather reporters talk about the wind, and what is usually said about it. Do the reporters mention the direction the wind comes from and how fast it is moving?

Wonder how weather reporters know that and talk about the instruments they use to measure wind direction and speed. Do they talk about *wind chill*? Explain what that means. Ask the children if they have ever noticed the wind carrying or moving things. Plan to go outside on the next windy day to observe.

### Demonstrate

Show a weathervane to the children (either one you bought or one you made). Blow on or fan the tail section of the vane to make it move, doing so from several different directions.

Explain that the tail section will move until it no longer feels force on either side, and the arrow will point directly to the source of the wind (you or the fan). Explain that this is pointing "into the wind," and is an indication of the direction from which the wind is coming. Wind direction is always reported in terms of where it is coming from. If the arrow on the weathervane points to the west, the wind is coming from the west and going to the east (the direction where the tail rests).

### Things to Bring

paper and a pen or pencil to record measurements and other observations ● weathervane, anemometer, streamers, wind skippers, parachutes, and paper planes (see the After the Walk section for instructions on building these and other wind-sensitive items) ● flags, balloons, pinwheels, and different kinds of kites ● bubble blowing liquid and wands ● Frisbee flying toys ● balls of different weights (such as beach balls, sponge balls, and rubber balls) ● plastic or paper bag for collecting things ● a camera

## On the Walk

### Observe

Look at trees to see if you can notice signs of the wind. Are the leaves and branches moving? Do they seem to move more at the top of the tree or near the bottom? Are some trees moving and some not moving? Notice how the movement of the trees relates to the wind's intensity.

Notice how the wind affects flowers, plants, and shrubs. Does the thickness of the leaves or clusters of branches make any difference? Which plants seem to be most affected by the wind? What does wind do to some of the flower petals?

Does the location of the trees or plants make any difference to how the wind affects them? Do things blow more if they are out in the open or up against a house or wall? Do they blow more on one side of the house (or building) or the other side? Wonder why that might be and if it would always be the same.

What other parts of trees or plants are blown by the wind? Do you see seeds or fluff from plant life being transported by the wind? Look for things you might pick to observe how wind will affect them. Try to find dandelion fluff, silk from milkweed pods, cotton fluff from trees, and other seeds.

Notice how the wind affects other objects in the environment, such as clothes hanging on lines; dust or debris along the walk; water from hoses, sprinklers, or in ponds; smoke from chimneys; flags; hanging planters; lights or wind chimes; and awnings. Look at the clouds and see if they are moving. Talk about what makes the clouds move.

Notice the wind blowing peoples' clothing, hair, or the items they are holding or using.

Let the children hold streamers in the wind and observe what happens. Have them hold the streamers in several different positions and directions to observe the wind's effect.

Take along a wind skipper. Lay it on the ground and observe the effect of ground breezes.

Blow bubbles in the wind and see what happens.

### SENSE

Listen to the sounds related to the wind. Ask the children what sounds they hear: leaves rustling, objects flapping, whistling, or humming. Decide if the wind itself makes the sounds, or if the things the wind is moving are making the sound? Do the sounds get louder, softer, or change in any way? What contributes to those changes?

Talk about how the wind feels blowing on your face, in your hair, and on your clothes. Have the children turn in different directions to see if the wind feels different. Run into and away from the wind to see how that feels. Are there sudden gusts of wind that feel different? Is it colder facing the wind?

Have the children shout into the wind to see what happens to the sounds of their voices. Are they as loud as usual? Can they hear each other over the wind?

Are there any other sensations the wind produces such as special aromas or gritty textures from dust?

Let the children imitate the sounds of the wind and make up short stories about the wind and how it feels.

### EXPERIMENT

Use your weathervane to decide on the direction of the wind. Does the wind's direction stay constant or does it change? Repeat this on several different days, recording the wind's direction.

Use the anemometer (page 150) to see how fast the wind is blowing. Count the number of times the spoons rotate in one minute, and use that as your own measurement of wind speed. Repeat several different times to see if the speed is the same or if it changes. Take some measurements when the wind is gusting so you can talk about what that means.

Have the children try holding different items in the wind, such as flags, balloons, pinwheels, and different kinds of kites. See what happens. On a very windy day, hold up white strips of textured cloth, such as terry cloth, to see if they pick up any dust from the wind. Do they catch any other objects, such as seeds, blowing in the wind?

Have the children experiment with objects of different weight to see how the wind affects them. What happens to things like balloons, feathers, papers, rocks, and blocks when they are left in the wind? Try tossing the homemade parachutes (page 149) around to see what the wind does to them. Try throwing Frisbees and balls of different weight. See if the wind has any effect on where they go or land. Practice flying paper and Styrofoam planes.

## After the Walk: Follow-up Activities

### TALK ABOUT IT

Talk about the things you observed and did on the walk. Let the children tell you the things they remember.

Write down a list of generalizations about the wind and use them for a book or chart.

Talk about how wind can be used for power, and show the children pictures of windmills. Think about how the wind blew the pinwheels and other things the children took outside. Explain that windmills have large blades on them to catch the wind. As wind turns the blades, the force is used to run a generator connected to the windmill. Long ago, wind was used in this way to turn wheels that milled or ground grain into flour, hence the name *windmill*. Windmills are now used mainly to pump water or drive electric generators for power.

Look at pictures showing the effect of wind on land and water. Talk about those effects. Include storm pictures and ones with people in them. Talk about the different types of windstorms such as hurricanes, blizzards, and tornadoes. Let the children share what they may have heard about those kinds of storms. Think about keeping safe during such storms and how weather forecasting helps people plan for safety.

### WIND AND SEASONS CHART

Make a chart showing the wind in different seasons.

Things to include: trees and leaves for fall, kites for spring, sailboats for summer, and blowing snow and bare branches or pine trees for winter.

## DEMONSTRATE

Talk about the relationship of the wind to the weather. Blow up a balloon and release the air in it to let the children feel the wind it makes. Explain that air always moves from a place where pressure is high (inside the balloon) to a place where it is low. The bigger the difference in the high and low pressure areas, the faster the air moves or the harder the wind blows.

Blow up the balloon again and hold a ball of cotton in front of it. This time when you release the air, let it catch the cotton ball and move it. Try this a few times, pointing the air in different directions. Discuss how the wind moves the clouds along and thus transports our weather systems.

## READ AND TALK ABOUT IT

Read *Feel the Wind*, by Arthur Dorros, or other books in the Resources section to find out more information about the wind. Dorros's book also has directions for making a simple weathervane. Several other books include delightful stories about things the wind can do. Add them to your library area while studying the wind so children can look at them and enjoy the great pictures.

## THINGS TO MEASURE THE WIND

**Weathervane, Version 1.** Make a simple weathervane using a straight pin, straw, pencil with an eraser, arrowhead shape cut out of tagboard, a long feather, and clay or gum.

Use the straight pin to attach the straw to the pencil eraser. Move the pin up and down a few times to make the hole in the erasure large enough for the straw to turn freely. Make a slit at one end of the straw. Slide the tagboard arrowhead into that slit. Pace the feather into the straw's opening at the other end, securing it with a small amount of a gummy substance such as the clay or gum. If you wish to hold the vane farther away than arm's length, tape the pencil to a stick.

**Weathervane, Version 2.** You can make a complex weathervane that includes direction indicators with two straws, scissors, clay or sealing wax, arrowhead and tail shapes cut out of tagboard, four toothpicks, a knitting needle, cork, a Styrofoam base, and small pieces of paper.

To make the vane part, cut a 2- to 3-inch section off a straw and seal one end with the clay or sealing wax. Place the remaining section in the clay or wax perpendicular to the first straw. Flatten the two ends of the larger straw section; glue the small tagboard arrowhead to one end and a larger tail section to the other end. Assemble the base of your vane by inserting the knitting needle through the small Styrofoam base and then through the cork. Slip the straw vane onto the knitting needle. Insert the four toothpicks into the cork so they are all at right angles. To the toothpicks, attach small cards with direction indicators (N, S, E, W) written on them. The important thing in making vanes is that the tail section be much larger than the arrow.

**Anemometer.** You can make an anemometer in much the same way as the weathervane, version 2. Set up the cork, knitting needle, and Styrofoam base as with the weathervane. Put gummy material on top of a drinking straw. Place three or four small plastic spoons (one of a different color) into the gummy material. Slip the straw over the knitting needle. Count the rotations per minute by counting the times the colored spoon passes a set mark.

You can measure the wind on several days, and keep a chart of your readings. Give your own weather reports using your own measures.

### THINGS TO FLY

**Airplanes.** Make airplanes from folded paper or from Styrofoam trays.

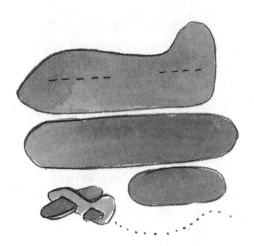

**Streamers.** Make streamers using different weights of paper, from strips of tissue paper to strips of heavy construction paper. Test how the wind affects them. Attach the strips to a dowel or stick. You can also make streamers from strips of corduroy, silk, and other cloths.

**Wind Skipper.** To make a wind skipper, cut a circle from a 10-inch tagboard square or use a 10-inch paper plate. Cut spokes from the center to 2 inches from the edge of the circle. Fold the wedges up and down in an alternate pattern.

**Parachute.** Use a 2-foot square of cloth, a small ball, and some string to make a parachute. Cut the string into four pieces of equal length and attach one piece to each corner of the cloth. Wrap the other ends of the strings around the ball so they enclose it, and tie securely. Toss in the air and let your parachute float down. Do this indoors and outdoors to see what difference the wind makes in the way the parachute moves.

### MUSICAL WIND INSTRUMENTS

Show the children pictures of wind instruments. Think about the sounds the wind makes. Explain that wind instruments are played by blowing into them. List all the instruments that are played by blowing. Explain that the ones made of wood are called woodwinds, while the others are called brass.

Have the children blow and make sounds like the wind. Have them try holding their mouths in different shapes to control the sound and also cup their hands around their mouths to see how that affects the sound.

Make kazoos by covering one end of a toilet paper tube with wax paper and securing it with a rubber band. Poke a hole near the covered end. Children hum into the kazoo's open end to see what happens. Make some with two or three holes to see if that changes the sound. Explain that the curves and number of holes on a wind instrument influence the way the sound will come out, and that the person playing the instrument can control the sound by opening and closing those holes (as the children can on their kazoos).

## WIND CHIMES

Make wind chimes to hang outside. Poke several holes in an aluminum pie tin. Knot several strings and suspend them through the holes in the pie tins. To these strings tie nails, bolts, nuts, bells, large metal paper clips, and anything else that will make noise when it is blown into contact with the other objects. Attach a heavier string to the center of the pie tin that can be used to hang the wind chime.

## SAILBOATS

Make sailboats from plastic dish detergent bottles. Poke a hole on one side of the bottle toward the top and cut a half-moon slit. Fold up the slit. Be sure the cap is in the closed position and glue it to the bottle.

For the sail, cut a triangle or rectangle from a plastic bleach bottle. Poke some holes along the longer edge of the sail and insert a skewer or dowel through those holes. Place the dowel into a small hole in the dish detergent bottle.

Float the sailboats in a large water tub. Make some with rectangular sails and some with triangular sails to see which shape sails better. Fan them or blow on them to make them sail. Use a balloon to create a bigger wind and see what that does to the sailboats. Try these boats outdoors in a pond or wading pool as well, attaching strings so they don't blow too far away.

You can also make sailboats from corks. Cut small paper triangles for sails. Insert a toothpick into one side of the sail and then into the cork. Use in a dishpan filled with water, and have the children blow on them through straws. You may want to have a few races. Number or decorate the sails so you can keep track of them during the race.

## LARGE MOTOR OR RHYTHMIC ACTIVITIES

Run with streamers or scarves to imitate what happens outdoors in the wind.

## WIND AND WEATHER MURAL

Make a mural showing different kinds of clouds and weather. Use cotton for the clouds. Toss some cotton balls in black powdered tempera in a paper bag to get some dark stormy clouds. Have the children draw on the mural or paste cutout magazine pictures onto it showing different types of weather.

## Related Trip Ideas to Explore

kite store ● area where people are flying kites ● area with windmills or wind turbine generators ● place to observe sailing ● wind surfing or other wind-related water activities ● watch hot air balloons or hang gliding

## Songs, Poems, and Finger Plays

### WIND IS BLOWING

*(to the tune of "Frere Jacque")*

Wind is blowing; wind is blowing.
All around, all around.
See the leaves go twirling;
(pretend to be leaves twirling)
See the dust it's swirling.
Blow, wind, blow—blow, wind, blow.

Wind is blowing; wind is blowing.
all around, all around.
See the kites go flying;
(pretend to run and fly kites)
Run and keep on trying.
Blow, wind, blow—blow, wind, blow.

Additional verses:
See the snowflakes twirling;
Into drifts they're swirling.

See the boats go sailing;
With their sails flailing.

### OH, HOW THE WIND DOES BLOW

*(to the tune of "Over the River and Through the Woods")*

Over the ground and through the trees
Oh, how the wind does blow.
It moves the leaves or clouds or snow everywhere it goes.
Over the ground and through the trees,
The wind keeps blowing so.
It bends the branches to and fro and hums so very low—oh.

Over the ground and through the trees
Oh, how the wind does blow.
It blows my hair and scarf around
And every other thing it's found!

### THE WIND

The wind is blowing very hard,
It's blowing things into my yard.
Papers, twigs, and all those leaves;
And many, many types of seeds.
It blows the clouds along the sky;
And flaps the clothes on the lines nearby.
It makes the smoke from chimneys curl;
And all the flags it does unfurl.

### FOUR LITTLE LEAVES

Four little leaves (hold up four fingers on one hand)
On the branch of a tree.
Along came the wind, (make flutter
   motion with other hand)
And then there were three. (hold up
   three fingers)
Three little leaves in the morning dew.
The wind fluttered by, (make fluttering
   motion)
And then there were two.(hold up two
   fingers)
Two little leaves
Waving in the sun.
A sudden gust of wind,
And then there was one. (hold up one
   finger)
One little leaf
Hanging up there,
The wind shook that branch, (make
   wind motions)
And now it is bare.

### WINDY DAY WALK

We went for a walk one windy day, (walk in one direction)
And found before too long
That if we turned the other way (turn around and walk
   in another direction)
The wind helped us along!

### WIND CHILL

As we went walking one winter day—(walk in one direction)
Into the wind so strong—
We turned around before too long
And walked another way! (walk backward)

## Resources

Barrett, Judi. (1977) *The Wind Thief*. New York: Antheneum.

Brewer, Mary. (1975) *Wind Is Air*. Elgin, IL: Child's World.

Broekel, Ray. (1982) *Storms* (A New True Book). Chicago: Childrens Press.

Carlstrom, Nancy White. (1993) *How Does the Wind Walk?* New York: Macmillan.

dePaola, Tomie. (1975) *The Cloud Book*. New York: Holiday House.

Dorros, Arthur. (1989) *Feel the Wind*. New York: Crowell.

Ets, Marie Hall. (1963) *Gilberto and the Wind*. New York: Viking (also available in
   Spanish).

Hutchins, Pat. (1974) *The Wind Blew*. New York: Macmillan.

Keats, Ezra. (1968) *A Letter to Amy*. New York: Harper & Row.

MacDonald, Elizabeth. (1992) *The Very Windy Day*. New York: William Morrow.

Schmid, Eleanore. (1992) *The Air Around Us*. Zurich, Switzerland: North-South Press.

Tresselt, Alvin. (1950) *Follow the Wind*. New York: Lothrop.

Ungerer, Tomi. (1982) *The Hat*. New York: Four Winds Press.

Zolatow, Charlotte. (1975) *When the Wind Stops*. New York: Harper & Row.

## OTHER GOOD RESOURCES

Taylor, Barbara. (1991) *Wind and Weather*. New York: Franklin Watts.

*Which Way Weather?* (video). (1994) Bo Peep Productions.

*Winnie the Pooh and the Blustery Day* (video). (1968) Walt Disney Educational Productions.

# Your Community

# Airport···················

Airports are busy places, making it crucial to carefully plan all logistical details in advance. Many airports offer tours, but may have specific age limits. But even an informal visit offers many interesting vehicles, people, and activities. Airports offer firsthand opportunities to

- observe planes taking off and landing;
- see how planes are guided to and from the gate areas, and how people get on and off the planes;
- watch all the vehicles that service the airplanes;
- observe how baggage is loaded on and off planes and delivered to passengers;
- learn about the people who work in the airport and what they do; and
- look at the many interesting exhibits or displays featured in the airport terminal, lobbies, and concourse areas.

If you plan to take a small group on an informal airport visit, be sure you have plenty of extra adult help. Consider using a distant parking lot that offers shuttle service to the main terminal. Use the shuttle ride to explain all the interesting sights the children may see, as well as to offer the children the experience of riding in the shuttle van. An alternative would be to arrange for another person to drive and park.

Visit the airport on your own before taking the children. Carefully plan which parts of the airport you are going to visit. If your airport has multiple terminals, find out which one is the least busy at the hour you plan to visit, and use this one for your trip. (Airports tend to be less busy in the early afternoon. International terminals are less busy in mid to late morning.) Be sure to check if special arrangements are needed to take the children into the gate area past security.

If your community has smaller auxiliary airports, consider visiting one of those. Remember to take a camera along to take pictures for use after the trip. Bring back two or more brochures from each airline, or other free materials (anything with logos on them) to use for follow-up activities.

## Before the Trip

### WORDS TO LEARN AND USE

terminal ● control tower ● air traffic controllers ● engine ● propeller ●
jet ● hanger ● ramp ● airline ● jetway ● rolling stairs ● conveyer belts ●
beltloader ● ticket counter ● ticket agent ● flight attendants ● pilot ●
runway ●  gate area ● car rental ● taxi ● fuel ● wings ● tail ● loading ● food
service  ● baggage check ● baggage claim ● carousel ● carry-on baggage ●
X-ray machine ● security ● sterile area ● helicopter ● shuttle ● boarding
pass ● flight number ● hoses ● fuel trucks ●  wheelchairs ● wind socks ●
take off ● landing ● arrival ● departure ● landing gear ● concourse ●
ground crew ● board

### TALK ABOUT IT

Ask the children if any of them have ever been on an airplane. Have other
members of their family been on an airplane? Have they gone to the
airport to meet anyone or to see anyone get on an airplane? Let them
tell you anything they know about airports, and write down the things
they mention. Ask if they would like to visit an airport to learn more
about how it works.

### READ AND TALK ABOUT IT

Read *Airports*, by Jason Cooper, *How an Airport Really Works*, by George
Sullivan, or *Inside the Airport*, by Mark Davies, and talk about the jobs
people do at airports. Do the children know anyone who works in an
airport? Plan to visit the airport in your community to observe people
doing the same jobs described in these books.

### THINGS TO BRING

paper and a pen or pencil to record observations ● money for snacks ●
compass to note directions ● plastic or paper bag for collecting things ●
a camera

## On the Trip

### APPROACHING THE AIRPORT

Are planes flying over your vehicle as you approach the airport? Are they
taking off or landing? Notice if the landing wheels are being raised or low-
ered. Do you hear engine noise overhead?

Look out the window for large buildings that look like huge garages.
Do any of these garages have their doors open? Are there planes inside
them? Explain that these are the storage garages, which house airplanes
when they are not in use or being repaired. They are called *hangars*. Do
you see any vehicles driving in or out of these areas? Wonder how the
airplanes get in and out of those hangars. Do you see vehicles pushing
or towing planes?

Notice all the special signs along the highway as you approach the
airport. Explain that these tell the location of different airlines in separate

terminal buildings. Arrows point to the departure and arrival areas as well as long- and short-term parking and rental car drop-off. Explain what all the words mean.

Is there a fancy entrance to the terminal area? Are there lots of flags? Do you recognize any of them? Is there a sign with the name of the airport? Most airports are named for people who were famous in their community or in the country. Some airports have names that are related to their location (either city or region). Explain the name of your airport to the children.

Notice if there is any construction around the airport. Point out any construction vehicles you may see. Talk about how the construction affects traffic around the airport. Are people directing traffic? Are they wearing anything special?

Notice all the bridges and ramps that lead into and out of the area and into the parking areas. Is there a large parking ramp? Why do airports need such large parking areas?

If you are riding on a shuttle van, notice the special places to store luggage. How do the people know where to get off? Notice all the other vans that are driving up to the airport and the signs that tell what company they are from. Tell the children which airline or terminal you are going to and ask the driver to be sure to announce that stop. Do people get on the van when it makes stops? Notice the drop-off area for

passengers and ways of handling baggage. Notice the many suitcases and packages people are carrying. Are there people or carts to help them?

Be sure to notice the control tower as you approach the airport. A control tower is easier to see from a distance. Why is it called a tower? Notice how it is located and constructed so that the controllers inside can see all the approaches to the airport.

### THE LOBBY AND CHECK-IN AREA

Point out airport maps or floor plans and discuss where you will be going.

Notice all the TV monitors along the wall as you enter the building. Explain that those list all the flights that are arriving or departing that day. There may be separate monitors for different airlines. Show the children that the information on the monitors keeps changing as flights arrive and depart. Count how many flights there are at any given time. If you can, figure out how many planes are coming or going every ten minutes (you will be surprised by the large number).

Notice any special exhibits or artwork on display in the terminal building. Some may be related to the famous person for whom the airport is named. Some artwork may convey feelings about flight or special features of your region. Ask the children what the paintings or sculptures make them think of. Along the concourses from the gate areas, the artwork may highlight famous sights in your region. Talk about why there are so many pictures of places in your community.

Notice the counters for flight check-in. Look at the airline names above the counters. How many agents are there for each airline? Are there names of airlines from other countries? Watch the people waiting in line to check their baggage and get their boarding passes. Is there a special line control system so people do not get mixed up? Are any people traveling with dogs? What happens to the dogs? Notice the stickers the ticket agents put on each suitcase before putting it onto a moving conveyer belt. These stickers tell the name of the airport where the suitcase is going. What would happen to a suitcase if its sticker got lost, or a wrong one was put on it? Are the people behind the counters (the ticket agents) wearing uniforms? Notice if the uniforms are the same or different for different airlines. Are people wearing badges? Notice people carrying walkie-talkies or phones.

Show the children the entrances to the gate areas where people get on and off airplanes. Notice that to get to those areas you have to pass through airport security. Large X-ray machines examine all carry-on baggage. Notice how the security staff places the bags on small conveyer belts made of rollers. The bags slide through the machine, which shows all the contents of the bag on a TV screen. People walk through large metal detectors, which make a noise if the person has anything made of metal in his or her pockets. The area beyond security is called a sterile area, meaning that everyone in it has been checked before entering.

## THE GATE AREA

As you enter the gate area, notice the number by each gate and the sign telling the flight using that gate. Listen for the announcements telling people when to board their plane or at which gate a flight is arriving. Do you hear many announcements over the loudspeakers? Are the announcements in other languages?

Notice the desk for additional check-in and the large door leading to the boarding ramp, which is kept locked except when people are deplaning or boarding. When the plane is ready to board, an agent will stand by the door to announce procedures and collect tickets.

Notice that there are many places to buy food, snacks, gifts, magazines, and books in the airport and along the concourse areas. There are also vending machines, phones, and restrooms. Point out the picture symbols that announce all these services. Can you guess why the signs are picture symbols? Can the children read the signs around the airport? Point out any signs in other languages and any different types of letters. Do the children recognize any of the fast-food restaurants?

Find a large window in a gate area and look out at the busy scene below. Notice the vehicles driving around to and from the planes. Discuss what they are loading onto the plane. Notice the food service trucks with the sections that lift up to the main cabin level for easy loading on and off the plane.

How do workers get fuel into the plane? Do you see gasoline trucks with hoses going into the plane? Do you see ground crew checking various parts of the plane?

Notice the many different sizes and shapes of service vehicles. Watch the tractors pulling different things to and from the plane, and forklifts with heavy chains that raise and lower objects to and from the plane. Do you see tractors pulling rows of baggage carts—looking almost like circus trains? Watch as the baggage handlers place each suitcase on a conveyer belt platform that tilts up toward an opening in the belly of the plane. This is called a belt loader and is used to help move the baggage from the carts to and from the terminal.

Do the people working on the ground wear uniforms? Are the crew members (flight attendants and pilots) waiting to board the plane in uniform?

How many planes do you see lined up along the side of the terminal? Do the planes in one section look alike? Point out the logos and coloring that identify planes belonging to the same airline. Do you see any different types of engines on the planes? Point out the difference between a jet engine and a propeller engine if you see them.

Watch the people signaling the planes to and from the gates. How do the workers tell the planes to turn, go forward, or stop? Wonder what might happen if the workers weren't there. What are they holding in their hands? Watch as a plane turns from the runway and taxies into the gate area. Does the plane have flashing lights? Talk about how the pilot knows where to go.

Can you see long runways with holding areas and planes lined up in them? Count how many planes are lined up. What are they waiting for? Watch as the first one taxies onto the runway, speeds up, and lifts into the air.

Notice the long ramps sticking out from all sides of the terminal building. Point out how these pull right up to the airplane so people can get on and off. Are there any other ways people might get on or off the plane and into the building, if the folding ramp didn't work? Notice any stairs that can be rolled up to the plane. Are there any wide buses or trams that take people to planes? If possible, walk onto a boarding ramp and notice the controls that move the connecting platform to the plane. Notice wheelchairs or special motorized carts used to transport people who need assistance.

There may be very long walks to and from gate areas or between terminals. Notice any moving walkways, escalators, airport trams, underground transit systems, buses, or monorails that move people around the airport. They can be fun to ride. (Be sure you have enough adults with you to help any child who is worried or frightened by walkways and escalators.)

### IN THE BAGGAGE CLAIM AREA

Leaving the gate area, proceed to the baggage claim section. Notice the flashing signs that direct you to that area, which may be on a different level. What else do you see in that area? Look for car rental desks, phones to nearby hotels and shuttles, and taxi services.

Notice more TV monitors. These tell you the number of the carousel, or claim area, that will receive baggage from each arriving flight. Watch as the carousel is turned on and begins to move. Watch suitcases start sliding down a pathway onto the rotating circular platform, which is known as the baggage carousel. Some airports may have a different system, such as a large moving conveyer belt that runs through a specific baggage claim area carrying suitcases along its path.

Notice all the different kinds of suitcases arriving in the baggage area. Some suitcases are on wheels, and people can move them easily. Other people may need help with their baggage. Notice all the special carts designed to help move baggage. Some are do-it-yourself carts like those in a grocery store. Others are used by skycaps who help people move large amounts of luggage.

# After the Trip: Follow-up Activities

## TALK ABOUT IT

Talk about your trip and let the children tell you what they noticed and learned. Write down what they tell you about the airport. Do this soon after you return, while the memories are still fresh. Compare this list to the one you made before the trip, listing the things the children knew before they left. Your new list will probably be much richer in detailed information. Ask if the children remember the name of your airport. If there are other airports in your area, tell the children their names. Are they people or place names?

Start an airport picture dictionary. Write down all the words the children learned on this trip. Try to find pictures to illustrate the items mentioned. Use travel magazines, airline brochures, or your own pictures as sources. Try to group the words by areas and describe what happens in those areas.

## AIRPORT MURAL

Have the children make a large mural of an airport. Use pictures, their own drawings, people, airplane and truck stickers, and paper cutouts. Besides the usual paper and wallpaper samples, add some silver wrapping paper to use for all the metal things found in airports. Foil wallpaper samples or aluminum foil may also work. The children can work on this over several days, and embellish the mural as they remember things or look in books for new ideas. Label items on the mural and give your airport a name. For additional information, read several of the books in the Resources section, and have others available for the children to look at.

## AIRLINE MATCH-UPS

Make a matching game using the logos of several airlines and airplane stickers. Cut two of each logo from the airline brochures you collected at the airport. Mount one of each logo on a master board, as in a picture lotto game. Use stickers of airplanes interspersed with the logos on each card to make a set of four to six master boards. Mount the matching second logo and stickers on a set of cards to play lotto. If you have pictures available, you can add cards showing people who work at the airport and items associated with airports. You can also make fun match-up games using flags, if you have two sets of small flags or pictures or stickers of flags.

## JOBS THEN AND NOW

Look at the book *Come to Work with Us in an Airport*, by Jean and Ned Wilkinson. Talk about how jobs at the airport have changed in recent years. Compare this book with *How an Airport Really Works*, which you read before the trip. Think about how improved computers and automation have changed the work at airports. Talk about the differences in baggage handling and getting on and off planes—from the past to the present day. Were there such things as boarding ramps in the older book? Today, airports have more involved security procedures; those jobs might not have even existed before. Airports now serve many, many more people, and have many more services available in them—more jobs have been added in those areas. Some jobs (such as directing planes) may not have changed as much.

### CONVEYOR BELTS

You can use the following methods to demonstrate how conveyer belts work.

- Show the children the tread of a toy tractor. Put a small object, such as a Lego building block, at one end of the tractor tread. Pretend it is a suitcase. Move the tractor wheels slowly and notice that the object on top moves. When the object comes to the end of the tread, stop the tread, and pretend to load it onto the next moving device, truck, or plane.

- Stretch a fat rubber band over two pens or large crayons, which you hold in your hands. Turn the pens and notice how the rubber band turns as well. Explain that this is the technique used to create most conveyer belt systems.

- To demonstrate the roller belt systems used in security check areas, line up five or six fat crayons in a row on a flat surface (be sure the crayons are very close together). Place a small object on the first crayon. Start rolling the crayons and notice that the small object moves across all the crayons as they turn. Be sure to keep the crayons close together so the object doesn't fall between them.

### DRAMATIC PLAY

Set up a dramatic play area of an airport. Let the children plan what parts they want to play, and what they will need for ticketing areas, baggage areas, and other airport areas. Use the block area to construct hangers to use for airplanes. Can some of your trucks be used to transport things to planes? Make airplanes out of paper or Styrofoam craft foam to use in various parts of your model airport. Add your homemade conveyor belts.

Dramatize going on an airplane. Set up two rows of chairs for the passengers. Have some children act as flight attendants and serve drinks or snacks to the passengers. Have a pilot and copilot fly the plane and announce where they are going. Use some of the resources to serve as models for this dramatizing.

Show the video or film of *Curious George at the Airport,* or read the story. How did George manage to get into all those adventures?

# Related Trip Ideas to Explore

train station ● bus terminal ● transportation center ● railroad yard ●
harbor or marina ● smaller airports or flying schools ● helicopter pad or
heliport ● small aircraft companies

# Songs, Poems, and Finger Plays

### AT THE AIRPORT

*(to the tune of "Down By the Station")*

Out at the airport
Early in the morning,
See all the airplanes
Lined up in a row.
The controller sends a signal:
Taxi to the runway.
Whoosh, whoosh, zoom, zoom;
Up in the air they go.

### THE BAGGAGE CAROUSEL

How many suitcases do I see
On the baggage carousel
Coming toward me?
Black ones, blue ones, and brown ones too.
I bet there are a hundred and two!
I wonder where my suitcase will be?
Oh, it's on the circle coming toward me.

### TO GRANDMA'S

I think I'll take a trip today
In an airplane and fly far away (make flying motions)
I'll pack my toys and teddy bear
And some clothes for me to wear. (pretend to pack)

I'll go to the airport at half past two (pretend to look
    at watch)
to catch a plane for Waterloo.
After a while the plane will land; (make plane
    landing motions)
I'll walk down the ramp
And take my Grandma's hand. (reach out for a hand)

# Resources

Barton, Byron. (1982) *Airport.* New York: Crowell.

Butler, Daphne. (1991) *The Airport.* Milwaukee, WI: Gareth Stevens.

Chart, Marjoram Heinemann  (1980) *Gila Monsters Meet You at the Airport.*
    New York: Macmillan.

Cooper, Jason. (1992) *Airports*. Vero Beach, FL: Rourke.

Davies, Mark. (1990) *Inside the Airport*. New York: Kipling Press.

Greene, Graham. (1974) *The Little Steamroller*. New York: Doubleday.

Jeffries, David. (1988) *Giants of the Air—The Story of Commercial Aviation*. New York: Franklin Watts.

Munsch, Robert N. (1991) *El Avion de Angela*. Willowdale, Ont: Annick Press.

Oechsli, Helen and Kelly. (1988) *Fly Away*. New York: Macmillan.

Peterson, David. (1981) *Airport* (A New True Book). Chicago: Childrens Press.

Radford, Derek. (1991) *Harry at the Airport*. New York: Aladdin Books.

Rayston, Angela. (1992) *Planes*. New York: Aladdin Books.

Rey, Margaret, and Alan J Shalleck (editors). (1987) *Curious George at the Airport*. Boston: Houghton Mifflin.

Rogers, Fred. (1989) *Going on an Airplane*. New York: Putnam.

Rutland, Jonathan. (1988) *See Inside an Airport*. New York: Warwick Press (revised edition).

Sauvain, Philip Arthur. (1988) *Airport*. Morristown, NJ: Silver Burdett.

Sullivan, George. (1993) *How an Airport Really Works*. New York: Lodestar Books.

Wilkinson, Jean and Ned. (1970) *Come to Work with Us in an Airport*. Milwaukee, WI: Sextant Systems.

Ziegler, Sandra. (1988) *A Visit to the Airport*. Chicago: Childrens Press.

## ANOTHER GOOD RESOURCE

*Curious George at the Airport* (video). (1988) Boston: Houghton Mifflin.

# Apple Orchard · · · · · · · · · · · ·

Nothing is more delightful than a trip to an apple orchard on a lovely fall day. At the orchard, you and your group can

- see where apples come from and how they are picked and packaged;
- learn about how an orchard works and how trees are cared for;
- observe how apples are sorted, graded, and stored or processed for other uses;
- taste different kinds of apples and learn something about the trees they grow on;
- learn about other products that are made from apples and see how some are made; and
- bring some apples back to eat or use.

Most orchards are well organized for field trips and can accommodate various size and age groupings—making them an ideal site to visit. Because of the popularity of this trip, reservations are a must and should be made early. When you call, check on facilities for snacks and what they provide or have available. (Make a timetable or schedule for your visit so you can plan for waits.) Find out if the children will be walking or riding in carts so you can let the children know what to expect.

There are many different types of orchards. Large working ones may have a lot of machinery to aid in their work, and they may also do much of their own processing and baking. Smaller operations provide opportunities to pick your own apples. Some orchards have other products available as well (such as pumpkins, other fruits, and apple products), while others have hayrides or other attractions.

Many of the procedures and activities suggested for this trip can be easily adapted to visiting similar places, such as a pumpkin patch, strawberry patch, orange grove, or other fruit orchard, adapting the vocabulary words to suit the fruit.

# Before the Trip

apple ● tree ● stem ● core ● skin ● peel ● seeds ● flesh ● pulp ● cider ● press ● ripe ● harvest ● apple crate ● apple picker ● bushel ● peck ● basket ● pie ● jelly ● apple butter ● juicy ● sweet ● tart ● grade ● picking ● sack ● ladder ● cooler ● juice ● dwarf tree ● branches ● grafting

### SHOW AND TASTE

Bring in several kinds of apples in different colors and shapes (for example, Granny Smith, Golden Delicious, Red Delicious, and Macintosh). Talk about their color and shape, and ask the children if they are all apples. After noticing their characteristics on the outside, cut the apples open and notice their core, flesh, and seeds. Do they look alike on the inside and do their seeds look alike? Cut the apples into small pieces and let the children feel their texture and taste them. Discuss the ways in which they are alike and different. Write down the children's observations about the apples and which ones they liked best. Explain that all apples grow on trees and that the type of apple depends on the type of tree. Plan to visit an orchard to see what types of trees and apples the orchard has and how their apples taste. Speculate about how apple growers can be sure they get the kind of apples they want. Do the apples ever get mixed up?

### TALK ABOUT IT

Ask the children what other things they like that might be made from apples. Bring in some apple juice and applesauce and discuss how these things might be made. Write down any questions the children have about things made from apples. Other things to ask at the orchard might be: Where do they keep all the apples until they sell them or use them? How long will apples stay fresh, and how do they take care of them during that time? Where does the orchard send its apples? What problems can happen to hurt the apples (for example, frost, too much rain or not enough rain, and insects or worms), and how do they try to protect them?

Plan to take the questions to the apple orchard to see if the people at the orchard can answer them.

### PLAY "WHICH CAME FIRST?"

Display an apple, some apple seeds, a picture of an apple tree, and a dish of applesauce. Ask the children which came first. Let children give their opinions and explain their associations and why they think that way. There will be many interesting opinions characteristic of children's level of thinking. Encourage children's thinking, but don't force a particular sequence on them (the idea may be too abstract). Wonder how the tree got there. Try this game again after your trip and see if the children's ideas have changed.

**THINGS TO BRING**

paper and a pen or pencil to record observations ● extra-large canvas bags or plastic buckets and plastic bags to help carry children's apples (paper bags often break) ● questions to ask orchard workers ● plastic or paper bag for collecting things ● a camera

## On the Trip

### OBSERVE

Notice how the trees are planted. Are they in rows? Are there differences in the trees' height, shape, fullness, branch structure, and color and texture of bark and leaves? Look carefully at the leaves to see how they grow. What happens to the branches when they are full of ripe apples? How are the trees organized? Are all the same kind of tree in one section? How many different kinds of trees does the orchard have? Watch how the apples are picked. Notice how careful the people are not to bruise or damage the apples. What special equipment is used to pick the apples?

How are the apples collected as they are being picked? How do they get from the trees to the buildings where they are sold or processed? Can you observe people or machines carrying apple crates to various places?

Are there apples lying on the ground? Discuss how they got there and ask what happens to them.

What buildings are there at the orchard? Is there a bakery where you can watch bakers making pies or other apple products? Is there a kitchen where you might see people making jelly, apple butter, or apple syrup? What machines do you see? What jobs do you see people doing?

What else do you see in the orchard's main building? Notice how products are displayed and organized. Are there displays of letters or pictures from children? What information about apples are on display?

Take photographs of the steps in the harvesting and sorting processes as you observe them, to use in your follow-up activities.

### SENSE

How do the orchard and the buildings smell? Do the areas around the trees have any special smells? Are they good or bad smells, and where do you think they come from? Can you smell things baking nearby, or are there other aromas in the processing and washing areas? Do the baskets of apples on display have any smell, and are there any differences among them?

Are there varieties of apples to taste? If possible, let the children taste several different ones. What differences do you notice? Talk about how the apples taste; use words such as tart, sweet, and not so sweet. Are there difference in how firm or soft the apples are, and does that affect the taste as well? Are there other things you can taste, such as apple cider, butter, or jelly? Talk about how those things taste, and ask what is added to them that affects the taste.

Does the orchard feel like a happy place? How can you decide? How do the people who work there look? Do the children think it would be fun to work there?

### CATEGORIZE AND MEASURE

Watch how the apples are sorted. How do the workers decide what group each apple belongs in? What are the grades of apples and what do they mean? Besides type of apple, are they sorted by size, shape, weight, color, marks on them, or any other characteristics? Which parts of the sorting process are done by machines and which by people? How are the different categories of apples priced? Do you see other evidence of sorting on the shelves and in other parts of the showroom? Are there different-sized baskets around? What does *peck* mean? How about *bushel*? Are there quarts and gallons or pints for some of the apple products?

### ASK

Bring out the questions you wrote down before the trip, and ask people at the orchard if they can answer them.

### PURCHASE

Bring back different types of apples—some sweet, some tart—to use in applesauce experiments.

Think about other items sold at the orchard that you might like to buy and taste later on, such as cider, apple jelly, butter, or syrup.

## After the Trip: Follow-up Activities

### TALK ABOUT IT

Talk about the trip and let the children tell you all the things they remember and what parts were most interesting to them. If they could work at the orchard, what job would they like best? See if they still have questions about controlling the types of trees or how bees help pollinate the blossoms to form the apple buds. Several books in the Resources section (especially those in the Other Good Resources section) have pictures and explanations of grafting and pollination and can answer many questions. Plan to look at and read some of the books in the next few days and encourage the children to look at them as well.

### ALL ABOUT APPLES

Write a story of an apple's cycle from blossom to purchase at the orchard or store. Include how long the various steps take, if you know. Describe how people and machines pick and sort the apples. Include in your story some of the photos you took.

### THANK YOU

Write a thank-you note to the orchard, and let the children tell you what to write. Use large newsprint and leave room for the children to add decorations, or include a separate sheet of things the children have drawn or made that reflect their reaction to the trip.

### MAKE BEFORE AND AFTER APPLE TREES

Look at pictures of apple trees in blossom and as the apples are growing. Make pictures showing that process—blossoming in the spring and full of apples in the fall.

For trunk and branches, trace a child's arm and hand with fingers spread out and have the children color the trunk and branches. You can also use paper cutouts or twigs pasted onto the paper for the tree trunk.

For blossoms, use bits of cotton glued to branches; white and pink tissue paper glued to branches; or spots made with Q-tip swabs dipped in Tempera paint.

For apples, use thumbprints from a red ink pad; red coding dots; red bits of tissue paper; cotton balls (shake them first in a paper bag with red powdered Tempera paint); small round apple-shaped sponges for printing (dip in red Tempera paint). You can also have the children add green or yellow apples to make a variety of trees—but remember that each tree must have all the same type of apples on it.

### READ AND DO

Look through the Resources section and pick one of the books titled *Fruit*. Talk about all the types of fruits and how they grow. Bring in samples of the fruits mentioned. Cut them open so the children can see the inside and examine the flesh and seeds. Afterward, wash the fruit and cut them up into a fruit salad for a healthy snack.

Look on page 24 of *The Life and Times of the Apple,* by Charles Micucci, and count the different types of apples mentioned (this book has many other interesting facts about apples). Plan to visit a grocery store to see how many different types of apples they have. (See the Grocery Store chapter later in this book for more ideas.) Ask the children to bring in apples and see how many different kinds you can collect. Look at a map of the United States and place a red sticker on all the states that grow apples.

### APPLE PRODUCT CHART

Make a list of all the products made from apples that were sold at the apple orchard. Can you think of other apple products? Find magazine pictures of these products and make a large chart that shows apples and their products.

### APPLESAUCE EXPERIMENTS

Make applesauce using different kinds of apples for each batch. Cook each type of apple separately and mash in separate bowls. Taste each type of applesauce to see which ones you like best. Mix some together and taste them again. Save some of the applesauce for further taste testing. Add sugar to one and cinnamon to another, and taste again to see the differences. (Some people say the best applesauce is made by mixing several different kinds of apples together. Does your group agree?)

### APPLE TREATS TO MAKE

**Baked Apples.** Remove the core of several apples, keeping the apples in one piece. Sprinkle a small amount of sugar and cinnamon (about 1/4 teaspoon) in the apple's center and dot with butter. Put a little water (about 1/2 cup) in the bottom of a shallow baking dish and place the apples in the dish. Bake them at 375 degrees for 45 minutes. Apples should be soft but not mushy. Let them cool. Cut in quarters for children to taste. Serve with a slice of uncooked apple, and talk about how baking changed the apples. What else changed the taste?

**Dried Apples.** Bring in dried apples to taste. If you have a food dehydrator, slice and make your own. How do dried apples differ from fresh apples? Talk about what's missing and what dehydration means.

**Apple Peel Snacks.** Take the peelings from several apples and place them on a cookie sheet. Sprinkle the slices with a small amount of sugar and cinnamon. Bake at 350 degrees for 30 minutes. Cool and eat.

**Uncooked Applesauce.** You'll need six apples, potato peelers, knife, 1/2 cup honey, a few drops of water, and a blender.

Have the children peel the apples. Cut them into sections. Put the apples, honey, and water into a blender. Blend until smooth. Enjoy!

**Fanciful Apple Treats.** Have children decorate slices of apple for a snack. Use toothpicks to hold cheese chunks, raisins, banana slices, celery pieces, and other finger foods onto the apples.

## Related Trip Ideas to Explore

other fruit farms or orchards ● pumpkin patch or berry picking ● food processors (for example, fruit canning, peanut butter, candied fruit, jam, or fruit drinks) ● farmer's market

## Songs, Poems, and Finger Plays

### TO THE ORCHARD

Hi Ho, Hi Ho, to the orchard we will go.
To see some trees, a lot of trees,
All standing in a row.

The apples we will eat
Are all so very sweet
Put some in the press
It looks like quite a mess
But when its done
We'll all drink some
And cider is the best!

Hi Ho, Hi Ho, to the orchard we will go.
For bushels full of apples sweet,
Hi Ho, Hi Ho, Hi Ho, Hi Ho.

## AT THE ORCHARD

*(to the tune of "Paw Paw Patch")*
The trees are full and the branches sagging,
The trees are full and the branches sagging,
The trees are full and the branches sagging,
Way o'er yonder in the old orchard.

Picking some apples and put them in a basket,
Picking some apples and put them in a basket,
Picking some apples and put them in a basket,
Way o'er yonder in the old orchard.

## FIVE RED APPLES

Five red apples in a grocery store. (hold up five fingers)
_____ bought one and then there were four. (name of child)
Four red apples on an apple tree. (hold up four fingers)
_____ ate one and then there were three.
Three red apples and what did _____ do? (hold up three fingers)
She ate one and then there were two.
Two red apples hanging in the sun. (hold up two fingers)
_____ ate one and then there was one.
One red apple and now we are done. (hold up one finger)
I ate the last one and now there are none.
(everyone pretends to eat apples)

## APPLES

Most apples are red, but some are green—
And even some yellow ones I have seen.
Apples are usually good to eat;
Some are tart, but most are sweet.
We put them all in a great big pot,
And stirred and stirred when they got hot (pretend to stir)
Applesauce is what we got!

## WHAT AM I?

First it was a pretty flower,
Dressed in pink and white.
Then it was a tiny ball,
Almost hid from sight.
Round and green and large it grew,
Then it turned to red.
It will make a splendid pie,
For your autumn dinner spread.

**TAKE A LITTLE APPLE**

*(to the tune of "I'm a Little Teapot")*

Take a little apple, cut it up
Put it in a pot and cook it up
When it gets all mushy, mash it up
Now it's applesauce, let's eat it up.


# Resources

Blocksma, Mary. (1983) *Apple Tree, Apple Tree.* Chicago: Childrens Press.

Bourgeois, Paulette. (1990) *The Amazing Apple Book.* Reading, MA: Addison-Wesley.

Bruna, Dick. (1984) *The Apple.* Los Angeles: Price Stern Sloan.

Gallimard, Jeunesse, and Pascale de Bourgoing. (1991) *Fruit.* (From the First Discovery Book Series) New York: Scholastic.

Gleiter, Jan, and Kathleen Thompson. (1987) *Johnny Appleseed.* Milwaukee, WI: Raintree Childrens Books.

Maestro, Betsy. (1992) *How Do Apples Grow?* New York: HarperCollins.

Micucci, Charles. (1992) *The Life and Times of the Apple.* New York: Orchard Books.

Moss, Miriam. (1994) *Fruit.* Austin, TX: Garrett Educational Corporation.

Patent, Dorothy Hinshaw. (1990) *An Apple a Day—From the Orchard to You.* New York: Dutton.

Pearson, Tracey Campbell. (1986) *An Apple Pie.* New York: Dial Books.

Rockwell, Anne. (1989) *Apples and Pumpkins.* New York: Macmillan.

Sanchez, Isidro, and Carme Peris. (1991) *The Orchard* (Discovering Nature Series). New York: Barrons.

Slawson, Michele Benoit. (1994) *Apple Picking Time.* New York: Crown Books.

Watts, Barrie. (1986) *Apple Tree.* Morristown, NJ: Silver Burdett Press.

## OTHER GOOD RESOURCES

Johnson, Sylvia. (1983) *Apple Trees.* Minneapolis: Lerner Publications.

Schnieper, Claudia. (1987) *An Apple Tree through the Year.* Minneapolis: Carolrhoda Books.

# Bank ·························

In a commercial society, even young children are aware of money and its uses. Most often, the preschooler's conception of the bank, if they have one at all, is of a money store. Studying a bank—and taking a trip there—can help children understand the real workings of this institution. A trip to the bank can also help children to

- learn about how and why people use banks;
- learn how checking and savings accounts work;
- meet the people who work in banks and see what they do;
- see where money and valuables can be kept for safekeeping;
- learn about saving; and
- observe the machines and other features of a bank.

When planning a bank trip, ask parents if they or anyone they know works at a bank. In arranging for the trip, explain what types of things you would like the children to see. You may be able to show and explain many things to the children yourself, but ask others to show them the vault areas and the workings of the machines and back office areas. Explain the purpose of the bank visit. As Ben Franklin would probably agree, it is never too early to start learning about saving money.

## Before the Trip

### WORDS TO LEARN AND USE

banker ● clerk ● secretary ● teller ● deposit ● check ● savings account● money vault ● safe ● guard ● computer ● bank windows ● bookkeeper● borrow ● withdrawal slip ● checkbook ● penny ● nickel ● dime ● quarter● dollar ● copper ● silver ● safety deposit box ● cash machine ● ATM ● pass card ● loan ● mortgage ● security ● calculator ● interest

### TALK ABOUT IT

Ask the children what they do with money they receive. Where do they keep it? Where do their parents keep money? Let the children suggest good places to keep money and talk about what a safe place should look like. Ask the children why people need money. What would we do if there were no money?

### SHOW AND TELL

Show the children your checkbook. Explain how checks work and that people use checks in place of paper money. Explain that banks issue checks; people keep their money in one of the bank's checking accounts. Plan to visit a local bank and find out what the banks do with the checks. Is there any other way people get money when they need it? If the children mention cash cards or getting money from machines, plan to ask the bank employees to explain how those cash machines work and what happens at the bank when people use those machines.

### THINGS TO BRING

paper and a pen or pencil to record observations ● plastic or paper bag for collecting things ● a camera

## On the Trip

### OBSERVE

Notice the appearance of the bank on the outside as well as inside. Is it old or new? What materials were used in its construction and furnishings? Are there pictures on the walls? Look at the people who work at the bank and notice if they are wearing special clothes.

Look at signs around the bank and tell the children what they say. What is the name of the bank? Is it part of a large bank system?

Notice the way the bank is organized with desk areas, offices, tellers' windows, and closed-in spaces. What do they see the bank tellers doing?

Point out machines you can readily see, such as typewriters, coin machines, computers, a money machine, and copiers.

Observe people transacting business in the bank. Are there different lines or places for different transactions?

Visit the vault area and notice the huge doors and automatic locking systems on the vault.

Peek inside to see the safety deposit boxes. Talk about what people would keep in those boxes, and why those things would be kept there.

Observe the auto-bank or drive-up window area and watch how that operation works.

## Ask

Ask several employees about the work they do at the bank. Learn as much as you can in the simplest terms possible about the different jobs in the bank, such as teller, receptionist, loan officer, president, and vice president.

Ask to see the safe and the back office area. Show the children the packages of coins and how the money is organized, sorted, and stored.

Let the children ask questions, too.

Ask an employee to show the children how various bank machines work. Children will probably be as fascinated by a photocopying machine as by calculators and money sorting machines. Perhaps the employee will make photocopies of some bank forms for you. Ask the employee to show you what happens to checks.

## Speculate

Wonder what the people talking to the bank personnel at various desks are doing. Are they opening new accounts or negotiating loans? Talk about what a loan is and explain that it is borrowing money from the bank that belongs to the bank. Why do the children think the bank lends money to people? Ask the children what people use loans for. Try to guess what these customers are planning to do with their loans. How does the bank get the money it uses for loans?

Guess where the bank president and vice presidents work. How can the children tell?

## Talk About It

Discuss the atmosphere in the bank and think about why it looks the way it does. Is it noisy, quiet, attractive? Would it be a good place to work?

Think about the way the bank works. Think about how people put money in the bank and then use it. How does the bank keep track of the money? How do people know how much money they have in the bank when they use it?

Talk about the way security boxes are protected. How do people get into that area? How are the lockboxes opened?

Talk about interest in terms children can understand. Explain that when people put dollars in the bank and keep it there, the bank pays them a few pennies for each dollar. When people borrow money from the bank, the bank charges them several more pennies for each dollar. Both of these are called *interest*.

### COLLECT

Bring back samples of deposit slips, checks, withdrawal slips, bank books, loan applications, bank statements, and anything else employees will give you to play bank.

## After the Trip: Follow-up Activities

### TALK ABOUT IT

Talk about the trip and let the children tell you what they found interesting. Write some of their comments in a thank-you note to the bank.

Talk about saving money and keeping it safe so it doesn't get lost. Discuss savings and checking accounts. Introduce the idea that savings accounts pay interest to encourage people to save money in the bank. Checking accounts do not pay interest because the people are using the money, and it keeps going out of the bank when people write checks.

Show and discuss checkbooks, bank books, and deposit and withdrawal slips. How is writing a check similar to paying cash and how is it different? Explain the deposit slips and how they are used. Make small deposit books and checkbooks to use in bank play.

### PIGGY BANKS

Make piggy banks out of baby food jars, cocoa or other small cans. Have children decorate them with construction paper, felt, or other materials.

### OUR BIG BOOK ABOUT BANKS

Make a group book about the things you saw in the bank. Look in newspapers or magazines for pictures of things seen at the bank, and put them in your book. Write the names by the items and talk about their uses.

### HOW MUCH IS IT?

Make "How Much Is It?" cards to help children discover which coin is worth more. You'll need four pieces of cardboard 6 1/2 by 7 inches, four pieces 3 1/2 by 6 1/2 inches, glue or tape, and coins (penny, nickel, dime, quarter).

Tape a larger and smaller card together so that the smaller one can fold over the larger one, and cover up the lower half of it. On the top of each larger card, glue or tape one real coin. Write the name of the coin below the coin and then the number of pennies in that coin. On the bottom half of the card, glue or tape the correct number of pennies.

When the smaller card is folded up, the real pennies and the numeral telling the correct amount should be covered up. For a dime card, show 10 pennies and 2 nickels. For quarters, make extra cards to show all the combinations that can make 25 cents. (You will need at least two extra card sets—one to show 5 nickels, one to show 3 nickels and 1 dime, and one to show 2 dimes and 1 nickel.)

## GAMES

With older children, play a simplified version of *Monopoly*. For younger children, play put-and-take type games, using play money or poker chips. Give some chips or coins to each child and place others in the center of the players. Make a spinner dial or use a stack of cards to tell each child how many chips or coins to take from or add to the center.

## COIN DISPLAY

Display various kinds of coins and bills. Note size, shape, and pictures. Display samples of coins from other countries. Talk about coins and their differences.

## PLAY MONEY MATCHING GAME

Make a play money matching game. Use poster board to create a master board with a penny, nickel, dime, and quarter on the left side of the board. On the right side, draw circles for amounts that correspond to each coin.

Make play money coins to use in the matching game by having the children lay paper over real coins and do rubbings. Cut out and laminate. If you want, mount the coins on copper- or silver-colored paper to look more realistic. Make enough play money for all combinations on your master board.

Children match the play coins using the circles drawn on the master board as a guide for the correct combinations equaling each coin. For a variation, make a similar set out of felt to use on the flannelboard.

## DRAMATIC PLAY

Set up a play money, checkers, or buttons bank. Children deposit the money. They can then write checks to friends for cash or they can make a withdrawal themselves. Children take turns being tellers and customers.

Add an old check-writing machine (if you can find one), stamp pad, cash register, and other props to your bank. Make a vault out of a large, heavy cardboard box or crate. Use a combination lock on it. Store extra money in it. Tellers can go to the vault to get extra money, checkers, or buttons for the day's business.

If you want, add a drive-up window area to your bank. Use small cans with plastic covers as your tubes to pass from car to window. Or customers can place envelopes on a dustpan that the clerk extends from the window.

## Related Trip Ideas to Explore

coin dealership ● credit union ● cashier's office at a department store

## Songs, Poems, and Finger Plays

### THE AUTO BANK

My Mommy drove to the bank today, (pretend to drive car)
To the drive-up window without delay,
Put checks in a tube which whooshed away. (pretend to
  fill a container)
Soon the whoosh was heard once more, (slip arm down
  and back)
And the tube was back with money for the store. (pretend
  to open container)
And then guess what I heard it say?
"Thank you" and "Have a nice day."

### IN THE BANK
*(to the tune of "Frere Jacques")*

In the bank, in the bank,
There's a safe, there's a safe.
Safe to keep our money, safe to keep our money,
Safe, safe, safe. Safe, safe, safe.

### THIS IS THE WAY WE SAVE OUR MONEY
*(to the tune of "Here We Go Round the Mulberry Bush")*

This is the way we save our money, (pretend to drop coins in bank)
Save our money, save our money.
This is the way we save our money,
We put it in the bank.

This is the way we write a check, (pretend to write)
Write a check, write a check.
This is the way we write a check
When we go to the bank.

This is the way we spend our money, (pretend to pay for something)
Spend our money, spend our money.
This is the way we spend our money,
When we go to the store.

## FOUR BRIGHT COINS

(Tape coins to large Popsicle sticks and have children
hold up the appropriate coin for each part of the verse.)

Four bright coins shining at me,
The first one said, "I'm a penny you see."
The second one said, "How do you do?
I'm called a nickel and I'm bigger than you!"
The third one said, "You're both small stuff,
If you want to buy something, you're not enough.
But look at me, I'm small and I shine,
I can buy something 'cuz I'm a dime."
The last coin looked at them all and laughed,
All of you together don't measure up to me,
'Cuz I'm a quarter, can't you see!"

### ONE-A-PENNY (CHANT)

One-a-penny, two-a-penny, three-a-penny, four,
Four-a-penny, five-a-penny, that's a nickel more.

Six-a-penny, seven-a-penny, eight-a-penny, more.
Nine-a-penny, ten-a-penny, that's a dime for the store.

# Resources

Adams, Barbara Johnston. (1993) *The Go Around Dollar*. New York: Four Winds Press.

Adler, David. (1985) *Banks: Where the Money Is*. New York: Franklin Watts.

Axelrod, Amy. (1994) *Pigs Will Be Pigs*. New York: Four Winds Press.

Berenstain, Stan. (1983) *Berenstain Bears' Trouble with Money*. New York: Random House.

Berger, Melvin and Gilda. (1993) *Round and Round the Money Goes*. Nashville: Ideals Children's Books.

Burns, Peggy. (1995) *Money*. New York: Thomson Learning.

Caple, Kathy. (1986) *The Purse*. Boston: Houghton Mifflin.

Davis, Mary. (1975) *Careers in a Bank*. Minneapolis: Lerner Publications.

Elkin, Benjamin. (1983) *Money* (A New True Book). Chicago: Childrens Press.

Gabriello, Vincent. (1982) *Bravo Ernest and Celestine*. New York: Greenwillow.

German, Joan. (1981) *The Money Book*. New York: Elsevier/Nelson Books.

Leedy, Loreen. (1992) *The Monster Money Book*. New York: Holiday House.

Maestro, Betsy and Guilio. (1988) *Dollars and Cents for Harriet*. New York: Crown.

Mitgutsch, Ali. (1985) *From Gold to Money*. Minneapolis: Carolrhoda Books.

Rockwell, Anne. (1978) *Gogo's Pay Day*. New York: Doubleday.

Schwartz, David. (1989) *If You Made a Million*. New York: Lothrop.

Smith, Maggie. (1994) *Argo, You Lucky Dog*. New York: Lothrop.

### ANOTHER GOOD RESOURCE

Maestro, Betsy. (1993) *The Story of Money*. New York: Clarion Books.

# Car Dealership··············

Looking at cars is a popular activity for many people; they are often fiddling with theirs in some way or coping with getting them fixed. Perhaps the adult fascination with cars contributes to young children's fascination with the small cars they all seem to love. Certainly everyone is exposed to promotion and advertising related to motor vehicles, so a trip to a car dealership can offer children firsthand experience with this great American pastime. This trip also can enable children to

- see all different kinds of cars and how they are displayed;
- learn about cars and their various parts, inside and out;
- observe the people who work there, both selling and fixing cars;
- see where people can go to buy cars; and
- learn what *sticker price* means and how it keeps changing, and see all the numbers written on the cars.

In choosing a car dealership to visit, check with parents to see if anyone has a connection with a specific dealer, or choose one closest to you. Although anyone can drop in at an open car dealership anytime, even with a small group of children, it is a good idea to talk with someone about your impending visit. This trip works best with a small group of children because showroom areas are usually not that large and there are not many different areas to tour. Car dealerships are usually not too busy in the late morning or early afternoon, but be sure to check their hours.

A note of caution: Remember when walking around outdoor lots to be extra alert for cars that may drive up or back out. Exercise extreme caution and stay away from the service area's entrances and exits where cars can pull in or out at anytime. A car backing up may not see preschoolers, who are below its sight line. View the service area from an inside entrance to avoid being in the way of traffic.

# Before the Trip

## WORDS TO LEARN AND USE

model ● sports car ● station wagon ● compact ● sedan ● two-door ●
four-door ● convertible ● hardtop ● hatchback ● new ● used car lot ●
showroom ● sticker price ● hood ● hubcap ● trunk ● fender ● wheels ●
tires ● rubber ● whitewalls ● radials ● car radio ● steering wheel ●
brakes ● stick shift ● automatic ● upholstery ● windshield wiper ● tinted
glass ● seat belts ● air bags ● bucket seats ● armrest ● dashboard ●
horn ● speedometer ● tachometer ● headlights ● bumper ● grill ●
hood ornament ● all-terrain vehicle ● minivan

## TALK ABOUT IT

Ask the children if their families have cars. If so, do they know what kinds
they are? Did they get their cars from a private person or a car dealer?
Have they ever been to see where people can buy cars?

Talk about cars that are made in this country. Name some of them.
Then talk about cars made in other countries, and name some of them;
explain that we call those cars *foreign* (meaning from other countries).

Bring in toy cars of many different types and a catalog from a dealership you plan to visit. Ask the children to bring in their toy cars. Talk about all the different models. Are those models still around or are they antiques from a long time ago? Ask if they would like to visit a place where people can buy cars. Show them the dealership catalog. Can the children tell what make of car is in the catalog? Ask how they know or recognize that make.

**THINGS TO BRING**

paper and a pen or pencil to record measurements and other observations ● toy cars for comparison ● book about cars and their parts ● tape measure ● plastic or paper bag for collecting things ● a camera

## On the Trip

**OBSERVE**

Notice the appearance of the building and any lots near it. Are there flags, balloons, or other decorations around? Are there big glass windows all around the building? Wonder why they have such big windows. Is there writing on the windows?

Look at the cars that are outside in the lot and see if you can tell whether they are new or used. Are there other vehicles besides cars for sale? Is there writing on the cars too? Look for any signs or information about the cars. Are they all the same make? How can you recognize different makes?

Notice all the different sections of the building. Is there a special area for looking at the cars (showroom) and other work areas like a service department or body shop? Notice all the different entrances into the building area. Are there entrances for cars as well as people?

Notice the cars or any other vehicles on display inside the building. Are they displayed in a special way? How can you find out what features those cars have? Are there sales tickets on them?

Point out and name specific parts of the cars on display: hood, bumper, fender, and so forth. Notice the parts that vary. There may be a trunk on some models, hatchback on others.

Look for special identifying features of cars and note especially the grillwork, hood ornaments, and names written on the car's body.

Notice the different clothes worn by the people working in different parts of the dealership. Are there special outfits for salespeople, service managers, and mechanics that identify them as working for a particular department?

Ask a salesperson to tell you something about the cars on display. How much do they cost? Have the salesperson point out the additional cost of things, called *special features*. Look at some examples of special features (such as electric windows, air conditioning, spokes in the hubcaps).

How do people arrange to pay for cars? Does the dealer take cars in trade?

Can the salesperson tell you what features are most popular with the public? What models are the biggest sellers? Is any color especially popular?

Ask if the children can sit in the cars and let them take turns trying out the front and back seats. Be sure to point out and name the inside parts of the car: steering wheel, brake, clutch, accelerator, glove compartment, dashboard, seat belts, and so forth.

Ask about the work different people do in the car dealership. What system do they use to keep track of the cars they have available and the customers whose cars are under guarantee? Ask to see the different work areas and name special machines or equipment used in those areas.

### COMPARE

Count the wheels, doors, windows, lights, seats, and other parts of cars. Are all of these the same on all models? How do station wagons or vans differ from other vehicles?

Compare the cars at the dealership with the top cars you brought. Look through the book about cars and their parts. Compare the parts in the book with parts of the real cars.

Compare color, paint finishes, and decorative trim on different models. Which colors and styles do the children like best?

Compare sizes of different models. Compare sizes of specific parts, such as tires and trunks. Look at how seating capacity changes with the size of the car. To aid in your comparison, measure some parts or ask the salesperson for dimensions of different models.

What other comparisons can you make that are less visible, such as engine horsepower and miles per gallon?

Look at pictures of other cars in catalogs the dealership may have. Compare those to the models you see on display.

### SPECULATE

Wonder why people decide to buy new cars. Wonder why people pick certain cars and not others.

Think about why the car dealership is decorated with all those balloons, flags, and bright colors.

Wonder where the word *horsepower* came from and what it means.

## After the Trip: Follow-up Activities

### TALK ABOUT IT

Ask the children again about their own family's cars. See if they can tell you more about them.

Write a story about which kinds of cars the children would like when they grow up. Use pictures cut from catalogs to help illustrate the story. Write a description taken from each child's idea about what kind of car the child would like. Have the child find a picture to accompany it. Put the pictures and descriptions together into a book or scroll.

### NUMBER OR COLOR MATCHING GAME: CARS AND GARAGES

Make garages by cutting the tops off milk cartons. Cover the cartons with paper and write a number on each, from one to five (ten for older children). Assemble a set of five plastic cars that will fit into the milk cartons.

For number recognition, mark each car with a numeral to match each garage. Have the children drive each car into the matching garage.

To teach the concept that each number represents a specific quantity, mark each car with coding dots ranging from one to five. Children can match the number of dots on a car to the corresponding numeral on a garage.

For a color identification game, use different-colored cars and cover the garages with paper in matching colors.

### DRAMATIC PLAY AREA

Set up a table-top dramatic play area to resemble a dealership showroom. Decorate with bright-colored flags or banners made by the children. Have model cars on display and lots of catalogs to look at. Write up signs for specials and signs that list features of the cars on display. During free play, children can pretend to order cars or take them out on loan.

### LARGE MOTOR ACTIVITY

Let the children sit on the floor with legs extended, pretending to be cars driving along the road. Have them move forward or backward by moving their buttocks and legs (an excellent exercise). Give directions such as "Go fast," "Go slow," and "Stop for stoplights." Have them pretend to steer, shift gears, or use turn signals as you direct.

### MATCHING GAMES

Make matching and lotto games using car stickers or wrapping paper with car pictures. Use catalogs from car dealers or from sets of toy cars. For simple matching or lotto games, children find the cars that are the same.

Make a model matching game. Cut out pictures of different models, such as a station wagon, sports car, two-door, four-door, and compact. Paste half of the pictures on small cards. On the left side of a master board, paste the matching pictures, one underneath the other. Leave room on the right side to place the cards. Children find the pictures that are the same model or type to match the first car in each row.

### CAR SHOWROOM MURAL

Make a mural of a car dealership. Show large car lots, the building, and all the decorations. Use cutout pictures of cars, or let the children draw their own. Use cutout paper shapes for flags and balloons.

### CUT-PAPER CARS

Cut out shapes of paper and let the children put them together to make cars. You will need small circles, larger-sixed half circles, rectangles that are curved on one side, and some different-sized rectangles.

### DIAGRAM OF A CAR

Draw a large diagram of a car, indicating its various parts. Cut out pictures of car parts from catalogs. Let the children match the parts (hood, tires, roof, trunk, windshield, windshield wiper) to the larger diagram. Mount on bulletin board and use pushpins to attach parts to the appropriate spots.

## Related Trip Ideas to Explore

motorcycle and snowmobile dealers ● jet ski or boat dealers ● trailer, camper, or recreational vehicle dealers ● antique car exhibits

## Songs, Poems, and Finger Plays

### FIVE NEW CARS

Five new cars on the showroom floor. (hold up five fingers)
Someone bought the compact
And now there are four. (hold up four fingers)

Four new cars that we can see.
Away goes the wagon
And now there are three. (hold up three fingers)

Three new cars the salesman shows to you.
Off goes the sports car
And now there are two. (hold up two fingers)

Two new cars: see a mother and her son.
They took the blue one
And now there is one. (hold up one finger)

One new car just as plain as can be.
But it's just right for
My family and me.

So we bought the last one
From the showroom floor.
And now we can't see anymore.

(You can use pictures of cars on a flannelboard.
Have children remove the cars, one by one.)

### THREE LITTLE CARS

*(to the tune of "Three Little Ducks That I Once Knew," or use a chant)*

Three little cars that I once knew, (hold up three fingers)
Hatch-back, and compact, that made two. (hold up two fingers)
But the one little car (hold up one finger)
With the stripes on its side,
It ruled the road with its overdrive.
Zoom, zoom, zoom. (put palms together and move hands forward in quick weaving motion)

### MY CAR

*(to the tune of "Mexican Hat Song")*

My car it has four tires (clap, clap)
Four tires has my car (clap, clap)
And had it not four tires (clap, clap)
My car couldn't go very far! (clap, clap)

### THE WHEELS ON THE CAR

*(to the tune of "The Wheels on the Bus")*

The wheels on the car go round and round,
Round and round, round and round.
The wheels on the car go round and round,
All through the town.

Additional verses:
The doors on the car go open and shut...
The wipers on the car go swish, swish, swish...
The lights on the car go blink, blink, blink...
The horn on the car goes beep, beep, beep...

## Resources

Aldag, Kurt. (1992) *Some Things Never Change*. New York: Macmillan.

Alexander, Anne. (1956) *ABC of Cars and Trucks*. New York: Doubleday.

Brandenberg, Franz. (1987) *What's Wrong with a Van*. New York: Greenwillow.

Burningham, John. (1976) *Mr. Gumpy's Motor Car*. New York: Crowell.

Cooper, Jason. (1991) *Automobiles*. Vero Beach, FL: Rourke.

Ets, Marie Hall. (1948) *Little Old Automobile*. New York: Viking.

Lenski, Lois. (1980) *The Little Auto*. New York: H. Z. Walck.

Maccarone, Grace. (1995) *Cars, Cars, Cars*. New York: Scholastic.

Newton, Laura P. (1987) *William the Vehicle King*. New York: Bradbury Press.

Osborne, Victor. (1989) *Rex—The Most Special Car in the World*. Minneapolis: Carolrhoda Books.

Parish, Herman. (1995) *Good Driving, Amelia Bedelia*. New York: Greenwillow.

Patrick, Denise Lewis. (1993) *The Car Washing Street*. New York: Tambourine Press.

Pinkerwater, Daniel. (1990) *Tooth-Gnasher Superflash*. New York: Macmillan.

Potter, Tracy. (1989) *See How It Works—Cars*. New York: Aladdin.

Radlauer, Edward. (1982) *Some Basics about Mini-Trucks*. Chicago: Childrens Press.

Rayston, Angela. (1991) *Cars*. New York: Macmillan.

Rockwell, Anne. (1986) *Cars*. New York: Dutton.

Scarry, Richard. (1989) *All About Cars*. Racine, WI: Western.

Shade, Susan. (1992) *Toad on the Road*. New York: Random House.

Wilkinson, Sylvia. (1982) *Automobiles* (A New True Book). Chicago: Childrens Press.

## OTHER GOOD RESOURCES

Cave, Ron and Joyce. (1982) *Automobiles*. New York: Gloucester.

Cole, Joanna. (1986) *Cars and How They Go*. New York: Harper & Row.

Lord, Trevor. (1992) *Amazing Cars*. New York: Knopf.

Spier, Peter. (1975) *Tin Lizzie*. New York: Doubleday.

Sullivan, George. (1991) *Cars*. New York: Doubleday.

*Uncle Wizzmo's New Used Car* (video). (1993) Think Entertainment.

# Construction Site ·········

Construction sites are probably everyone's favorite as a potential people- and place-watching experience—especially if the site is in a neighborhood location where you can frequently visit and see progress. Watching a building go up—from excavating the foundation to raising the roof beam—is a fascinating process and one that will easily spill over into the children's play experiences and conversations. Frequent visits to a construction site offer children an ideal opportunity to

- observe firsthand each step in the building process;
- see how a large number of machines work and what various things they can do;
- learn about the work of the various people involved in the construction process and how they work together;
- see the materials used in the process and how they are put together; and
- see what can cause problems for the construction project.

If the site is within easy walking distance, the best way to observe is to take small groups of children at different times to allow everyone a chance to watch this process without crowding. The most complicated part will be finding the best vantage points that allow you to observe things without being in the way or being in any danger. Construction workers are wary of letting anyone get too close to construction sites without hard hats, although if you have several small ones you could let the children wear them. Sometimes a neighboring driveway or a spot across the street will work out well for viewing the action. In some cases, taking a group in a car if you have one is easiest (even if the site is close by) because the children can watch from inside a vehicle and not be in the way. Friendliness, admiration, interest, and possibly cookies for the work crew may help the construction workers to understand and be open to your visits.

# Before the Trip

## WORDS TO LEARN AND USE

digging ● excavate ● contractor ● electrician ● steamfitter ● ducts ● wiring ● plumber ● pipes ● blueprints ● carpenter ● builder ● cement ● concrete blocks ● foundation ● basement ● bricks ● shingles ● bricklayer ● framing ● roof beam ● rafters ● hard hats ● plasterboard ● girders ● tractor ● bulldozer ● dump truck ● power shovel ● back hoe ● crane ● wall ● skyscraper ● grade ● scraper ● prefabricated ● insulation

## READ AND TALK ABOUT IT

Read *Mike Mulligan and His Steam Shovel*, by Virginia Lee Burton. Talk about the kind of excavators used in construction today, and think about how they avoid the problem Mike Mulligan faced. Plan to visit a construction site and ask.

Ask the children if they have noticed any buildings being built. What did they see at the construction site? List some questions the children raise and plan to talk to someone in construction to get some answers. Arrange to have the children visit and to ask the questions themselves.

## THINGS TO BRING

paper and a pen or pencil to record measurements and other observations ● plastic or paper bag for collecting things ● a camera

# On the Trip

## OBSERVE

Notice the collection of machinery and materials assembled at the site. Are they arranged in any particular way? Who seems to be telling people where to put things and what to do?

Watch any machines being used, such as bulldozers, power shovels, dump trucks, and cement mixers. Stay well out of the way of machines in use, but find a spot where you can see them work. Talk about how the machines move and who operates them. When machines are parked and not in use, it may be possible to observe them more closely to see how they work. Notice, for instance, that many machines are made up of special parts like a bulldozer blade or a crane attached to a tractor.

Try to observe various phases of construction, such as workers pouring cement for a foundation, framing the building, raising the roof beams and rafters, grading and finishing the yard, connecting the wiring, laying the pipes, and adding floors to apartment buildings.

If possible, observe the different ways workers use cranes. For tall buildings, workers often use them to deliver materials to places where they are needed. Notice hooks, magnets, and all other types of parts added to cranes to aid in this process.

Notice any special ways the work site is prepared. Are there temporary structures on the grounds for the workers to use? Is the area fenced off in any way?

Observe the mounting pile of debris and trash accumulating as work progresses. Is it hauled away? If there are useful pieces of lumber tossed on that pile, ask if you can take some for the children to use.

Observe the work various people do. Notice how the people work as a team to get tasks done. Do they give directions to each other?

Do the workers wear special clothes? Do they use anything to protect their head or eyes?

Notice hand or power tools in use in addition to the larger machines. If power tools are in use, where does the power come from?

## ASK

Ask someone to show you specific machines and tell you about them. Be sure to consult with the general contractor about suitable times to ask questions. For example, there are times when workers are waiting for something or taking a break and can answer questions without interrupting their work. If appropriate, ask how workers avoid having a power shovel get stuck in the bottom of the hole it digs for the foundation.

If someone is mixing cement, ask how it's made. Observe how it comes out of the mixer and is transported. Ask how long it takes to harden and how quickly the person has to work. Are different cement types or consistencies used or is all cement the same?

Tell the children as many of the names of machines and materials as you can. Ask someone to tell you the names of those items you don't know. Ask someone to show you the plans for the building. Do people keep consulting those plans?

### SPECULATE

Can you tell what kind of building is being built? Try to guess what it might be, based on location and what you have observed so far. Does it look like any other building you have seen? Fast-food restaurants tend to look alike as they go up, but they often put up signs in advance, so there's not much left to imagine. Let the children guess anyway, as it is fun to make up ideas for the building and its use.

Wonder how much it is costing to build the building. Perhaps you can get some estimates from the builders.

Think about what would look nice around the building when it is finished.

### COUNT

Count the number of people working, the number of trucks or machines you see, the stacks of materials, bags of cement, and other visible items.

Count features you can see related to the building, such as the number of openings for windows or doors, floors, roof beams, and corner posts.

You might also keep track of the number of trips the dump truck makes, or the number of times the cement mixer is loaded.

Time how long each batch of cement is mixed or how long other specific tasks take.

## After the Trip: Follow-up Activities

### TALK ABOUT IT

Talk about all the things you saw on the walk. Comment on what things are added each time you visit a site. Keep a record of how the building is progressing. Add to your running account after each visit. Keep your comments in a diary or log so you can review them from time to time.

Collect pictures of buildings being built and a variety of construction sites and stages. Show the children the pictures, and talk about what is going on in them.

### DRAMATIC PLAY IN THE SANDBOX

Set up a construction site in the sandbox. Fence off a part of the sandbox to use for construction. Excavate in that area, using a steam shovel or plain shovels.

Fill dump trucks with sand and haul to the other side of the sandbox. Collect stones and rocks to use for a foundation. Mix plaster or use clay to cement rocks together as needed; insert stir sticks to use for framing your building. Attach pieces of cardboard to the sticks for walls.

To make a homemade scoop, mount a soup ladle onto a pulley with one piece of string tied at the ladle end and one at the handle. Attach one of the strings to a pulley and raise and lower the ladle. (If you don't have a pulley, make a simple one using hanger wire and empty thread spools. Insert the wire through the hole in the spool and bend the wire to make a bracket holding the spool.) Turn the ladle by the handle to scoop up sand. This will probably be harder to use than plain shovels, but will show how complex it is to design and use machines.

Collect a variety of toy trucks used in construction to use in your dramatic play area. Demonstrate how they work and talk about their uses. Put signs up around the dramatic play construction area and let the children plan what they want to build and how long they want to pursue this activity.

### TABLE TOP BUILDING ACTIVITIES

Use Lego, Lincoln Log, and Tinkertoy building blocks and other building material sets to construct houses or buildings.

### PEOPLE-IN-CONSTRUCTION SCROLL

Talk about all the jobs that are part of construction, and design a scroll that tells about the work each person does. Use builders' supply catalogs for pictures to use. Some occupations to include in your scroll are: architects and engineers who design buildings and materials; carpenters who work with lumber; bricklayers and masons who work with bricks; plumbers who put in the sewer pipes and plumbing; electricians who do the wiring; steamfitters and sheet metal workers who put in the heating or cooling systems and the duct work; and painters who finish the wood. Mount the scroll on paper towel rollers. If you wish, use your scroll for a pretend TV series called "Building Our City." Cut up a large box for a pretend TV set.

### PICTURE PERFECT

Encourage the children to make paintings and drawings of the construction in process. Write comments about the building that the children dictate on each picture. Save these for a while, and if appropriate, take them on a later visit to the construction site for comparison.

### FOUNDATIONS YOU CAN EAT

Illustrate the bricks-and-mortar concept with a variety of food combinations that offer fun in the making and eating. The sticky substances hold together the solid substances to construct a foundation or a whole house. After the building process, the builders can dismantle their creation and eat it if they wish.

Some materials to use for bricks include Jell-O gelatin squares, crackers, graham crackers, toast, pieces of banana and apple, or marshmallows.

For the mortar, you can use cream cheese or whipped cream, peanut butter, applesauce, or soft cheddar cheese.

### INVITE VISITORS

Invite parents or friends who work in construction to visit your group. Ask them to bring along the tools they carry or a specially equipped truck. Have them tell the children about their work.

### ROLLER PAINTING

Bring out paint rollers, brushes, and water, and let the children pretend to paint with them. Indoors, they can paint on a blackboard; outdoors they can paint on walls or sidewalks.

### A BOOK ABOUT CONSTRUCTION

Make up a book about different types of construction. Include pages on highways, bridges, skyscrapers, shopping malls, tunnels, airports, and as many other settings as you wish. Think about the problems each kind of building presents and what would be needed for each site. Look for pictures to use in your book. Write the children's comments about how to solve design and construction problems. Encourage the children to look in books about construction to get ideas for your book.

## Related Trip Ideas to Explore

road or sidewalk construction or repair ● neighborhood repairs such as sewer repair ● excavation work (for example, tree removal) ● house painting and other repairs and improvements

## Songs, Poems, and Finger Plays

### THIS IS THE WAY WE BUILD A HOUSE
*(to the tune of "Here We Go Round the Mulberry Bush")*
This is the way we dig the basement, (use arms to imitate digging)
Dig the basement, dig the basement.
This is the way we dig the basement,
When we build a house.

Additional verses:

This is the way we make the basement... (pretend to stack concrete blocks and smooth cement around them)

This is way we make the walls... (pretend to hammer boards in place)

This is the way we hoist the roof beam... (pretend to lift very heavy beams)

This is the way we put on the shingles... (pretend to nail shingles onto a roof)

This is the way we paint the house... (move arms up and down in a painting motion)

This is the way we lay the carpet... (get down on hands and knees and pretend to smooth out the carpet)

### THE SKYSCRAPER

Build a floor, and add a floor
And another floor I see.
Do you know how many?
I bet it's fifty-three. (hold up five fingers on one hand
   and three on the other)
Build levels, start low and go up, up, up

Have you ever seen a building
That went up so high? (look way up and point to the sky)
They call it a skyscraper
Can you tell me why? (or 'Cuz it seems to touch the sky.)

### THE CEMENT MIXER

See the mixer turning, round and round, (twirl hands)
Mixing up cement, pound after pound.
Fill the wheelbarrow, hurry to the site, (pretend to push
   heavy wheelbarrow)
Smooth on the bricks, to hold them right. (pretend to build
   a brick wall)

### DOWN AT THE CORNER

*(to the tune of "Down by the Station")*

Down at the corner, early in the morning,
See all the workers gathering their things.
See all the trucks, moving to and fro.
What are they building? Do you know?

**Who Builds Our House?**

*(to the tune of "The Muffin Man")*

Oh, do you know an architect,
An architect, an architect?
Oh, do you know an architect,
To draw the plans for our house?

Additional verses:
Oh, do you know a carpenter...
To build the frame for our house?

Oh, do you know an electrician...
To bring light and power to our house?

Oh, do you know a plumber...
To bring water and heat to our house?

# Resources

Alterman, Lee. (1991) *Girders and Cranes.* Morton Grove, IL: Albert Whitman.

Barton, Byron. (1981) *Building a House.* New York: Greenwillow.
———. (1987) *Machines at Work.* New York: Crowell.

Base, Coleen Stanley. (1992) *This Is a House.* New York: Cobblehill Books.

Burton, Virginia Lee. (1939) *Mike Mulligan and His Steam Shovel.* Boston: Houghton Mifflin.

Gibbons, Gail. (1990) *How a House Is Built.* New York: Holiday House.
———. (1983) *New Road.* New York: Four Winds Press.
———. (1986) *Up Goes the Skyscraper.* New York: Four Winds Press.

Gliori, Debi. (1992) *My Big House.* Cambridge, MA: Candlewick Press.

Hennessy, B. G. (1994) *Road Builders.* New York: Viking Press.

Hoban, Tana. (1975) *Dig, Drill, Dump, Fill.* New York: Greenwillow.

Mitgutsch, Ali. (1981) *From Clay to Bricks.* Minneapolis: Carolrhoda Books.

Neville, Emily Cheney. (1988) *The Bridge.* New York: Harper & Row.

Olney, Ross Robert. (1984) *Construction Giants.* New York: Atheneum.

Radford, Derek. (1992) *Building Machines and What They Do.* Cambridge, MA: Candlewick Press.

Robbins, Ken. (1984) *Building a House.* New York: Four Winds Press.

Rockwell, Anne. (1986) *Big Wheels.* New York: Dutton.

Rockwell, Anne and Harlow. (1972) *Machines.* New York: Macmillan.

Royston, Angela. (1991) *Diggers and Dump Trucks.* New York: Macmillan.

Scarry, Richard. (1968) *What Do People Do All Day?* New York: Random House.

Watanabe, Shigeo. (1985) *I Can Build a House.* New York: Philomel.

Wilkinson, Jean and Ned. (1970) *House Construction: Come to Work with Us in Construction.* Milwaukee, WI: Sextant Systems.

## OTHER GOOD RESOURCES

Adkins, Jan. (1980) *Heavy Equipment.* New York: Charles Scribner's Sons.

Jennings, Terry. (1993) *Cranes, Dump Trucks, Bulldozers, and Other Building Machines.* New York: Kingfisher Books.

Sobol, Harriet Lansam. (1978) *Pete's House.* New York: Macmillan.

Wilcox, Catherine. (1990) *A Skyscraper Story.* Minneapolis: Carolrhoda Books.

*Heavy Equipment Operator: Cranes, Dump Trucks, Dirt Movers* (video). (1993) Big Kids.

*Mighty Construction Machines* (video). (1994) Noda Films.

*Road Construction Ahead* (video). (1991) Focus Video Productions.

# Farm · · · · · · · · · · · · · · · · · · · · · · · · · · ·

For the vast majority of children who live in cities and suburbs, food comes from stores, not farms. Even the few who have been to farmers' markets have no way of connecting the produce they are buying to the farm that produced it. Children have seen pictures of farms in books and on TV, but the real sight of large cows walking around, peas growing inside pods, and corn on those very tall stalks is vastly different and amazes young children. Not many children get to visit farms with their families, so a group experience may be the only way for many children to do so. A trip to a farm offers children an opportunity to see for themselves

- the animals that live on farms, what size they are and where they live during the day and at night;
- how animals are fed, what they eat, and where their food is kept;
- the food farmers grow for both their animals and for people;
- farmers doing chores, such as milking cows or goats and collecting eggs;
- various crops growing and being harvested;
- the machines farmers use, their size, and perhaps how they work; and
- the land and buildings on the farm and what they are used for.

Although some farms are set up for visiting groups and they welcome children, it can be difficult to find a farm to visit. To find a farm, ask parents, friends, relatives, and other teachers if they have a farm connection to pursue. The extension agent of your county agricultural extension service may list farms that welcome visitors. (Even urbanized counties may have outlying areas that have farms, or call a rural neighboring county's extension service.) Other resources to contact are 4-H clubs and youth programs in your own or neighboring counties or the state office. A college, university, or vocational school with an agricultural program may also have its own farm or animal barns and may have some experimental sites or farm connections. Another possible source would be to ask the people selling produce at farmers' markets. Ask where their farm is, what type of farm it is, and if they would consider letting children visit.

Some dairy farms that also make cheese welcome visitors and have many interesting things to see. You can also ask at county fairs about farms in the area that might welcome visitors. County fairs are usually held in the summer and are good places to visit, to line up interesting resources as well as to see all the things on display. If all else fails, drive around the countryside and stop at a farmer's stand by a large- to medium-sized farm and ask if they ever have children's groups visit their farm or know of a farm that does.

If it is not possible to previsit the farm, ask specific questions in your phone interview. Ask if there is mud or wet grass so you can have the children dress appropriately. Ask what type of animals are on the farm, what products the farmer raises, and what machines are used. Also ask about bringing a snack for the children, and if the farm has a place for snacking and toilets. Perhaps the farmer can recommend a nearby park where you can take the group for a pit stop en route.

As with all trips, have some extra help. Some young children may be reluctant to proceed to areas that get close to the animals and should not be forced to do so. You will need enough people to ease the transition for those children, while the more enthusiastic participants go full steam ahead.

## Before the Trip

### WORDS TO LEARN AND USE

crops ● soil ● harvest ● machinery ● seed drill ● plow ● harrow ● tractor ● combine ● compost ● wheat ● corn ● oats ● barley ● barn ● grain ● hayloft ● silo ● chicken ● hen ● rooster ● pigs ● calf ● herd ● cows ● udder ● horses ● pony ● sheep ● lambs ● goats ● kid ● fence ● hay ● pitchfork ● meadow ● pasture ● foal ● eggs ● donkey ● dairy farm ● cheese ● milk ● yogurt ● soybeans ● milking machine ● creamery ● pasteurizer ● curds ● whey ● farmers' market ● culture ● straw ● bales ● seeds ● kernels ● stems ● flour mill ● bread ● dough ● food processors ● ice cream

### SHELL PEAS

Bring in a pound of fresh peas. Show the children the pods and ask them if they know what they are. Pop one of the pods open and show the children what is inside and see if they know what it is now. They may not recognize the contents as peas until you pull them off and put them in a bowl. Let the children shell all the peas and talk about where the peas and other foods grow.

The book *Growing Food*, by Claire Llewellyn, shows how many different foods grow. The book *What's on My Plate?*, by Ruth Gross, is a humorous version of the same idea.

Ask the children if they would like to go see food growing on a farm. Talk about what else they might see on the farm, and have them think of questions to ask about growing food. Taste the peas raw, and cook the rest for lunch or snack.

## A Look at Farms

Read one or two books from the Resources section. If you are visiting a dairy farm, *700 Kids on Grandpa's Farm* (*Kids* meaning goats), by Ann Morris, or *Extra Cheese, Please*, by Chris Peterson, offer wonderful introductions to producing cheese to finished product. *Farms*, by Jason Cooper, *All About Animals*, by Brenda Cook, and *Farming*, by Gail Gibbons are good general introductions to the topic. The videotapes listed in the Other Good Resources section also offer excellent introductions, particularly to the animals on farms. Ask if any of the children have ever lived on a farm or been to a farm, and if so, what it was like. Again, assemble a list of questions the children have about the animals or other aspects of farm life.

## Things to Bring

paper and a pen or pencil to record measurements and other observations ● a blanket and some books in case you need diversion ● a tape recorder to tape sounds ● list of questions ● tape measure ● plastic or paper bag for collecting things ● a camera

## On the Trip

On the way to the farm, point out the changing landscape. Do you see fewer houses and stores and more open spaces? Can you tell if the land belongs to anyone? Do you see fences around parcels of land or just open fields and woods? Do you see animals in the fenced-in areas, and what kind are they? Do you see fields that are planted with crops? Point out how crops seem to be planted in rows whereas, plain woods do not have an organized look.

Children will not automatically know the difference between woods with brush and bushes growing on them and planted fields of grain, unless you point it out to them. You may see some houses that have a few horses in a fenced-in corral and a small stable. Explain to the children that those are not real farms, but houses that have made room for horses for the family or other people to ride.

When you see cows, goats, or sheep in a pasture, you are getting to farm country. Notice the really large areas of land that have some kind of fencing around them for the animals, and the large tracts of planted fields or plowed fields waiting to be planted. Do you see any silos or barns in the distance? Point them out to the children and talk about their shape and color and what they are used for. Since they are usually quite large, they are easier to see in their entirety from a distance. Do you see some smaller buildings as well? Plan to find out what is in all the buildings you see. Can you tell where the people on the farm live?

Notice the mailboxes along the road and how far apart they are and how far from the houses they may be. Think about how the people get their mail each day.

At the farm, notice how all the buildings are laid out. Are there fenced-in areas next to each building that house animals so the animals can go outside? Are there any animals roaming around outdoors? Do you see animals eating or people feeding them? Where is the animals' food stored or prepared? Are there separate buildings for different animals?

Look in the barn to see what is there. Are there stalls for animals? Are there open spaces and a hayloft? Notice special features and everything else in the barn—from a rope swing to bales of hay, pitchforks, implements, or feeding areas. In all the buildings, observe the arrangements and procedures for feeding the animals and notice how each trough is adapted to the animal's size and way of eating. Do you see milking machines for cows or goats and egg collection areas by the chickens? Can someone show you how cows are milked? Is there a special place for milking?

Observe as many food crops growing as you can. (Before approaching a field, ask the farmer if it has recently been sprayed with insecticide, herbicide, or fertilizer. If it has been, be careful not to expose the children to the area.) Notice vegetable patch areas and corn or grain fields; try to take the children close to these areas so they can see how high the corn is and see the ears on the plants. Point out how vegetables grow, either on plants, vines, or in the ground. What else do you see growing (flowers, grains)? Show the children as many different types of grain as you can. Talk about where they have heard these names before. The wheat and oats they see will not look much like the cereals they eat, so you will have to explain the connection later.

Watch equipment in use and talk about the jobs machines do on the farm. Notice how large and complicated many of the machines are, and how some machines attach to tractors to do their jobs. Does the farmer have his or her own equipment or is some equipment shared with other farmers? Where is the equipment stored? Do you see fuel tanks for use on the farm? (Farmers usually cannot take their machines to a gas station.) Are there gas pumps or hoses attached to the tanks? Point out where the gas goes into the tractor and think about how it gets there. How much gas can the tractor hold and how often does the farmer have to fill it ? How long can it run on a tank of gas? Does the size of the tractor have anything to do with how much gas it can hold and how much gas it uses? Do you see different-sized tractors?

## Sense

Listen to the sounds on the farm. Do the animals make sounds like the ones we always say they make? What animal sounds do you hear? Tape record some of the sounds you hear to play when you get home. What other sounds do you hear besides animal sounds? Try to identify as many as you can.

What smells do you notice on the farm? Are there different smells in the different animal areas? Can you smell the hay either in bales, in the barn, or as it is being cut? Is there a smell to the animals' feed as it is being mixed or served? Which animals seem to have the strongest odor? Are there different smells indoors and outdoors in the animal areas?

Are there any animals the children can touch? What do their coats feel like? Do the baby animals feel different than the grown ones? What does hay feel like?

## Identify

Tell the children the names of as many different kinds of farm implements, machines, and animals as you know. Explain that animals are called different names when they are young than when they are grown up (just like boys and girls become men and women) and have different names if they are male or female as well. Ask the farmer to help you with the identification if you are not sure what things are called.

Identify the separate buildings and parts of buildings, such as *chicken house* or *coop*, *granary*, *silo*, and *hayloft*. Again ask the farmer to tell you the correct names for parts of the farm. Do the feeding areas have names? Do the working areas, such as the milking stations, have special names? What about places where eggs are collected or hatched?

Don't be embarrassed to ask what things are called. Farming has become highly technical and mechanized and people not involved in farming have no idea what many things are. Point out the few familiar implements, such as a pitchfork, which may be similar to things children have seen before.

### COUNT AND MEASURE

Count all the buildings you see and the number of doors into some of the buildings. Ask why there are so many doors. Count the stalls for different animals and the number of areas for baby animals. Count how many fenced-in areas you see.

Count how many people you see working and the number of different machines you see. Are there large and small versions of some of the machines? Count wheels or other machine parts.

Can you count any of the animals, or is it too hard because they keep moving? Maybe you can count baby animals. Take photos of clusters of animals to count and identify later.

Measure how high the plants are. You can measure how high plants come up on you and on the children. Do the children have to reach over their heads to measure some things? What plants grow the tallest? Write down some of the size comparisons of the different plants as well as your other findings. Count how many ears of corn are on a corn stalk, or pumpkins on a vine. Let the children think of other things they would like to count or measure.

### WONDER

Wonder what it must feel like to be up in the hayloft. If there are children who live on the farm, they may be able to tell you. Wonder how the hay gets up there and how people get up there.

Wonder what it feels like to ride on a tractor—especially a very big one. Wonder if the farmer gets tired of having to take care of the animals every single day, since there are no weekends or time off from feeding or milking animals. Does the farmer ever take a vacation? What happens to the animals if he or she does leave for a while?

Wonder if the animals ever get lost and how does the farmer find them? Wonder how they keep the animals from climbing over fences and getting out. Are there different kinds of fences for different animals?

Wonder what can make problems for the farmer. What does he or she do in really bad weather? What things can harm the crops?

### COLLECT

Bring back a collection of dried grains, corn, straw, corn shafts, and any other dried weeds or plants to use in collages.

# After the Trip: Follow-up Activities

## TALK ABOUT IT

Talk about the trip and ask the children to tell you what they liked about the farm. What things impressed them the most, and what things surprised them? Write down the things they tell you. Also discuss the things they didn't like so much and what things would be hard for them if they lived on a farm. Do they think they would like living on a farm? After the discussion, create two lists. Title one list "Things I would like about living on a farm"; title the second "Things I would not like about living on a farm."

## WRITE A THANK-YOU NOTE

Have the children draw pictures about the farm to send to the farmer with a thank-you note. Write a collective note from the group and include individual comments the children want to include on their pictures.

## FARM ANIMAL PUPPETS

Make paper bag or paper plate puppets of various farm animals. Put out a collection of small paper plates; construction paper; scrap pieces of wallpaper in browns, pinks, and other animal colors and textures; small pieces of yarn; curls of crepe paper; cotton balls; crayons and markers; and glue. Encourage children to make farm animal puppets. Let the children use their puppets to make up and present farm stories or to give information about the animal to the group.

## MAKE FARM BUILDINGS

Cover a table with newspaper. Find several medium-sized boxes (such as shoe boxes, round oatmeal boxes, and half-pint milk cartons). Use the materials to make the farm buildings you saw. Ask the children what color paints they need to paint the buildings and what other boxes or materials they might need. Let them paint and decorate the buildings over several days. When the buildings are dry, let the children use them in the block area. Add sets of plastic farm animals and farm machinery to encourage dramatic play about life on the farm.

## MAKE COLLAGES

Make collages using the grains, corn seeds, and other plant parts you brought back from the farm. If you want, add pictures of foods or flowers from magazines (let the children tear or cut them out) to your collages.

## FARM SOUNDS

Listen to your tape recording and see if you can identify the sounds of the animals and any other sounds. Read books that use farm sounds, such as versions of *Old MacDonald Had a Farm*, by Nancy Hellen, *Barnyard Banter*, by Denise Fleming, or *Over on the Farm*, by Gwenda Turner. Let the children join in using the farm sounds in the stories.

## FROM FARM TO TABLE

Read *Little Red Hen*, by Byron Barton, *Extra Cheese, Please*, by Chris Peterson, *Cows in the Parlor*, by Cynthia McFarland, *How Bread Is Made*, by Neil Curtis and Peter Greenland, or books about milk. Talk about how plants and animals give us the foods we eat. Think about the names of the grains and the names of the cereals the children eat. Start a large chart of plants or animals and the foods and other food products they become. Bring in magazines with food pictures, farm magazines, and seed catalogs that show plants. Some examples for your chart include:

Cow: milk, cheese, pizza
Corn Plant: corn on the cob, creamed corn, popcorn, corn flakes, cornbread
Tomato Plant: fresh tomatoes, soup, ketchup, juice
Potato Plant: whole potatoes, mashed potatoes, French fries, potato chips, potato salad

Add items to your chart as you find pictures or as the children think of food to add. This should stimulate discussion about vegetables and foods in all their different forms. Ask the children if they know or remember where pickles come from. Encourage them to figure that out. Put books about growing food on display to help the children come up with more ideas for this chart.

Bring in items from your chart to taste in their various forms. Notice if vegetables seem to belong to families like fruits do. See if you can decide on some vegetables that might be related and what characteristic they share.

## ALL ABOUT FARM IMPLEMENTS AND MACHINES

Set up a display of the books about farm machines (some of the general farming books have machines in them too). Get some catalogs from a farm implement store or a tractor dealer (John Deere catalogs are impressive) and add those to the display. Make up a book of things used on a farm and put in it pictures of the machines you saw. Write in the name of the machine or implement and what it does. If you have toy versions of farm machines, add those to your display as well.

## What Is It?

Play guessing games using vegetables, grains, animals, or machines seen on the farm. Give a short description of the item and see if the children can guess it. If not, add more information until they do. For example: What grows on a plant and is round and soft and red? We eat it with lettuce or it can be made into juice or ketchup. The answer is a tomato.

## Milk the Cow

Make a cow to demonstrate how farmers used to milk cows by hand. Wrap a cow-colored bathroom carpet around a sturdy sawhorse and tie it on to hold it in place or attach Velcro strips in a few places. Attach a shoe box to one end of the sawhorse using tacks or nails. Decorate the lid of the shoe box to look like the cow's face, using cut-paper eyes, ears, eyelashes, horns, nose, and tongue. Glue the lid onto the box. If you want, cut several pieces of rope to attach to the other end of the cow for her tail.

Make pinpricks in the fingertips of a rubber glove (don't make the pricks too big or the water will just drip out), and fill the glove with water. Tie it at the top and attach it with rope to the bottom of the cow to form its udder. Put a pail under the glove.

To milk the cow, squeeze from the top of the fingers downward toward the tips. You must wrap your thumb and index finger around the top of the finger part to prevent the water from going upward into the hand part of the glove, and then gently squeeze with your other fingers, pressing into your hand. It takes practice, but it works and water should be squeezed out through the pricks in the fingertips.

# Related Trip Ideas to Explore

university animal barns ● community vegetable gardens ● farm implement store ● county fairs that have animals ● cheese factory ● dairy ● food processors including ones that use grain to make cereals, noodles, or soy products ● flour mill ● bakery

# Songs, Poems, and Finger Plays

## Farm Animals

Animals live on the farm
We love them every one.
The cow goes "moo," that's what they do
Her big brown eyes just stare at you.
Our visit was such fun.

Animals live on the farm
We love them every one.
The pig says "oink" and points his snout
He looks at you as if he wants to get out.
Our visit was such fun.

Additional verses:
The horse says "neigh" and runs away
But he'll come back if you give him hay.

The sheep says "baaa," just look at me
My fleece is curly as can be.

The goat says "naah," don't bother me
'Cuz I'm as grouchy as can be.

### THE FARMER

*(to the tune of "The Farmer in the Dell")*
The farmer milks cows each morn. (act out milking)
The farmer milks cows each morn.
Hi Ho, the derry oh
The farmer milks cows each morn.

The farmer plants some corn. (act out planting)
The farmer plants some corn.
Hi Ho, the derry oh
The farmer plants some corn.

It's time the sheep are shorn. (act out shearing)
It's time the sheep are shorn.
Hi Ho, the derry oh
It's time the sheep are shorn.

Get the animals before the storm. (act out rounding up the animals)
Get the animals before the storm.
Hi Ho, the derry oh
Get the animals before the storm.

Look! A new calf is born. (act surprised)
Look! A new calf is born.
Hi ho, the derry oh
Look, a new calf is born.

### PLANTS GROW

Cornstalks grow high, up toward the sky. (reach up towards the sky)
Pumpkins are round, and sit on the ground. (make a circle with arms)
But under the ground where we cannot see, (point to the ground, shake head)
Grow carrots, potatoes, and onions—All three! (hold up fingers, 1-2-3)

## Resources

Aliki. (1992) *Milk from Cow to Carton*. New York: HarperCollins.

Allen, Thomas. (1989) *On Grandaddy's Farm*. New York: Knopf.

Barton, Byron. (1993) *Little Red Hen*. New York: HarperCollins.

Brown, Margaret Wise. (1989) *Big Red Barn*. New York: Harper & Row.

Carrick, Donald. (1985) *Milk*. New York: Greenwillow Books.

Clayton, Gordon. (1992) *See How They Grow—Lamb*. London: Dorling Kindersley (also in this series: *Pig*, *Foal*, and *Calf*).

Cook, Brenda. (1988) *All About Animals*. New York: Doubleday.

Cooper, Jason. (1992) *Farms* (Discovery Library of Great Places to Visit). Vero Beach, FL: Rourke.

Curtis, Neil, and Peter Greenland. (1992) *How Bread Is Made*. Minneapolis: Lerner Publications.

deFelise, Cynthia. (1994) *Mule Eggs*. New York: Orchard Books.

Duffy, DeeDee. (1992) *Barnyard Tracks*. Honesdale, PA: Bell Books.

Flanagan, Terry. (1980) *Snoopy's Facts and Fun Book About Farms*. New York: Random House.

Fleming, Denise. (1994) *Barnyard Banter*. New York: Henry Holt.

Fowler, Allan. (1993) *Woolly Sheep and Hungry Goats*. Chicago: Childrens Press.

Gibbons, Gail. (1988) *Farming*. New York: Holiday House.

Gross, Ruth B. (1990) *What's on my Plate?* New York: Macmillan.

Hellen, Nancy. (1990) *Old MacDonald Had a Farm*. New York: Orchard Books.

Kightley, Rosalinda. (1989) *The Farmer*. New York: Macmillan.

Kundhardt, Edith. (1990) *Which Pig Would You Choose?* New York: Greenwillow.

Llewellyn, Claire. (1991) *Growing Food* (First Look Series). Milwaukee, WI: Gareth Stevens.

Maris, Ron. (1986) *Is Anyone Home?* New York: Greenwillow Books.

McDonald, Flora. (1994) *I Love Animals*. Cambridge, MA: Candlewick Press.

McFarland, Cynthia. (1990) *Cows in the Parlor*. New York: Antheneum.

McPhail, David. (1990) *Ed and Me*. San Diego: Harcourt Brace.
———. (1985) *Farm Morning*. San Diego: Harcourt Brace.

Miller, Jane. (1989) *Farm Noises*. New York: Simon & Schuster.

Morris, Ann (1994) *700 Kids on Grandpa's Farm*. New York: Dutton Children's Books.

Otto, Carolyn. (1990) *That Sky, That Rain*. New York: Crowell.

Peters, Lisa Westberg. (1995) *The Hayloft*. New York: Dial Books.

Peterson, Chris. (1994) *Extra Cheese, Please*. Honesdale, PA: Boyd Mills Press.

Pryor, Bonnie. (1991) *Greeenbrook Farm*. New York: Simon & Schuster.

Tafuri, Nancy. (1994) *This Is the Farmer*. New York: Greenwillow Books.

Turner, Gwenda. (1993) *Over in the Farm*. New York: Viking.

Wykeham, Nicholas. (1979) *Farm Machines*. Milwaukee, WI: Raintree.

## Other Good Resources

Bial, Raymond. (1991) *Corn Belt Harvest*. Boston: Houghton Mifflin.

Jacobson, Karen. (1981) *Farm Animals* (A New True Book). Chicago: Childrens Press.

*Farm Animals—Close Up and Very Personal* (video). (1994) Stage Fright Productions.

*Farm Animals* (See How They Grow Videos). (1993) Sony Kids' Video.

*Good Morning, Good Night! A Day on the Farm* (video). (1988) Bo Peep Productions.

# Fire Station••••••••••••••

Most visits to fire stations will be part of a scheduled tour, since fire departments everywhere offer extensive community outreach programs. One local department in a small community reported that thousands of preschoolers and kindergartners visit every year, and that the department also offers a fire prevention curriculum. Many firefighters will demonstrate their specialized equipment to children. Looking at this huge equipment up close is impressive and so is seeing how everything is carefully planned for quick action. Trips to the fire station give children an opportunity to

- see several types of emergency vehicles up close and standing still so they can look inside;
- learn about the work that firefighters do and see their uniforms and fire fighting clothes up close;
- see the various parts of the equipment such as hoses, hooks and belts, ladders, and oxygen tanks;
- learn how the equipment is stored, taken care of, and made ready for action; and
- see what the inside of the fire station looks like and perhaps hear the emergency alarms, loudspeakers, sirens, walkie-talkies, and other equipment.

Arrange trips to visit fire departments by calling your local fire department or the nearest fire station. Their busiest time is fire prevention month (usually in October), so you might want to choose another time (although during that time they are all geared up for visits). A few family child care providers might want to get together to schedule a trip so that you can share taking care of babies and toddlers while older children participate in the more organized tour. You'll find many introductory activities for this trip because children will get more out of their visit if they have more prior information. The fire station is not a place you and your group can drop in for follow-up visits and questions. It is a good idea to have all your questions in mind before your trip so you can get them answered by the firefighter who shows you around.

# Before the Trip

## WORDS TO LEARN AND USE

firefighter ● fire truck ● volunteer ● full time ● chief ● company ● crew ● rigs ● engine company ● ladder company ● pumper engine ● hose ● nozzles ● lines ● pumps ● ladder trucks ● hooks ● fire hydrant ● pole ● aerial ladder truck ● elevating platform truck ● tanker truck ● ambulance ● alarm ● siren ● rescue unit ● boots ● packs ● gauge ● dials ● dispatcher ● oxygen tanks and masks ● searchlight ● sledge hammer ● beeper ● hydraulic boom ● snorkel bucket ● foam ● tiller cab ● turntable ladder ● fire extinguisher ● Dalmatians ● ax ● stop, drop, roll ● pike pole ● soft suction hose ● hard suction ● mini-pumper ● turnout coats ● gloves ● helmets

## READ AND TALK ABOUT IT

For several days before the trip, read and discuss books on firefighters and fire stations. *Fire Stations*, by Jason Cooper, and *I Want to Be a Firefighter*, by Edith Kunhardt, are good general introductions. *I Want to Be a Firefighter* is about a girl planning to be a firefighter like her dad and

shows something of the daily work involved. *Fire, Fire*, by Gail Gibbons, has wonderful information about fighting fires in a variety of settings and shows the vehicles in action. Both this book and Gibbons' book *Emergency* label parts of the fire trucks and other vehicles to help you point these things out to the children. Many other books also have good pictures of vehicles and would be good to have on display. The book *Firehouse*, by Katherine Winkleman, has interesting information. It's good for your own background information; and has wonderful pictures. *Fire Trucks*, by Hope Marston, has clear information about all the different kinds of trucks. Fire trucks are specially designed according to what each fire department needs. Use words on the list in reference to parts of the trucks and show the children the pictures of those parts. In the books, point out all the things including the firefighter's clothes and equipment.

Talk about how firefighters have special jobs to do and how they work as a team. Even after reading all these books, you will have questions, so start assembling a list to ask at the fire station. Plan to ask how they decide what kind of trucks they need. Wonder if all the trucks have their own water, how the hoses go up with the ladders, or if the ladders have pipes on them. Become familiar with the large variety of equipment in use today; this will help the children recognize some of it and assimilate what the firefighter shows and tells them. It will also help you to notice things to point out to the children, focus attention, and reinforce the things you discussed and saw in the books.

## LOOK AND SEE

Look for the fire hydrants in your area and take your group to examine them. See if you can figure out where the fire hoses attach and where the controls might be. Wonder how the firefighters open the hydrants and make them work. How far apart are the fire hydrants? Are all fire hydrants the same? If not, what are the differences? Can firefighters use the water from several hydrants to fight a big fire?

Look around your building or home for any fire extinguishers, smoke detectors, alarm systems, or anything else that seems to be connected to fire safety or prevention. Think of any question to ask the firefighters about these items. Do they use anything like the fire extinguishers that are found in homes or schools? Wonder when those type of chemical or foam materials should be used, and when you should just use water. Do the firefighters ever get false alarms from building alarm systems that go off when there is not a real fire? What can make alarm systems go off by mistake?

## DO ALL FIRE STATIONS HAVE POLES?

Think of other questions you may have—believe it or not, not all fire stations have poles, especially some of the newer ones where the living quarters are not above the station, or stations that do not have living quarters because they use volunteer or part-time firefighters. If you are visiting a station that looks like it is on one level, don't expect to see a pole. What safety procedure do they have in stations that have poles to make sure no one falls down the hole?

Will they have a Dalmatian dog at the fire station? Some fire stations still have dogs as mascots as some books suggest, but not for the jobs that the Dalmatians used to do when horses pulled fire wagons.

Why are the colors of fire engines changing? Write down all the questions you can think of to ask on your trip.

### THINGS TO BRING

paper and a pen or pencil to record observations ● questions for the firefighters ● plastic or paper bag for collecting things ● a camera

## On the Trip

### OBSERVE

Look at the fire station building as you arrive and notice objects that tell you it is a fire station. Is there a name or number on the building and are there any vehicles outside? Are there large garage-type doors and are the driveways kept clear? Do you see any writing on the vehicles that tell you what it is or whose it might be? Are there loudspeakers, lights, alarms, or sirens on top of the building? Can you tell how many floors there are in the building and if it looks new or old; guess whether or not it has a pole. Are there other doors besides the garage-type doors?

When you enter the building, notice how huge the fire engines look and all the equipment lined up around the room. Notice the firefighters' working suits (coats and pants) hanging, ready to use. Are there pants with boots inside them already to be jumped into? This system of the pants placed over the boots is called a Quick Hitch—it might work well for preschoolers snow pants and boots.

Notice belts, hooks, packs, helmets, gloves, oxygen tanks, and anything else that is ready to go. A tour leader will probably tell you about the things you are seeing and may demonstrate how quickly firefighters dress into their work clothes. He or she may let your group feel the helmets, coats, boots, and gloves. They are heavier than they look. They will also tell you all about the equipment and point out the hoses, ladders, and parts of the fire trucks and other vehicles. Look at the dials and gauges on the trucks and have the firefighter explain what they tell or do. Look at the controls on the truck and any other special equipment. Notice the lights on the engines. How many of the engines are like ones you looked at in the books? Do you see an ambulance or rescue unit, and are there stretchers, splints, and other emergency equipment on or near it? Notice any extra ladders and hoses around the station. Do they load those on the trucks or are there extra sets to use when hoses are being cleaned? Ask how the hoses are cleaned and dried, and ask all the questions from your list.

Notice other things inside the station. Are there living quarters in this station? Is there a kitchen or lounge area, lockers for storage, an office, and, a pole? Do you see people working in an office or taking care of equipment? Are there any pictures, posters, or information about fire prevention on display?

## COUNT

There are many things to count all over the station, starting with the number of doors. Count the number of vehicles in the station, tires on each vehicle, lights, ladders, hoses, bells, horns, dials, windows, and seats. Talk about why there are so many lights on the fire engines. Count the number of working outfits and ask how many people ride on each engine. Are all the outer garments hung near the engines or stored in other places as well?

## SENSE

Talk about how shiny all the fire engines look. Touch them and feel the slick metal of the panels. Feel the bumpy parts on the steps and climbing areas; explain that the bumpy ridges on steps will make the steps less slippery for climbing in and out.

If the firefighter turns on any of the alarms, have the children cover their ears. Talk about how loud they sound. Talk about any scary feelings children might have being close to fire engines, but emphasize how firefighters work hard to keep people safe and save lives when there is a fire.

## KEEP SAFE

The firefighter may tell the children a little about keeping safe and preventing fires and have special information on good rules for being safe. They may talk about Stop, Drop, and Roll if children's clothes catch fire. Collect all the fire safety materials they have available to use in follow-up activities. Some fire departments have fire safety curriculum especially for young children, and if yours does you may want to use it. Fire prevention education is an important part of firefighters' job of making our communities safer. They know better than anyone how dangerous playing with matches and fire can be and welcome your help in getting that message out.

## After the Trip: Follow-up Activities

### TALK ABOUT IT

Talk about the trip and let the children tell you their reactions to the fire station. On one sheet, write down their observations and comments about the vehicles. On another sheet, write down the children's comments about the work of firefighters. Talk about how exciting it might be to ride on the fire engines, but how scary to run into someplace that is burning. Ask how many children think they would like to be a firefighter when they grow up. (In the days before astronauts, fire fighting was the number one career choice of four year olds.) Use the information from your discussion to write a group thank-you note to send to the fire station.

### DEMONSTRATE AND TALK ABOUT IT

Add hand water pumps to your water table. (You can find plastic pumping toys or hand pumps in water and sand toy kits.) Add a small piece of plastic tubing to the pump to work like a hose. Have the children pump slow and fast to see what happens to the water coming through the small plastic tube. If the pumping was even stronger and faster, what would happen? If you have an aquarium with an electrical water pump in it, watch how the pump works. Explain to the children that the pumper fire engines have powerful mechanical pumps built into them that pump the water from hydrants, water tanks, or lakes through the hoses to the fire, just as you pumped water in your water play table. Also demonstrate and use the pumping nozzles that come on cleaning materials. (Clean the nozzles thoroughly before adding them to your water play table). In summer, use these items outdoors along with real hoses and nozzles.

### BLOCK PLAY

Encourage the children to convert some of your trucks to fire engines by adding toy ladders (or handmade ladders) and small pieces of plastic tubing. Add the new fire engines to your block corner to put out any pretend fires that happen in the buildings the children build.

### DRAMATIC PLAY PROPS

Bring in slicker raincoats and large boats to dress up like firefighters.

Add plastic fire helmets or make paper ones: round off one end of a piece of construction paper; cut two slits in the opposite end about 2 to 3 inches long and fold over the center; staple together to make a hat. Attach a large silver or gold round sticker in the center as a badge.

Make air tanks out of large plastic 2-liter bottles or large oatmeal containers: tie a wide piece of ribbon around each bottle or container and leave enough ribbon for the children to wear them like a backpack, tying the ribbon behind their backs. Add pieces of thin plastic tubing to look like a breathing line.

Use empty and cleaned air freshener containers as handheld walkie-talkies.

Add plastic tubing and nozzles to make hoses (without water this time) to put out fires. Encourage the children to make up dramatic situations in their play and work as a team of firefighters to help save the day.

## FIRE STATION MURAL

Make a large mural of the fire station. Use colored construction paper shapes for the fire engines. Add circular coding dots to use for lights, dials, and gauges. Use string or narrow ribbon for hoses; dark-colored plastic for coats, boots, and helmets; and silver ribbon for ladders. Encourage the children to make many different trucks, and provide paper in all the new fire engine colors to see if they get used. Add firefighter stickers or pictures from magazines, toy catalogs, or fire safety brochures. Add a section with buildings, a fire, and the fire trucks in action.

## FIRE SAFETY

Read books on fire safety and make up a chart of fire safety rules. Look at the fire safety brochures for more ideas, and add pictures or picture symbols from the brochures to your chart. Read it over frequently with the children.

Practice the Stop, Drop, and Roll technique. Explain that fires need air to burn so drop and roll are ways to smother the fire by taking away the air.

Encourage the children to make their own book about fire safety to take home. Let the children pick rules from your group chart to put in their books. Make the books from folded, stapled construction paper. Use the fire prevention brochures and other materials for pictures.

## READ AND WRITE

Reread books about the fire station that you read earlier to see if all your questions have been answered. Talk about the other types of fire fighting vehicles besides trucks, such as fire boats, helicopters, and trucks for airport fires. Add them to your mural and label them. Make up a big book about fighting fires and include pictures of all the different kinds of vehicles. Write up brief descriptions of the equipment and the fires they fight.

## Related Trip Ideas to Explore

police station ● city hall or courthouse ● village parade with fire engines in it ● mall fire prevention displays ● post office ● service sites, such as utility and telephone repair, snow removal, street cleaning, and recycling

## Songs, Poems, and Finger Plays

### FIGHTING FIRES

Fire engines shiny and bright;
Ready and waiting day and night.
Standing by is its faithful crew;
Each one with a special job to do.
They rush to the fire at the sound of the alarm;
And try to save the people from any harm.

### FIRE ENGINES

How many fire engines do I see?
A pumper, a ladder, and a tanker are three. (hold up three fingers)
A rescue truck makes number four. (hold up four fingers)
The fire chief's car and some vans add more.
Sirens blasting, red lights flashing.
There they go—
1-2-3-4-5 in a row. (hold up a finger for each number)

### WHAT COLOR IS IT?

Our town's fire engines all used to be red;
But now they have a yellow one instead.
They say there are white ones and green ones too;
I don't like the idea, do you?
Fire engines are supposed to be red!

## Resources

Barrett, Norman. (1990) *The Picture World of Fire Engines*. New York: Franklin Watts.

Bridwell, Norman. (1994) *Clifford the Firehouse Dog*. New York: Scholastic.

Brown, Margaret Wise. (1993) *The Little Fireman*. New York: HarperCollins.

Bundt, Nancy. (1984) *The Fire Station Book*. Minneapolis: Carolrhoda Books.

Carter, Kyle. (1994) *Safety With Fires*. Vero Beach, FL: Rourke.

Cooper, Jason. (1992) *Fire Stations* (Discovery Library of Great Places to Visit). Vero Beach, FL: Rourke.

Elliott, Dan. (1983) *A Visit to the Sesame Street Firehouse*. New York: Random House.

Flagin, Clairece. (1991) *Safe at Home*. Chicago: Contemporary Books.

Gibbons, Gail. (1994) *Emergency*. New York: Holiday House.

———. (1984) *Fire, Fire*. New York: Crowell.

Hankin, Rebecca. (1985) *I Can Be a Firefighter*. Chicago: Childrens Press.

Johnson, Jean. (1985) *Firefighters A–Z*. New York: Walker and Company.

Kuklin, Susan. (1993) *Fighting Fires*. New York: Bradbury Press.

Kunhardt, Edith. (1995) *I Want to Be a Firefighter*. New York: Scholastic.

Maass, Rob. (1989) *Firefighters*. New York: Scholastic.

Marston, Hope Irvin. (1984) *Fire Trucks*. New York: Dodd Mead.

McMillan, Bruce. (1988) *Fire Engine Shapes*. New York: Lothrop.

Rius, Maria. (1985) *Fires*. New York: Barron's.

Rockwell, Anne. (1986) *Fire Engines*. New York: E. P. Dutton.

Smith, Betsy. (1981) *Firefighter: A Day in the Life of*. Mahwah, NJ: Troll Associates.

Smith, Dennis. (1990) *The Little Fire Engine that Saved the City*. New York: Doubleday.

Winkleman, Katherine. (1994) *Firehouse*. New York: Walker and Company.

Yee, Herbert Wong. (1994) *Fireman Small*. New York: Houghton Mifflin.

## OTHER GOOD RESOURCES

Bester, Roger. (1987) *Fireman Jim*. New York: Crown Publishers.

Broekel, Ray. (1981) *Firefighters* (A New True Book). Chicago: Childrens Press.

Stephen, R. J. (1986) *Fire Engines*. New York: Franklin Watts.

# Grocery Store··········

Most preschool children have probably been to a grocery store many times—but most likely they have gone on hurried shopping trips and not educational experiences. Grocery stores, however, are literally stocked with wonderful learning opportunities. A grocery store is a living laboratory of categorization. It offers opportunities to observe and learn about likenesses and differences among similar things as well as to see multiple transformations of the same things (for example, fruits and vegetables that are whole or cut up in various ways, canned, dried, or frozen). Trips to the grocery store also offer opportunities to

- observe what people do who work in these stores;
- learn how grocery stores work and how foods are packaged and items arranged for display and sale;
- buy some things for later use;
- see demonstrations of foods being cooked or processed;
- see the large variety of things sold in these stores; and
- learn about the different departments and what types of things are in each one.

Many large grocery stores offer wonderful tours for preschool groups, but there are also many things to see and explore on your own. Indeed, you can take frequent trips to the store with different objectives for each excursion. You play a crucial role in using the language and other learning opportunities a grocery store offers. Anyone—young or old—can only absorb so much at a single exposure, so revisits and on-going follow-up activities offer the best chances to reinforce old and add new learning.

## Before the Trip

### Words to Learn and Use

vegetables ● fruits ● meat ● produce ● bakery ● section ● department ● delicatessen ● dairy products ● racks ● counters ● shelves ● paper products ● cereal ● canned goods ● freezer ● frozen foods ● condiments ●

spices ● check-out ● express check-out ● manager ● stock clerk ● carry out ● conveyer belt ● butcher ● aisle ● soft drinks ● returnable ● cash register ● cashier ● cart ● bulk ● generic ● organic ● brand ● gourmet food ● coupon

### READ AND DISCUSS

Read the book *Bread, Bread, Bread*, by Ann Morris, and ask the children if they have eaten any of the breads shown in the book such as pita, French bread, or tortillas. Ask them if they think breads like those in the book can be found in nearby grocery stores. Plan to go to the store to look for as many of the breads as you can find to buy and bring back to taste.

### TALK ABOUT IT

Ask the children if they go to grocery stores with their families. Do they know which store they have been in? What can they tell you about the stores they have been in? What have they noticed? Write down the things they tell you about the store. Plan to see if the store you visit is similar or different from the ones they describe.

paper and a pen or pencil to record observations ● list of breads to look
for ● list of items to buy (including citrus fruits and fresh vegetables) ●
plastic or paper bag for collecting things and for carrying purchases ●
a camera

## On the Trip

### OBSERVE

Notice the general appearance of the building. Is it small, large, new, old,
busy, or quiet? What features around the building are part of the store's
operation, such as an area for deliveries, a grocery pickup area, and areas
for grocery carts? Is there advertising on the windows or around the
store? Observe people delivering products to the store. How are they
unloaded and moved into the store? Notice the loading docks in back and
point out that the height of the docks is the same height as trucks (if
there are no trucks there).

Notice the entryway to the store. Are there double doors, automatic
doors, or separate entrances and exits? Is there a bulletin board with
notices or other items on display to catch people's attention?

Look at the store arrangement and notice the different sections. How
much can you see from the entrance area? Talk about the way things are
grouped and read signs that tell what is in each area, such as meat
department, produce, and bakery.

Observe the check-out procedures. Are there several counters or just
one? Are there special counters if shoppers have just a few items or for
bagging your own groceries? How do people know which check-out to go
to? Are there lines? Notice the equipment in use. Are there conveyor
belts, computerized cash registers, laser scanners, or any other special
features? Watch the cashier and the people bagging the groceries. Do they
follow any system in doing their jobs? Do people carry out their own groceries, or is there a pickup arrangement? What system do the employees
use to keep track of people's groceries? Are there places to return bottles
or other returnable containers? What other services are available in the
grocery store?

Explore a few sections of the store, such as the produce department
and the meat department, pointing out and naming as many items as you
can. Notice how things are displayed, with the same type of items being
grouped together. Talk about categories (or groupings) and different ways
of packaging the same items, such as cans or boxes of soup and bags or
cans of coffee. Observe anyone who may be grinding coffee beans or making oranges into juice, and talk about these procedures. How are the display racks and counters especially suited to the items they contain? Look
at the many different types of the same things: different types of apples,
lettuces, ground meat, and steaks.

Notice how items are packaged and marked. Call attention to how
things are sold and priced. Is it by the item or by the pound? How can

people decide what is a good buy? Look for signs that give price information and tell the children what different things cost. Are there sections for bulk foods? Explain that idea to the children. Show them bulk cereals and their price and the same kind of cereal in a box and its price.

Notice the jobs people do at the store. Do people have special tasks? Do you see employees marking items for sale, replenishing shelves, or packaging foods?

Notice some of the specialized sections the store may have, such as gourmet foods, diet foods, ethnic foods, and natural foods. Talk about the large areas for frozen foods or baked goods. Notice the areas that have things kept cold and the different types of display cases in sections like the meat department, deli, or bakery sections.

### COUNT AND COMPARE

Count the number of aisles, check-out counters, wheels on the carts, people working in each area.

Count the number of different types of the same thing such as different kinds of grapefruits, carrots, packages of bacon, brands of paper napkins, and types of pizza.

Count the different-sized containers of milk and other dairy products. Talk about the amounts in each container such as pint, quart, half-gallon, and gallon.

Compare the different sizes and types of some produce items such as oranges, grapefruit, tomatoes, potatoes, and carrots. Be sure to note when something is a different item even though it may resemble something else. For instance, cabbage may look like lettuce, but it is actually a different vegetable.

### ASK

If you are not on a special tour:

Ask the department managers to show you the back room work areas where items are received, wrapped, or sorted. Ask them to tell you about their work.

Ask to see special equipment employees use for packaging or marking products. Have them demonstrate the equipment for the children.

Ask to see the bakery kitchen or receiving area, if there is one. Notice the huge pans and storage racks for holding baked goods. If they do baking on the premises, look at the huge mixers, pans, and ovens. If there is a cake decorator at work, ask for a demonstration.

### SENSE

Stand in different sections of the store; close your eyes and listen. Stores are such visually stimulating places, it may be necessary to close off one sense to really use another. Do you hear cash registers, carts slamming or moving, music, phones ringing, babies crying, announcements, or pages? List all the sounds the children tell you.

What smells do you notice in the store? Again, move around to different sections. Can you smell coffee beans grinding, fresh juice being made, things baking, or chickens on the spit? Are there smells in the deli section, fish department, and produce sections? Sniff particular items such as onions, herbs, or garlic, and talk about strong smells. Are employees giving out free food samples? Talk about why some stores give out tasting samples.

## SPECULATE

Wonder why there are so many different brands of items.

Think about why so many areas of the store have things kept cold. How is that done? Why is it done? Wonder what happens in stores that don't have items kept cold. How do people shop in places without refrigeration? Does it feel cold in the store? Why is that?

What happens to the baked goods that don't get sold each day? Think about the differences of baked goods in boxes and fresh baked goods. Why can one be kept while the others have to be sold each day? Discuss the idea of preservatives.

What would it be like to work in a grocery store?

## COLLECT

Ask store employees to give you pictures of foods, old displays, or any other potential throwaways you might find useful.

Buy items to use in follow-up activities: breads; citrus fruits (at least one of each kind); assorted fresh vegetables (for tasting or to make soup); assorted other fruits and some that may not be familiar to the children (such as pineapple or some melons); dried fruits; rice and frozen bread dough.

# After the Trip: Follow-up Activities

## TALK ABOUT IT

Talk about the trip and ask the children what they remember about the store. How does the store you visited compare to ones they have been to before? Where else do people shop for food? Talk about special stores that have foods from other cultures, called ethnic food stores, that may have some of the breads you could not find. Mention also farmer's markets, which have fresh things from farms or special shops such as bakeries, coffee shops, and co-ops.

Ask the children if they still have questions about stores. Write down a list of things they are still curious about related to grocery stores or things they saw in the store. Find out the answers. If appropriate, plan another trip to the store to find the answers or plan to visit a different kind of food store.

### FRUIT IN MANY FORMS

Show some examples of dried fruits, fresh fruits, canned fruits, and frozen fruits. Try to figure out what has to be done to fresh pineapple to make it look like canned pineapple. Cut the fresh pineapple in various ways, similar to how it appears in cans (such as slices or chunks). Take the fresh pineapple and let it cook for a while in a little water to see what happens. What happens if you add sweetener to the water? Wonder if other canned and fresh fruits are related. How are they treated and packaged? Read the labels on the cans to see if sugar is added.

Compare dried and fresh fruits and decide what has happened to the fruit to make it dried. Try dehydrating some banana slices by baking them at a low temperature. Taste fresh fruits and their dried counterparts.

Make a chart showing pictures of fresh fruits and their dried counterparts. Include fresh and dried apricots; prune plums and prunes; grapes and raisins; apples and dried apple slices; and any others you can find. Besides dried fruits, include in your fruit chart pictures of fruits and their other forms such as juices, sauces, and jams.

### FRUIT FAMILIES: TASTE AND TELL

Examine the citrus fruits you bought at the store. Cut them open and notice their structure, seeds, texture, and taste. Decide what things are similar among all of them and what are different. Can you decide why they are a family of fruits, or why they are called citrus fruits? Write a description of each one, giving its name and distinguishing characteristics. Be sure to include how they taste. Squeeze juice from each fruit and let the children taste it. Conduct similar examinations of other fruit families, such as peaches, nectarines, and other fruits with a single seed. Decide what they have in common, and if they are a fruit family.

### CITRUS FRUIT PRINTING

Use remaining halves of citrus fruits for printing with paints. Mix bright-colored paints and line paper plates or pie tins with paper towels. Pour different colors of paint on each towel so the paint is absorbed and can be used as a stamp pad. Dip the fruit halves in the paints and make prints on dark-colored construction paper.

## GROCERY STORE DRAMATIC PLAY

Set up a grocery store dramatic play area. Have the children
bring in empty boxes, cans, and other food packages. Sort
them on shelves and mark prices on them (cut out grocery ads from the newspaper to get an idea of prices).
See if the children can find ads for any of the items for
which you have empty packages. The children can
decide on specials for the day and so forth.

## VEGETABLE EXPLORATION

Bring in a batch of fresh peas and green beans.
Let the children shell the peas and taste them.
Try cutting the green beans as they are cut before
being frozen: French-cut, sliced plain, and sliced on an
angle. Taste them raw; then cook and eat them. Which way do the children like them best? Use the empty pea pods as paintbrushes if you wish.

Compare other vegetables as well, such as cucumbers and zucchini
squash, corn on and off the cob, varieties of tomatoes, and varieties of
potatoes.

## STORE BULLETIN BOARD

Divide a bulletin board into areas and use corrugated strips of paper to
represent shelves within each area. Put names over each area to correspond to the areas you visited in the store: bakery, produce, meat department, paper products, and so forth. Cut out pictures of store items from
magazine ads. Let the children pin them up on the bulletin board in the
proper section. Encourage the children to organize the items on the
shelves as they were in the store. Put one item in each area to get them
started.

## ALL ABOUT BREAD

Taste the breads you brought back from the store and talk about their
origin. Talk about how the same ingredients (flour, water, yeast—either in
or out) can result in different types of bread depending on the kind of
oven used and the way bakers roll and shape the dough.

Let frozen bread dough thaw and give each child some dough. Let
them decide how to shape their dough: flat like a pizza or tortilla or puffy
like a roll. Bake their breads to see what happens and how they taste. Be
sure to look in the oven frequently to make sure the flat breads do not get
too crisp. If the bread rises somewhat despite being pounded flat, explain
that this dough has yeast in it that makes dough rise.

If you wish, experiment with making your own dough.

## WE ALL EAT

Ask the children about their favorite foods and list them. Think about what the foods they listed are made of and how those foods are like foods eaten in other places. Most likely the list will include things made out of noodles, such as macaroni, ravioli, or pastas. These all come in different forms in many cultures, and may taste a little different related to how they are cooked and served. Bring in frozen ravioli, wontons, pierogi, and other stuffed dough foods and experiment with them. Chicken soup, vegetable soup, and rice are other foods that almost every culture eats in some version. Read the story *Everybody Cooks Rice*, by Norah Dooley, and plan to try some of the recipes for cooking and tasting rice.

## EVERYBODY SHOPS COLLAGE

While everybody shops, not everybody shops in grocery stores. While many places in the world have big grocery stores, many places do not. Most places in the world have markets and special days that people come to markets to sell the things they grow or make and buy things they need. These markets are like very large farmer's markets combined with flea markets and craft markets; they take place usually twice a week on set days in specific locations.

The book *It Takes a Village*, by Jane Cowen Fletcher, offers a glimpse of this type of market and is a good way to introduce the idea of the different ways people shop for food. Travel brochures will have colorful pictures of markets in various countries as will magazines such as *National Geographic*. Pictures taken at farmers' markets, flower markets, and other fairs also show the flavor of this worldwide phenomenon. After looking at pictures and talking about all the ways people shop, create a large collage using these pictures and ads or pictures from supermarkets or specialty food stores.

## CATEGORIZING GAMES

Create a "Do We Eat It?" game. Use two containers (for example, small boxes or halves of milk cartons). On one box, draw or paste a picture of a person eating. On the other box, paste the same type of picture with a big "no" or "X" over the person. Cut out grocery products, both edible and inedible. Let the children sort them by which can be eaten and which cannot. This is a good way to talk about not tasting poisonous or dangerous things that come from stores.

Create a "Food Sort" game. Make up master boards marked with each of the major food categories: fruits, vegetables, meat, dairy, and cereals and grains. Paste a picture of a food from that category on the board. Cut out food pictures and mount on cards. Children take turns picking cards and deciding on which master board it belongs. This is a good way to help children learn about food groups and eating foods from each group each day. Are there some foods that do not fit in any food group (candy, for instance)? What does that suggest?

# Related Trip Ideas to Explore

ethnic food stores ● fish or meat markets ● bakery ● bottling plants
(water or soda) ● candy factory

## Songs, Poems, and Finger Plays

### SHOPPING

*(to the tune of "Twinkle, Twinkle, Little Star")*
The grocery's shelves are piled high;
Almost reaching to the sky.
Busy people hurry by;
Wondering what they should buy.
See the carts all in a row;
Through the check-out,
Out they go.

### AT THE STORE

Up and down the aisles we go, (pretend to push cart and fill it with items)
Pushing our grocery cart to and fro
Filling it up with good things to eat:
Fruits and vegetables, cereals and meat.
Cheese and eggs and milk to drink,
And ice cream for a treat, I think
We always buy good things galore,
Whenever we go to the grocery store.

### FIVE FRUITS

(Use with felt cutouts or pictures of fruits; children take turns eliminating
each fruit as appropriate; substitute their names and the fruits)

Five different fruits at the grocery store.
_____ chose an _____ and now there are four. (substitute child's name and
 let each child pick a fruit)

Four different fruits we all can see.
_____ picked an _____ and that leaves three.

Three different kinds left for you.
_____ chose a _____ and now there are two.

Two yummy fruits will soon be done.
_____ took the _____ and now there is one.

One bunch of _____ for everyone. (for the
 last fruit use cherries, box of berries, or
 any fruit that comes in bunches)
We will all share them
and now there is none!

## THREE GROCERY STORES

A little neighborhood store, (form a partial rectangle shape by joining
   thumbs and extending fingers upward)
A medium-sized store, (enlarge the shape)
And a great big supermarket, (spread hands to form a large, large shape)
I see.

Shall we count them?
Are you ready?
One, two, three (repeat the three motions; indicate size of building)

## Resources

Burningham, John. (1980) *The Shopping Basket*. New York: Crowell.

Carle, Eric. (1995) *Walter the Baker*. New York: Simon & Schuster.

Dooley, Norah. (1991) *Everybody Cooks Rice*. Minneapolis: Carolrhoda Books.

Fletcher, Jane Cowen. (1994) *It Takes a Village*. New York: Scholastic.

Gordon, Margaret. (1984) *The SuperMarket Mice*. New York: Dutton.

Grossman, Bill. (1989) *Tommy at the Grocery Store*. New York: Harper & Row.

Hausherr, Rosemarie. (1994) *What Food Is This?* New York: Scholastic.

Hautzig, David. (1994) *At the Supermarket*. New York: Orchard Books.

Morris, Ann. (1989) *Bread, Bread, Bread*. New York: Lothrop.

Oxenbury, Helen. (1988) *Tommy and Pippo Go Shopping*. New York: Aladdin.

Parenteau, Shirley. (1981) *I'll Bet You Thought*. New York: Lothrop.

Pearson, Tracey Campbell. (1988) *The Store Keeper*. New York: Dial Books.

Rockwell, Anne and Harlow. (1979) *The Supermarket*. New York: Macmillan.

Ross, Pat. (1981) *M & M and the Big Bag*. New York: Pantheon Books.

Schick, Eleanor. (1982) *Joey on His Own*. New York: Dial Books.

Smith, Barry. (1989) *Tom and Annie Go Shopping*. Boston: Houghton Mifflin.

### ANOTHER GOOD RESOURCE

Schwartz, Alvin. (1977) *Stores*. New York: Macmillan.

# Hardware Store·········

Some people love hardware stores and would rather browse there than anywhere else. Those people tend to like to fix or make things. Other people never go into hardware stores except to have keys made. If you fall into the second category, look again—hardware stores present wonderful learning opportunities. Your follow-up activities can use real supplies purchased from hardware stores that are sturdy and appeal to children. On a trip to a hardware store, children can

- see a large variety of tools in all sizes, and see how they are organized and displayed;
- learn about all the different small hardware items people use to fix things or hold things together;
- learn how this store works and what people do there;
- watch keys being made;
- buy things to use in many projects; and
- see all the things hardware stores sell that are used every day in our homes.

Hardware stores have many interesting items available—usually on low shelves that present enormous temptations to young children. Therefore, take only a small group of closely supervised children on this trip, and give them specific instructions about picking out things the group will be buying. For example, they can pick out so many nails or screws of such and such a size. Before venturing into this type of store, children must be able to follow directions and understand which things they can touch and handle. This trip is not recommended for toddlers because there are too many small, dangerous objects that are too accessible. If you have a toddler among older children, be sure the toddler is in a stroller or with you at all times.

## Before the Trip

nails ● screws ● nuts ● bolts ● tools ● hammer ● wrench ● screwdriver ● pliers ● saw ● tape measure ● crowbar ● pulley ● wedge ● lever ● drill ● power tools ● sandpaper ● lumber ● pegboard ● hinges ● pipes ● kitchen ● appliances ● metal tubing ● glass ● storm windows ● dowels ● plugs ● sockets ● electric wire ● doorknobs ● latches ● locks ● keys ● paint ● paintbrush

### TALK ABOUT IT

Read *Toolbox*, by Anne Rockwell. Ask the children where their family gets tools, what kinds of tools they have at home, and what tools they use.

Show some tools you have and talk about them.

Ask the children if animals use tools and talk about their answers. Talk about what life would be like if there were no tools.

### SHOW AND TELL

Examine your blocks and select some that have rough edges. Select toys that need repair. Show them to the children and ask them what to do about them. When they suggest fixing or sanding them, ask where your group can get the things needed to fix them.

Plan to take a trip to buy tools and materials used to repair toys.

### THINGS TO BRING

paper and a pen or pencil to record measurements and other observations ● ruler or tape measure ● shopping list (including items such as sandpaper, nails, small tools, plastic tubing, large-sized washers, and nuts and bolts) ● plastic or paper bag for collecting things ● a camera

## On the Trip

### OBSERVE

Notice the general organization of the store. Make the children aware of the categories of items in the store, and how the things that are used for similar purposes are put in the same section: paint, plumbing supplies, tools, and so on.

List the different items available in the store. Point out items such as doorknobs, hinges, light switches, handles, and all types of items children may not have seen unattached. Point out lightbulbs, appliance parts, hooks, trash cans, water stoppers, and other household items.

Browse one section of the store at a time, noticing the tremendous variety of hardware items and the varying sizes of those items. Name and describe the uses of as many items as you can.

Call attention to different types of familiar tools such as screwdrivers, hammers, and wrenches.

Notice how the storage space, shelves, walls, and counters are adapted to accommodate the types of items sold in the store. How are large things and small things arranged and displayed?

Point out how items are labeled. Talk about what those fractions or inch marks on the hardware items mean.

Notice the prices of various items in the store, especially the different range of prices for some items.

If possible, watch specialized activities in the store such as employees operating machines to shake paint cans and make keys.

Watch the way employees check out customers' purchases. Do the clerks get items for customers, or do customers help themselves and take them to a central check-out?

Notice seasonal items the store may carry. Notice large equipment the hardware store has available for rent such as floor polishers, rug cleaners, and tillers. Talk about what each machine does and how much it costs to rent. Does the store rent many things? Talk about why people rent these things.

## COUNT

Count the different sizes of the same type of item. How many sizes of nails, washers, and screws are there? How many different sizes of screwdrivers, hammers, and paintbrushes?

Measure several items and match the measurements to the store's signs.

Count the different brands of the same item such as paint, mops, toasters, and irons.

Call attention to container sizes such as gallons, half-gallons, quarts of paint, and other liquid items.

Measure tools to note the differences in sizes of things such as the heads of hammers, blades of saws, and sizes of screwdrivers.

Compare the long- and short-handled versions of tools and cleaning implements. Talk about all the uses of these items.

## SENSE

Feel the variety of textures of items such as the different kinds of sandpaper, ridges on screws, bristles of brushes and rollers from mops, and smooth metals of items.

Notice the shades of colors in paint and the paint charts.

Listen to the sounds of the hardware store. Do you hear grinding or cutting sounds or noises from moving heavy equipment?

Are there particular smells in the store, such as smells related to oiling machines, from paint or cleaning items, or from bags of things sold in the store?

### SPECULATE

Guess what some of the unfamiliar items might be used for. Ask the children to guess the uses of some of the more familiar items, but ones the children may not have noticed before.

Think about what the store does with seasonal things it doesn't sell.

If the store sells toys, wonder why it does.

What would happen if the store didn't have separate spaces for all the small hardware items? Think about how the store got its name.

### ASK

Ask the owner or clerk how they keep track of everything in the store. How do they know when they need some things?

Do they have other things you can't see, such as in a catalog?

How do they decide what something should cost or what things to put on special sales?

How do they decide what things to sell and where do they get them?

Ask for or collect paint sample color cards to use later.

### PURCHASE

Buy different kinds of sandpaper to sand blocks or make sandpaper letters.

Buy some large nails and small tools to use at the workbench. Buy plastic tubing and large-sized washers to make stringing toys.

Buy large nuts and bolts and plumbing joints to use for fit-together games.

## After the Trip: Follow-up Activities

### TALK ABOUT IT

Talk about the trip and write down the children's impressions of the hardware store.

Look at hinges on cupboards and doors and talk about how they work. Look for other items in your room that you saw in the hardware store (such as light switches and cupboard handles), and call attention to how they are used. Look inside closets and hidden spots for other things you saw, such as cleaning supplies, tools, and hooks. Make up lists of things you find, the rooms they are in, and their uses.

Look at plumbing and other pipes at home or school and talk about their uses. Notice faucets and other such items. Make up some generalizations about the hardware store and its importance and usefulness.

### WORKBENCH

Organize a workbench area using different-colored cans or boxes for different-sized nails, screws, washers, and so on. Draw outlines for tools.

Obtain scrap lumber, and let the children pound nails to make simple objects. Use soft lumber or acoustical tile so the children can pound the nails easily. *Closely supervise children when they use tools.*

### FIX-IT CORNER

Bring in real tools and materials to use, and set up a fix-it corner to repair toys. Children can sand blocks, form puzzle pieces from plastic wood, replace hinges, and tighten loose screws. Talk about the idea of recycling: fixing things instead of throwing them away.

### SANDPAPER

Make sandpaper letters in different grades of sandpaper.

Sand blocks using all different textures of sandpaper. Note any differences in results with the different kinds of sandpaper.

Cut bits of different sandpaper and paste on a collage with bits of smooth paper. If you want, paint over the collage to see how the different textures absorb paint.

### FEEL AND TELL

Place common tools in a sack. Let each child reach in and try to describe or name the tool without looking at it. Show the tool and talk about what kind of tool it is and what it is used for.

### FIT TOGETHER

Provide a box of large nuts and bolts and let the children find ones that fit together.

Provide a box of pipes and fittings for the children to fit together.

Provide a ready-made lock box or make one yourself.

### HARDWARE MATCH-UPS

Make a matching game of hardware store items that are used together. From magazines or catalogs, cut out pictures and their match, such as paintbrush and paint, screwdriver and screws, hammer and nails, wrench and nuts, saw and large pieces of wood, sandpaper and small rough wood, keys and locks. Mount one picture of each pair on stiff cardboard. Paste the other picture on one side of a master board, leaving an empty square next to it for the picture of the item that goes with it.

### HARDWARE LACE-UPS

Cut thin plastic tubing into 2-foot lengths. Tie a washer to one end and use the tube as a bead lace. String washers (rubber or metal) bolts, small spools, or other small items with holes in the center.

### SHADES OF COLOR PICTURES

Let the children paint pictures that use shades of the same color. Use one color paint at a time and a container of water. Start at the top of the paper and make a stripe of paint after dipping the brush in the vivid color. Dip the brush in water and make another stripe. Dip the brush in water again and paint another stripe. Repeat until the paint color has become pale. The picture will produce various shades of the same color and look much like the paint sample cards. After the children understand how they can make shades of the same color by using water and paint, have them create their own designs and pictures.

### WHAT MAKES IT WORK?

Discuss tools that are worked by hand (muscle power) and by electricity (power tools). Make a sorting game using a master board with a category for hand tools on one side and a category for power tools on the other. Have the children sort pictures of tools (cut from catalogs or magazines) into the appropriate category.

### COLOR SAMPLES MATCHING GAME

Using sets of paint color samples, make a matching game. Cut the samples into individual pieces and mount four or five shades of the same color onto a 5-by-5-inch master board (make separate master boards for six different colors). Put the second set of colored pieces into a small box. Children match the pieces to the same colors on the master board. One child at a time can use this game, or you can use it as a small group game.

## WHAT DOES IT DO?

Make a categorizing game that organizes hardware store items by the functions they serve. Cut out pictures of items from Sears or hardware catalogs. Have three small containers (boxes, envelopes, or paper plates) with a picture on each that illustrates one type of category. Samples of categories include:

- things that cut: all types of shears, saws, scissors, utility knives
- things that hold things together: nails, screws, nuts, bolts, hinges
- things that make things smoother: sanders, polishers, sandpaper, file, rasp

Children sort the small cut-up pictures into the appropriate container. This game could be done with an adult at first.

## Related Trip Ideas to Explore

fix-it shops ● repair shops (for televisions, lamps, small appliances, and other items) ● gadget shops ● clock stores

## Songs, Poems, and Finger Plays

### THIS IS THE WAY
*(to the tune of "Here We Go Round the Mulberry Bush")*

This is the way we hammer a nail,
  (make hammering motions)
Hammer a nail, hammer a nail.
This is the way we hammer a nail,
So early in the morning.

Additional verses:
This is the way we sand our blocks…
  (make sanding motions)
This is the way we saw our wood…
  (make sawing motions)

### THE TOOL SONG
*(to the tune of "Did You Ever See a Lassie?")*

Did you ever see a hammer, a hammer, a hammer?
Did you ever see a hammer
Pound this way and that? (imitate up and down pounding motions
  with wrists)
And this way and that way,
And this way and that way.
Did you ever see a hammer
Pound this way and that?

Did you ever see a saw, a saw, a saw?
Did you ever see a saw
Cut this way and that? (imitate sawing motions with arm)
And this way and that way,
And this way and that way.
Did you ever see a saw
Cut this way and that?

(Add other tools and the accompanying motions)

### THE TOOLS

I have a little hammer
That can pound nails all the day; (imitate pounding)
And a funny little monkey wrench
That can turn things any way. (imitate turning)
And a saw too. (imitate uses of each tool)
Is there anything you'd like me
To fix for you?

### WORKS WITH ONE HAMMER

*(to the tune of "Mary Wore a Red Dress")*

_____ works with one hammer, (make pounding motion with one fist)
One hammer, one hammer.
Johnny works with one hammer
All day long.

_____ works with two hammers, (add pounding motion with second fist)
Two hammers, two hammers,
_____ works with two hammers,
All day long.

(Continue with up to five hammers. After fists, add feet, one at a time, and head for the pounding motions; vary the names as you start each verse, and have that child start the motion.)

Last verse:
_____ works with five hammers,
Five hammers, five hammers, (all parts making hammering motions)
_____ works with five hammers,
Now he (or she) puts them down. (stop all motions)

# Resources

Gibbons, Gail. (1982) *Tool Book*. New York: Holiday House.

Kalman, Bobbie. (1992) *Tools and Gadgets*. Niagara Falls, Ont: Crabtree.

Kelley, True. (1994) *Hammers and Mops, Pencils and Pots*. New York: Crown.

Miller, Margaret. (1990) *Who Uses This?* New York: Greenwillow.

Morris, Ann. (1992) *Tools*. New York: Lothrop.

Pluckrose, Henry. (1989) *Join It*. New York: Franklin Watts.

Robbins, Ken. (1983) *Tools*. New York: Four Winds Press.

Rockwell, Anne. (1988) *Handy Hank Will Fix It*. New York: Henry Holt.
———. (1971) *Toolbox*. New York: Macmillan.

Schwartz, Alvin. (1977) *Stores*. New York: Macmillan.

Shone, Venice. (1990) *Tools*. New York: Scholastic.

## ANOTHER GOOD RESOURCE

Gibbons, Gail. (1980) *Locks and Keys*. New York: Crowell.

# Hospital••••••••••••••••••••••••

Children's experiences with hospitals are apt to be of a sudden nature, involving their own emergency needs or those of a parent who may disappear to a "strong place." In such cases, prior educational experience can be enormously helpful to a child. A trip to a hospital can help children by

- letting them see what a hospital is and what the building looks like inside and out;
- showing them what people who work in the hospital do;
- relieving anxiety and fear that could be caused by having a sudden experience with an unknown place; and
- showing them items found in hospitals, such as special beds, wheelchairs, and X-ray machines.

Many hospitals have special tours for preschool children. If this service is available, take advantage of it; but call in advance as space fills up quickly. If a local hospital does not offer this service, plan to visit anyway and explore the public areas, conducting your own tour using the suggestions in this chapter. Your example will model the importance of this experience to hospital staff. Also try to work with volunteer services of your hospital to establish a tour program for children.

If you are not taking a tour offered by the hospital, but doing it on your own, a previsit is essential. Hospitals can be confusing places, and you will want to know exactly where you will be taking the children and what things you will be showing them. Check the visiting hour schedule and hours when the new baby nursery is open for viewing. Visiting during regular visiting hours offers more access to various parts of the hospital, but it also means the hospital is more crowded. Be sure to arrange for extra help to assist in parking and breaking up into small groups for parts of the visit. Give your helpers a map of the hospital and a rough outline of the order of places to visit so you are not all crowding into the same places at the same time. Set a regrouping time. It is extremely helpful to have parents who may work in the hospital accompany you, since their input can make the visit much more personal and informative.

# Before the Trip

WORDS TO LEARN AND USE

doctor ● intern ● resident ● nurse ● aide ● name tag ● receptionist ● volunteer ● technician ● patient ● waiting room ● gift shop ● admitting office ● emergency room ● elevator ● ambulance ● siren ● wheelchair ● litter ● laboratory ● blood ● lancet ● blood pressure ● thermometer ● stethoscope ● otoscope ● stitches ● cast ● tongue depressor ● operation ● adjustable beds ● nursery ● X-ray ● pharmacy ● pills ● medicine ● sterilize ● ward ● tray ● dietitian ● physical therapy ● reflex hammer ● anesthetic ● vaccine ● oxygen tank ● scales ● scanner

## TALK ABOUT IT

Ask if anyone has been to a hospital and what they did or saw there. Let the children share their knowledge and experience about hospitals. Find out if any parents have been to the hospital or work in hospitals. If parents have been in the hospital, ask what happened to the parent at the hospital and what he or she said about it. Talk about the feelings the children had while their parents were in the hospital.

Ask the children about the people who work in hospitals. If they mention doctors and nurses, ask where else they see doctors and nurses. Talk about differences between a doctor's office, clinic, and hospital. Explain that hospitals see outpatients, just like an office or a clinic, but they also have inpatients who stay in the hospital for a few days. Hospitals have beds for people to sleep in and special rooms for operations, delivering babies, taking X-rays, and caring for new babies.

## READ

Read *Curious George Goes to the Hospital*, by Margaret and H. A. Rey. Talk about Curious George's adventures at the hospital, and wonder which things in the book would be found at a nearby hospital. Plan to go and see. Ask the children if a monkey would go to a hospital. If the children wonder about that, plan to ask at the hospital.

## MAKE CARDS

If anyone has a friend or relative who is a patient in the hospital, make get well cards to take to them. Talk about making these cards bright and cheerful to help make the person feel better.

## THINGS TO BRING

paper and a pen or pencil to record observations ● list of questions ● get well cards ● plastic or paper bag for collecting things ● a camera

# On the Trip

**OBSERVE**

Look around outside. Notice if there are several entrances and if one is an emergency or ambulance entrance. How are the entrances set up to offer easy access to the building? Are there special signs or clues that tell you this is a hospital?

Notice special equipment near the entrance area or emergency room that might be needed to assist people. Are there wheelchairs, litters, oxygen tanks, portable X-ray machines, or blood pressure measurement devices on wheels?

Look at the lobby area and waiting rooms. Is there a large and small lobby, and special waiting rooms by the business office, emergency room, outpatient area, as well as a main lobby area? How are they all decorated? Are some nicer than others? Notice the furniture, plants, artwork, or other decorative touches. Are there plaques, special tributes, or names engraved on walls honoring people who have been involved with the hospital?

What other areas do you see in the general lobby section? Is there a gift shop, coffee shop, reception area, chapel, business office, telephone operator, elevator, or a hospital directory or map?

Walk down the corridors of the hospital and notice their composition. Are the floors easy to care for and very clean? Do you see anything

special along the walls such as mirrors, loud speakers, dumb waiters, or systems for sending information or medicines from one area to another? Are there glass-enclosed areas with hospital personnel visible inside?

Notice special features in some halls or offices such as the doctors' call board, X-ray viewing boxes mounted on walls, clipboards and charts, flip card files of patients in the hospital, plants, or the items to be delivered to patients.

Observe the people working in the hospital. Do they wear special clothes, name tags, or coats that indicate their department or the work they do? Do you see any people who are patients either arriving or leaving the hospital? Do you see doctors or nurses working with patients in some way?

Notice food being served in the hospital. Are there big carts with stacks of trays on them?

Look at how the rooms are arranged. Are they organized around a central service station with desks and a clerk and places for doctors and nurses to work? Does that station have TV monitors showing things from the rooms or receiving messages when patients call for help? Point out the numbers on the rooms and charts and doctors' names by the rooms.

Notice the size of the elevators. Are they much bigger than the elevators the children have seen before? Talk about why they have such big elevators in hospitals. Do you see beds or litters being moved around or big carts filled with trays or other types of equipment going to different floors or rooms?

### Ask

Ask the receptionist to show you how a record is kept of who is in the hospital and where their room is located. Ask how the plants and other items get delivered to the patients.

What duties does the receptionist have? Are there passes to give visitors or special visiting hours to monitor?

Ask the telephone operator to show you how the doctors' call board and the hospital's paging system work. Do all the announcements over the public address system come from the same central area, or can anyone talk on the system from anyplace in the hospital?

Ask the people in the gift shop to tell you about their work. Are they volunteers helping to raise money for the hospital by the gift shop sales? What items do people buy most frequently? Talk about the types of things they sell in the gift shop, and who decides what things they will carry in the gift shop.

Ask people in the emergency room area to explain some of the equipment you see. What are things called, and what do the various machines do? Ask to see an X-ray clipped up on the lighted viewing box. Perhaps someone can explain what part of the body is visible in the X-ray.

Ask to see the food service area or how food is served to people in the hospital. Do people get to choose what they want? How do patients know what they can have to eat? Who prepares the meals and who decides which patients can have what? Perhaps you can see sample menus. Do they have special menus for children?

Ask for demonstrations on adjustable hospital beds, self-guiding wheelchairs, and adjustable litters. Let the children notice all the different items on wheels and the sizes of the wheels.

## SENSE

Listen to the sounds of the hospital. Do you hear continual sounds over the public address system? What is the person saying and how does he or she sound? Do you hear sirens, noises from TV sets, and conversations? Is the overall atmosphere quiet with some intruding noises?

What smells do you notice in the hospital? Are there smells from cleaning, disinfectant and sanitizing, medicine, and food? Do different areas of the hospital have different aromas?

Talk about how it might feel to come to the hospital in an emergency. Talk about feeling scared or worried about what might happen along with the physical problem of pain or sickness that brought you there.

## COLLECT

Bring back anything you can from the trip. Collect free tongue depressors, clean tubes from syringes, sample syringes, sample of bandages, surgical masks, gloves, and any kits the hospital may give out to children.

Take pictures of the children at the hospital to use after the trip.

## After the Trip: Follow-up Activities

### TALK ABOUT IT

Let the children talk about the trip. Encourage discussion in groups and on an individual basis. Be sure you are hearing all their comments and concerns. Generate several lists based on their comments. These should include: Things we learned about the hospital, questions we still wonder about, our feelings about going to the hospital (for ourselves or others).

Talk about cheering people up when they are not feeling well, as Curious George did in the story. Think about what you could do to cheer up some children who might be in the hospital. Plan to send some things to the hospital such as pictures, homemade floral decorations, and perhaps homemade games or books about your trip.

Talk about reasons why people go to the hospital: to have an operation, have a baby, have a cast put on, or get stitches. Talk about anesthetics and how they are used to help people not feel the pain of some procedures.

Look over the items you brought back and discuss them. Explain why hospital workers wear surgical masks and gloves. Look over the syringes and talk about their uses. Explain that syringes and needles are used for many different things: to draw blood for blood tests; give medicine; give local anesthetics so people won't feel something that might hurt; give inoculations to prevent diseases. Read *No Measles, No Mumps For Me*, by Paul Showers, to explain inoculations.

### MEDICAL INSTRUMENTS CHART

Look over diagrams of body systems in books or encyclopedias and talk about how they work. Talk about things that happen to our body and cause us problems such as infections, cuts, or fractures. What does the doctor do to find out what the problem is and how to treat it?

Make a chart that shows the body system and problems; instruments used to measure the problem; and possible treatments. (Use pictures cut out from medical magazines available from doctor offices or hospitals.) Some examples for your chart include:

| Body System and Problem | How to Measure | Treatment |
| --- | --- | --- |
| Circulatory (heart trouble) | Stethoscope, EKG, take pulse | Rest, medicine, oxygen, diets |
| Infection | Thermometer, blood tests (for virus) | Rest, medicine, shot |
| High blood pressure | Blood pressure cuff | Medicine, low-salt diet |
| Respiratory (sore throat, cold, ear infection, pneumonia) | Thermometer, blood tests, otoscope, X-ray | Rest, medicine, shots |
| Skeletal (broken bones) | X-ray | Cast, crutches |
| Digestive (stomachache) | X-ray, examination | Rest, medicine, shot |

Talk about the fact that some illnesses, such as the flu, can affect more than one system. Also notice that some tests, such as blood tests and X-rays, can be used to look for many different problems.

### MAKE A HOSPITAL BOARD GAME

For older children, make a hospital game. On a large piece of tagboard, trace a path and mark off spaces along the path. Draw special symbols by some spaces to indicate places or procedures seen in the hospital. Make the hospital entrance the start space; draw a house for Return Home at the end of the game.

Make a set of playing cards to use with the board. Have some cards read "Move 1 space," "Move 2 spaces," and "Move 3 spaces." Put pictures on other cards, indicating that the player has to go to the appropriate space. Examples for special cards: "Ride in wheelchair," "Buy gift in gift shop," "Go to the business office," "Visit babies in nursery," "Have X-ray taken." For each of the special cards, the player stays on the spot for one turn. Keep the game simple with a low number of spaces to move at one time.

Have children pick the cards and move along the path. Use spools with faces drawn on them for players.

## MAKE UP STORIES

Make up stories about situations involving a hospital. If you wish, let the children dramatize the stories. Let the children tell you stories about their own experiences with hospitals. Write the stories up in a book and title it "Our Own Hospital Book." Let the children illustrate it.

## DRAMATIC PLAY

Set up a hospital dramatic play area. Doll beds can become hospital beds. Cover surfaces with towels to look like examining tables or storage space for medical kit materials and items brought back from the hospital. Ask parents from the health field if they have supplies to contribute to your hospital corner. (One parent contributed a cast for a large Raggedy Ann doll's leg.) Use large cardboard tubes to make pretend casts; paint them white if you want them to look more realistic. Children can pretend to be doctors, nurses, patients, office personnel, telephone operators, visitors, volunteers, and a variety of people observed on your trip.

## BOOK AND MATERIALS DISPLAY

Put out several hospital-related books for the children to look at. Also put out books with pictures of the body and diagrams of all its systems: respiratory, circulatory, skeletal, lymphatic, digestive, excretory, and reproductive. Encyclopedias often have colored diagrams (with overlays) of the human body. Science museums, pharmaceutical houses, or toy stores may have body parts models you can borrow to add to your display. Include some X-rays and hospital-related play equipment in the display for children to look at and manipulate. Encourage making a Lego building block hospital for your table display and add emergency vehicles to use with it.

Read and discuss several of the books and explain any of the other materials in the display. Be sure to answer any of the children's questions about items on display.

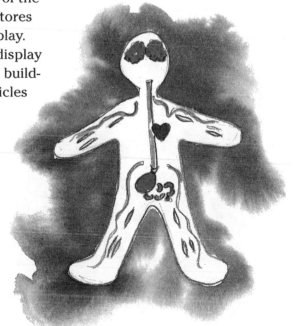

## BODY SYSTEMS DIAGRAM

After talking about systems of the body and the internal organs, let the children make a body diagram or collage using various materials to represent organs and systems. Paste items on a torso shape cut from tagboard.

Some items to use include: thin wooden skewers or toothpicks for bones; pieces of sponge for lungs; plastic packing bubbles for kidneys; heart-shaped stickers for the heart; packing peanuts for small intestines; thin plastic tubing or straws for large intestines; telephone wire or yarn for circulatory systems (arteries and veins); steel wool, clay, or a sponge for the brain; a straw for the esophagus; small balloon for the stomach and bladder; thin rope for muscles.

## Related Trip Ideas to Explore

doctor's office ● dentist's office ● nurse's office in a school or clinic ● eye doctor or optometrist ● physical therapist or rehabilitation center

## Songs, Poems, and Finger Plays

### TO THE HOSPITAL
*(to the tune of "Here We Go Round the Mulberry Bush")*
This is the way we go to the hospital, (pretend to drive to hospital)
Go to the hospital, go to the hospital.
This is the way we go to the hospital,
If we are sick in the morning.

Additional verses:
This is the way we wait at the hospital... (children sit and fidgety and
   wiggling movements)
This is way they take our pulse... (put fingers of one hand on wrist of other
   hand)
This is the way they check our blood... (pretend to prick finger)
This is the way they hear our heart... (put on pretend stethoscope and
   move it around)
This is the say they take an X-ray... (pretend to take picture)
This is the way they put on a cast... (pretend to wrap a leg)

### THIS LITTLE CHILD
*(to the tune of "This Old Man")*
This little child, he felt sick.
Drove to the hospital quick, quick, quick.
They checked his ears and throat and head;
And sent him home to go to bed!

This little child, broke her toe.
Oh my dear, it hurt her so.
Rushed to the hospital, X-rayed the little bone;
Taped it up and sent her home.

This little child had a pain.
What is was, was not so plain.
They did some tests so they could tell;
What medicine would make him well.

## AT THE HOSPITAL

I went to the hospital and what did I see?
I saw some babies looking at me.
The littlest babies, all nice and new,
Sleeping and eating is what they do.

### A HOSPITAL TRIP

I like to ride in a wheelchair
And turn it round and round. (pretend to work wheelchair with
    hands)
I like to take the elevator
And ride it up and down. (stretch up and bend down)
I like to see the flowers and toys
They have in the gift shop, (pretend to smell flowers or play with
    stuffed animal)
But there's one thing I do not like,
That's when I get a shot! Ouch! (children pretend to give themselves
    a shot)

## A HOSPITAL BED

A hospital bed can do some tricks. (lie down flat on floor)
It moves up and down by a button that flicks. (raise and lower heads)
Its head goes up, (lift heads off floor)
Its feet do too; (lift feet too)
It's amazing what that bed can do! (sit all the way up)

## FOUR LITTLE BABIES

Four little babies in the nursery I see, (hold up four fingers)
The nurse gives one to a mommy;
And now there are three. (hold up
    three fingers)

Three little babies crying boo hoo,
The nurse picks up one;
And now there are two. (hold up
    two fingers)

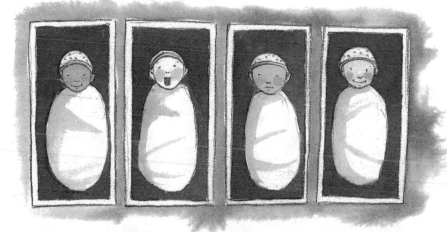

Two little babies cooing for fun,
Along comes a daddy,
And now there is one. (hold up one
    finger)

One little baby is all that I can see,
But that is the one for my family.
    (pretend to rock baby)

# Resources

Balestrino, Philip. (1989) *The Skeleton Inside You*. New York: Crowell.

Bemelmans, Ludwig. (1960) *Madeline*. New York: Viking (also available in Spanish).

Bucknall, Caroline. (1991) *One Bear in the Hospital*. New York: Dial Books.

Carlstrom, Nancy White. (1994) *Barney Is Best*. New York: HarperCollins.

Ciliotta, Claire, and Carole Livingston. (1981) *Why Am I Going to the Hospital?* Secaucus, NJ: Lyle Stuart.

Davison, Martine. (1992) *Kevin and the School Nurse* (AMA Kids Series). New York: Random House (also in the series: *Maggie and the Emergency Room, Rita Goes to the Hospital, Robby Visits the Doctor*).

De Santis, Kenny. (1989) *A Dentist's Tools*. New York: Putnam.
———. (1985) *A Doctor's Tools*. New York: Dodd Mead.

Hautzig, Deborah. (1985) *A Visit to the Sesame Street Hospital*. New York: Random House.

Hill, Eric. (1987) *Spot Visits the Hospital*. New York: Putnam.

Keller, Holly. (1989) *The Best Present*. New York: Greenwillow.

Kuklin, Susan. (1988) *When I See My Dentist*. New York: Bradbury Press.
———. (1988) *When I See My Doctor*. New York: Bradbury Press.

Linn, Margot. (1988) *A Trip to the Doctor*. New York: Harper & Row.

Martin, Charles E. (1985) *Island Rescue*. New York: Greenwillow.

Pace, Betty. (1987) *Chris Gets Ear Tubes*. Washington, DC: Kendall Green.

Reit, Seymour. (1985) *Some Busy Hospital*. Racine, WI: Western.

Rey, Margaret and H. A. (1966) *Curious George Goes to the Hospital*. Boston: Houghton Mifflin.

Rockwell, Anne and Harlow. (1985) *The Emergency Room*. New York: Macmillan.

Rogers, Fred. (1988) *Going to the Hospital*. New York: G. P. Putnam.

Showers, Paul. (1980) *No Measles, No Mumps for Me*. New York: Crowell.

Steel, Danielle. (1989) *Max's Daddy Goes to the Hospital*. New York: Delacorte Press.

Suhr, Mandy. (1991) *How I Breathe*. Minneapolis: Carolrhoda Books.

Wolfe, Robert. (1983) *Emergency Room*. Minneapolis: Carolrhoda Books.

## OTHER GOOD RESOURCES

Broekel, Ray. (1984) *Your Skeleton and Skin*. Chicago: Childrens Press.

Cole, Joanna. (1985) *Cuts, Breaks, Bruises and Burns: How Your Body Heals*. New York: Crowell.

LeMaster, Leslie Jean. (1984) *Your Heart and Blood* (A New True Book). Chicago: Childrens Press.

Vaughan, Jenny. (1988) *Hospital*. Englewood Cliffs, NJ: Silver Burdett.

Witty, Margot. (1980) *Emergency Room Nurse*. Mahwah, NJ: Troll Associates.

# Hotel / Motel ● ● ● ● ● ● ● ● ● ● ● ●

In our mobile society, adults are often on the go, and many think of staying in a motel or hotel as a routine activity. Young children, however, may have no idea what kind of place the parent is referring to either as a potential vacation stop or a stopover on a business trip. A visit to a hotel or motel expands the children's firsthand knowledge of a place they may have heard about. This knowledge may help ease anxiety associated with family member's travel. This type of trip can also offer opportunities to learn about

- the jobs people do in hotels;
- where people eat and sleep in such places;
- how the building and the rooms look and how they are taken care of;
- what other services or facilities are available in hotels;
- how various things work such as room keys, elevators, and luggage carts; and
- how hotels may be similar to homes and how they are different.

In choosing a place to visit, consider the ease of getting to and from the facility and the parking arrangements. If you travel by public transportation, a hotel near a bus or train stop may be the most convenient choice. In fact, the distinction between a hotel and motel (according to the dictionary) is based on that provision of parking for the traveler's vehicle (a motel) as opposed to just room and meals for the traveler (a hotel). We tend, however, to use the words interchangeably along with several others that refer to accommodations for travelers.

While specific items of interest will vary from site to site, a previsit will give you an idea of the special features to look for and point out to the children. Look for hotels with suites and special attractions (in one hotel, glass elevators over an atrium garden proved a hard-to-beat attraction for the preschoolers).

Since this type of facility may not be used to hosting field trips for young children, the staff may not realize they have anything of interest to offer. Explain to the manager why you want to visit and what you would like to show the children.

## Before the Trip

### WORDS TO LEARN AND USE

hotel ● motel ● inn ● bed and breakfast (B & B) ● reservation ● registration desk ● check-in ● check-out ● key ● key card ● room number ● lobby hallway ● elevator ● escalator ● suitcase ● luggage cart ● bell boy ● bell captain ● cashier ● manager ● coffee shop ● gift shop ● room service ● house phones ● atrium ● garden ● fountain ● decorations ● chandeliers ● housekeeping ● linens ● single ● double ● suite ● catering office ● meeting rooms ● ballroom ● set-up ● swimming pool ● game room ● vending machines ● ice machine ● entrance ● exit ● parking lot ● schedule ● vacancy

### TALK ABOUT IT

Ask the children how many of them have stayed in a hotel or motel or have visited a relative who was staying in a hotel. Let them tell you all they remember about it. Where else do people stay when they go on trips? Think of several questions about places to stay. What things do you need to take with you? Do you need to take blankets, pillows, sleeping bags, towels, or just things you want to have? Can you bring pets? How will you get everything into your room? Write down all the questions and plan to visit a hotel or motel to see if you can answer them.

### SHOW AND TELL

Look at the pictures in *Hotel/Motel*, by Carol Wright, or read *Buzby* or *Buzby to the Rescue*, both by Julia Hoban. Talk about the jobs people do in hotels. Plan to look for people doing those jobs when you visit a hotel.

### THINGS TO BRING

paper and a pen or pencil to record observations ● list of questions ● plastic or paper bag for collecting things ● a camera

## On the Trip

### EXPLORE THE GROUNDS

As you arrive, notice the parking areas and how they function. Is there a covered area for loading and unloading near the entryway, parking near rooms, and extra lots for cars and large vehicles. Point out the lines that show people where to park. Are there signs telling about special parking spaces? Are there vehicles with names or logos on them? Do these vehicles match other signs you see around the building? Point out signs announcing special events or celebrations at the hotel.

How can people tell if there is room to stay in this motel? Is there an outdoor sign or do they have to go in and ask? Notice plantings, decorations around the building, flags, or banners. Is there any theme to the decoration? Is there a play area, pool, or other special attractions outdoors? Who uses them? Talk about why motels offer all these things.

Do you see people arriving or leaving the motel? Does anyone help them? How do travelers transport their luggage? Point out special luggage carts (if you don't see them in use) and how they are suited to carrying all different types of baggage, from hanging garment bags to bulky duffel bags.

Notice the size and shape of the building. How many floors does it have? How can you tell?

## OBSERVE INSIDE

Notice the lobby and reception area and talk about how it looks and feels. Notice the decorations and furniture. Is the style of decoration related to the hotel's name? Point out any bulletin boards, monitors, or computer directories that tell about things happening in the hotel or nearby. Is there a display area with brochures and information for visitors? Take some of each brochure for use in your follow-up activities. If there is a map showing other locations in this chain, point it out. Point out maps or diagrams that show where things are in the building.

Notice all the jobs people are doing to serve the guest and to keep the hotel clean and efficient. Look at the housekeeping carts the housekeepers use to bring supplies to each room. Notice the large bags for trash and dirty linens, the cleaning supplies and all the clean things on the cart. Talk about what a big job it would be to clean all these rooms every day.

Watch people check in and out at the reception desk. Notice the large panel of numbered boxes behind the desk. Explain to the children that each box is for a room key with a matching number. Watch to see if any people are asking for room keys or turning them in. Some facilities have switched from keys to key cards, but they are still stored in the same manner. Ask at the desk to visit a room and demonstrate the use of keys or key cards.

Notice any other machines that are in the desk area. Talk about the work the people are doing. Do the phones ring a lot? Can you observe or learn how the phones are connected to phones in the rooms. Are people paying bills?

Walk around the public areas of the hotel and point out all the things that happen in the hotel. Point out small and large meeting rooms, places to sit, eat, shop, swim, play, or exercise. Notice the decorations and artwork in all these areas. Are there fancy chandeliers? Do you see extra furniture or coat racks? Are people setting up or changing room arrangements? Notice special tables set up for food or coffee by meeting rooms.

Look in the rooms. Notice the furniture, lamps, pictures, closets, TV, telephones, and special items such as coffee service and ice buckets. Look in several rooms if possible. Is each one different?

See where you can find ice and show the children how the ice machines work. Are there other vending machines in the same area as well?

Notice the long hallways, exit signs, stairways, elevators, room numbers, numbers in Braille, as well as anything else of interest along the hallways. Are there big windows into the rooms along the hallways or just doors?

### SENSE

Stand in the central atrium area and look around. Look up and notice where the light is coming from and what effect that has. Talk about skylights and all the light that can come in that way. Do the children see other lights? Notice the plants, the uses of water, the places to sit, and other decorations. Let the children tell you what it feels like to be in this area.

Close your eyes and listen to the sounds around you. Talk about what you hear. Can you hear the water fountains, the elevators, and people sounds?

Watch the elevators going up and down and imagine how it feels to be up high. Take some rides in those elevators and talk about those feelings.

### COUNT

Count the number of floors. Check your answer by looking at the number of floors in the elevators.

Count the number of rooms on one side of a corridor. Are there the same number on the other side?

Count other things you see. How many planters on each side of a floor? How many benches in the garden area? How many fountains, coins in the fountain, tables in an eating area, telephones, desks, and high chairs? How many meeting or special rooms are there and how many are being used that day? Check the bulletin board to see.

## WONDER

Where does all the laundry get washed? Where do they keep all the linens and supplies? Do they have extra beds or special cribs for baby guests? Perhaps the housekeepers can show you.

Why might there be trays outside some of the rooms? How do they know how much food to make? Where is it cooked? Perhaps the catering office or food service staff can tell you.

# After the Trip: Follow-up Activities

## TALK ABOUT IT

Talk about the trip and write down the things the children noticed and remembered. Did they think it would be fun to stay in that hotel? Use the material they mention to compile a group thank-you note to the hotel. Have the children draw pictures about the trip and jot notes for each child about the picture as he or she dictates. Send or take the pictures and the group note to the hotel manager. Since hosting a tour group may have been a new experience for the hotel, letting them know what the children appreciated and learned is important. Try to include pictures or comments about the people who work in the hotel.

## READ AND FIND OUT

Read *Blumpoe the Grumpoe Meets Arnold the Cat*, by Jean Okimoto, *Do You See a Mouse?*, by Bernard Waber, and several other books about staying in or running hotels. After several stories and discussions related to your trip, write up some summaries in list form, such as:

- Bad Things About Staying in Hotels
- Easy Jobs to Do in the Hotel
- Hard Jobs to Do in the Hotel
- Things about Hotels that Are Like Home
- Things about Hotels that Are Different from Home

## WHAT WOULD YOU DO IF...?

Play a problem-solving game using problems you or the children make up related to staying in a hotel. Think of solutions for each problem. Try to be creative problem solvers. Possible questions include What Would You Do If

...you forgot the number of your room?
...you lost your room key?
...your suitcase went to the wrong room?

…you forgot your toothbrush or teddy bear?
…the TV set was not working properly?
…there were four people in your family and only three beds?
…you got hungry before bedtime?
…the room was too hot or cold or noisy?

### DESIGN YOUR FANTASY HOTEL

If Disney can design fantastic hotels, why not your group? In a display area, put out the brochures and pictures of hotels and resorts you collected on the trip or cut out pictures from ads, magazines, or travel brochures. Ask parents for brochures or postcards of places they have stayed. Let the children look at the materials and decide what things they would like to add to their fantasy hotel. Use a large sheet of paper to design this great place. Draw it or make a large collage using samples cut out of your brochures. Show all the special features the children want to include in their hotel.

Write up a description to put next to the drawing or collage. Let the children decide on a name for their hotel and where it is located. Remember to include the people who will work there and what they will do. Will they wear special clothes?

Plan to take an imaginary trip to your fantasy hotel. Plan what you will need to pack, how you will get there, when you will go, and how long you will stay.

### BUILD IT

Use your block corner to build a hotel or motel. Plan the building and the surrounding areas including parking lot or garage, swimming pool, and play area. Will it be a low, spread-out motel or a tall hotel? Put labels on the parts of the building. Think about props to add to the construction. Use Tinker toys or your small construction sets to create luggage carts.

Make suitcases out of small gift boxes covered with construction paper. Add elastic strips or pipe cleaners for handles or straps. Toy cars can drive up in front of the motel or park by the rooms or in the lot. Larger vehicles could be the hotel vans.

### MATCH THE KEY

Make up a key matching game using a collection of twelve or more old keys. Ask parents to send you old odd keys. Attach a tag to each key and write a number on the tag. Make a key-holding panel by stapling together an equal number of small jewelry-type boxes and writing corresponding numbers inside the boxes. As an alternative, use a hardware sorting box with the numbers written on labels on each drawer.

## Related Trip Ideas to Explore

bed and breakfast ● other places people stay (college dormitory, YMCA or YWCA, spa, campground, resort) ● places to stay that people take with

them (recreational vehicle dealer, camping store, marina or yacht dealers) ●
places pets stay (kennel, pet inn)

## Songs, Poems, and Finger Plays

### THE HOTEL
A hotel has so many floors.
On each floor are many, many doors.
And each door has its own special key.
Behind the door is a room with a TV.
And beds for all my family.

### GOING AWAY

Sometimes it feels scary to go away
And not know where you are going to stay.
It might be a big place we call a hotel
Or a drive-up version that's called a motel.

In both of these there are fun things to do.
There may be an elevator you can see through;
Things to climb on and a swimming pool, too.
There are places to eat to get snacks for you.

### A SUITE HOTEL

It's so much fun to go away, (pretend to drive)
And check in to the place we stay. (sign paper and get key)
I like to jump on the great big bed. (pretend to jump)
I'm careful not to bump my head. (hold head)

One room has a couch instead, (pretend to sit on couch)
But it opens up into a bed. (pretend to pull it out)
It's just perfect for my brother and me.
We climb inside and watch TV.

## Resources

Brewster, Patience. (1991) *Rabbit Inn*. Boston: Little Brown.

Cushman, Doug. (1992) *Aunt Eater's Mystery Vacation*. New York: HarperCollins.

Graham, Alastair. (1991) *Full Moon Soup or The Fall of Hotel Splendide*. New York: Dial Books.

Hoban, Julia. (1990) *Buzby*. New York: Harper & Row.
———. (1993) *Buzby to the Rescue*. New York: Harper & Row.

Lewin, Hugh, and Lisa Kopper. (1985) *An Elephant Came to Swim*. London: H. Hamilton.

Okimoto, Jean. (1990) *Blumpoe the Grumpoe Meets Arnold the Cat*. Boston: Little Brown.

Quackenbush, Robert. (1985) *Funny Bunnies*. New York: Clarion Books.

Vaughn, Marcia, and Patricia Mullins. (1992) *The Sea Breeze Hotel*. New York: HarperCollins.

Waber, Bernard. (1995) *Do You See a Mouse?* Boston: Houghton Mifflin.

### ANOTHER GOOD RESOURCE
Wright, Carol. (1979) *Hotel/Motel*. Morristown, NJ: Silver Burdett.

# Library••••••••••••••••••••••••

Your neighborhood public library is a valuable community resource and
a great one to use for field trips. It is a child-friendly place with many
interesting items to observe and explore. The library can serve many
purposes, and on your visit the children can

- attend story hours, puppet shows, or special programs;
- get a library card and check out books and other items;
- look up specific information you want to know;
- look for something in magazines or newspapers from other
  places; and
- learn about how the library works and what the people who
  work there do.

A library is a perfect site to use for an initial field trip. It is appropriate
for most age groups and for mixed age groups. Small groups can visit a
library informally using many of the ideas suggested in this chapter (there
are enough suggestions here for several trips). If you bring a large group or
want to visit special parts of the library, schedule a more formal tour.
Many libraries have community rooms they can schedule for your group's
use if you have made an appointment. Libraries can and should be visited
many different times to fully explore the rich resources they offer.

## Before the Trip

### WORDS TO LEARN AND USE

librarian • book • author • check-out • return • story hour • puppet
stage • card or computer catalog • shelves • stacks • racks • reference •
encyclopedia • dictionary • almanac • atlas • map • globe • exhibit •
display • files • fiction • nonfiction • biography • circulation system •
laser beam • scanner • book drop • overdue fine • call and catalog •
numbers • bar code • newspapers • magazines • microfilm • microfiche
reader • photocopier • media • audiovisual • pictures • videos •
records • cassette tapes • bookmobile • repair • book jacket • browse

Read *Armando Asked, "Why?,"* by Jay Hulbert. Let the children ask questions about things they would like to know. Write down questions and plan to go to the library to find the answers.

**SHOW AND TELL**

Show the children your library card, and ask if any of them have library cards. Explain that a library card allows you to check out books and other materials from the library to take home or to your group. Plan to take a trip to the library to find out about getting library cards for children who may want them.

**THINGS TO BRING**

paper and a pen or pencil to record observations ● questions to look up and find answers for ● plastic or paper bag for collecting things ● a camera

## On the Trip

**OUTSIDE THE BUILDING**

Notice the setting of the library and its building. Is it a big, imposing building with many steps and statues around it, or a more modern structure with large glass windows? Talk about artwork you see around the building. Are there inviting places to read outside by the building? If so, think about bringing a blanket on your next visit to have an outdoor story time.

Notice the name of the library and explain any significance it might have. Is this the main library or a branch? Explain that libraries are so important and helpful that there are many of them in communities to make them easy for people to get to and use.

Look for a cornerstone on the building to see the date when the library was built. Why is there a flag in front of the library?

Look at the hours printed on the door. When does the library open? Can people bring things back to the library when it is closed? Notice drop boxes people can use when the library is closed.

Wonder how people get to this library. How can you tell? Is there a parking lot for cars and bike racks for bikes, or is this library in a big city with bus or transit stops nearby?

Take photographs of the library both on the outside and inside.

**INSIDE THE BUILDING (GENERAL AREAS)**

Once inside, notice special displays, exhibits, artwork, or decoration. Are there themes to the displays you can help the children understand? What kinds of things are on the walls? Are there special books on display? Is there information about the library and a library map or guide to show the children? What other information is available for people to take?

Notice how the library is organized. Look at the central checkout and return area, the computer or card catalogs, and the information desks where you can get help. Point out the equipment on the checkout counter and how the people behind the counter handle each book. Many libraries have an automated circulation system that uses a laser beam. Explain that the laser beam records the number of the book and the number on the library card and tells the computer system that the book is being checked out. Some libraries still use photocopying equipment to keep track of who has checked out each book. Show the children where to put books that are being returned and explain that the librarians will copy the number again to show that the book has been returned.

Visit the reference area of the library and show the children all the encyclopedias, dictionaries, almanacs, and other reference books. Look up the topic of your questions in an encyclopedia, or ask the reference librarian for help. Show the children the many volumes of the *Readers' Guide to Periodical Literature*, which lists all the articles in magazines by topics. Explain that reference materials stay in the library so anyone can come to look for answers to their questions. Notice that there are many places to sit and work in the reference area.

Visit the newspaper and magazine area (called periodicals) and notice how everything is displayed. Are there comfortable chairs to sit in and read? Look at the newspapers hanging on their special racks and notice the name of the city in the heading. If there are maps or globes in this area, point out some locations. Show the children the special machines that people can use to read newspaper and magazine articles stored on microfilm or microfiche. Copying information on microfiche helps the library save old newspapers and other periodicals in very little space.

Compare all the different types of library shelves, racks, and containers, and think about how they are suited to the items they hold. Some examples of shelves include: the newspaper and magazine racks; small paperback book racks; big, solid shelves for heavy reference materials; smaller shelves for videos and CDs; bins for records; tall shelves in the adult area; and lower shelves in the children's area.

Notice the signs around the library that tell what is in each section. Read them to the children and discuss what they mean. Particularly notice the signs on shelves that say *fiction* and *nonfiction,* since those are the categories that are crucial to how libraries are organized.

Explain that *fiction* means stories that are made up, such as the Curious George stories. *Nonfiction* means books about real things in the world, such as the Let's Read and Find Out books. Storybooks (fiction) are organized by the author's last name. They are in alphabetical order on the shelves. All other books are organized by number and kind of book. The librarian can explain how your library is organized.

### VISIT THE CHILDREN'S AREA

Wonder how people find the books they want when they go to the library? Do they browse around until they find something they like, or look up a book in the catalog and go find it?

Let the children browse in the children's area and choose books to look at. Show the children the letters on the shelves and see if they match the first letters of the author's last name. Those must be fiction books.

Point out the numbers on the books. There may be both numbers and letters printed on the edge of the book. This is the book's call number and is something like a person's address. It is how libraries keep track of their books. Look at the back inside cover of the book. Is there a book pocket with a card in it with numbers printed on it, or is there a label with a bunch of black stripes and numbers on it? If the book has those zebra stripes, your library is computerized and is using a bar code system. Many books will have both; pockets left from their older system and the bar code labels of their new system.

Notice if there are special sections in the children's area for very large books, books and cassette tapes, and records. Are there any toys, stuffed

animals, or puppets to play with? Is there a place for storytelling or puppet shows? Are there machines such as computers, tape players, and filmstrip viewers? Is there a picture file?

Notice how the area is decorated and if there are special displays. Does the library have programs for children?

Explain to the children that in the library they may leave books on the table or put them in a special bin. They should not try to put them back on the shelf because each book has its own place on the shelf. Librarians can put the books back for them.

### WONDER

How do people reach things that are high up? Are there step stools, ladders, or special tools to reach things?

How does the library take care of its books to help them last? Notice the paper or plastic jackets that cover many books. Can a library employee show you how they make the book jackets and put them on books, or do the books come already covered?

How do people repair books that get torn? Is there a special work area for fixing books? What do the employees use? What does the library do with the books that are too old or out-of-date? Do you see any books for sale?

What happens when people don't return their books on time? Are there fines for overdue or damaged books? How do the librarians decide what books to order for the library? Where do the books arrive and how do they get them ready to put on the shelves?

## After the Trip: Follow-up Activities

### TALK ABOUT IT

Talk about your trip and ask the children to tell you all the things they noticed and remembered. Write down their comments on a large sheet of paper. Write a group thank-you note to the library and include in your note the list of all the things the children noticed.

Read the book *Librarians A to Z*, by Jean Johnson, and discuss the things you saw that are like those in the book. This is a good way to help the children review what they saw and understand the work librarians do.

### LETTER DISPLAY

Start a letter display table using small objects that begin with a particular letter. For example, for "B," display a small ball, plastic baby, bib, and blue beads. Store the objects in small boxes. When you have done several letters, set up a letter file system in a hardware organizer case (a thirty-drawer case works well). Put a letter sticker on each drawer and keep it on the letter display table. Encourage the children to put the objects in the appropriate letter drawer after they have used them.

### FILE THIS

Bring in interesting magazine pictures and show them to the children. Decide what topic each picture is about and put them in file folders with the name of the topic on it. Find a place to keep your picture file so the children can look through it. Use letters or a picture or number code system to organize your picture file so the children can learn to find the picture they are looking for.

### OUR OWN LIBRARY

Look at your library area to see if it looks like a library. Talk about how you can arrange it to look more like the library you visited. Can you put pictures on the walls? Choose a librarian of the day who helps keep the book area neat and helps children find books. Set up a repair area for your book corner to fix any books that need it. Decide if you want to make book jackets for your books.

### ALL ABOUT THE LIBRARY

Check out books about libraries and read them during the week following your trip. Talk about the ideas in the books and what new information they give you about libraries.

Begin a big book about your library trip. Put in the book what you saw on display, what program you attended, and something you learned about the library. Add to your book each time you go to the library and date each entry. Include pictures you took of the library and add children's drawings, if you wish. After several trips and the accompanying entries, take it with you on a future trip to show to the librarian.

## Related Trip Ideas to Explore

bookstores with story hours ● newspaper publisher ● book bindery ● toy library ● school library ● book mobile

## Songs, Poems, and Finger Plays

### TO THE LIBRARY WE GO

Hi Ho, Hi Ho, to the library we will go.
To find some books.
Oh, lots of books;
We see them row by row.

Let's chose some books to read
A card is all you need
Then they can let them go
Hi Ho, Hi Ho, Hi Ho.

### AT THE LIBRARY

How many books on the shelves do you see?
Hundreds and hundreds for you and me.
The library is an amazing place;
So many things in each special space.

But the thing I like best at the library,
Is they always seem to like to help me
Find just the perfect book I need
To take to my house to read and reread.

### THREE BOOKS

A great big book, (pretend to hold a big book in your hands)
A medium-sized book, (hold a medium sized book)
And a little book I see. (hold a small book)
Shall we read them
Are you ready?
1, 2, 3 (repeat the motions from big to small)

### SOME BOOKS

*(to the tune of "Here We Go Round the Mulberry Bush")*
This is the way we find some books, (pretend to take books)
Find some books, find some books.
This is the way we find some books,
At the library in our town.

This is the way we look at the books, (pretend to look at books)
Look at the books, look at the books.
This is the way we look at the books,
At the library in our town.

### THE READING FAMILY

A book about planes for Tom; (hold up one finger)
A book about sailing for Mom. (hold up two fingers)
A book about dinosaurs for Tad; (hold up three fingers)
A book about fishing for Dad. (hold up four fingers)
A book about dogs for Amy, (hold up five fingers)
A book about trains for me. (point to self)
Six great books for my family; (hold up six fingers)
And we found them all at the library!

### IN THE LIBRARY

*(to the tune of "My Darling Clementine")*
In the library, in the library
In the library down the street,
There are books, so many books
About things that are so neat.
There are stories about people
Who would be so fun to meet;
In the library, in the library
To read stories is a treat!

# Resources

Alexander, Martha. (1983) *How My Library Grew*. New York: Wilson.

Dauer, Caroline Feller. (1984) *Too Many Books*. New York: Frederick Warne.

Casley, Judith. (1993) *Sophie and Sammy's Library Sleepover*. New York: Greenwillow.

Fujimoto, Patricia. (1984) *Libraries* (a New True Book). Chicago: Childrens Press.

Furtado, Jo, and Frederic Joos. (1988) *Sorry Miss Folio*. New York: Kane/Miller.

Gibbons, Gail. (1985) *Check It Out*. San Diego: Harcourt Brace.

Hautzig, Deborah. (1993) *Una Visita a la Biblioteca de Sesame Street*. New York: Random House/Children's Television Workshop (also available in English).

Houghton, Eric. (1989) *Walter's Magic Wand*. New York: Orchard Books.

Huff, Barbara A. (1990) *Once Inside the Library*. Boston: Little Brown.

Hulbert, Jay. (1990) *Armando Asked, "Why?"* Milwaukee, WI: Raintree.

Jaspersohn, William. (1994) *My Hometown Library*. Boston: Houghton Mifflin.

Johnson, Jean. (1988) *Librarians A to Z*. New York: Walker and Co.

Kimmel, Eric A. (1990) *I Took My Frog to the Library*. New York: Viking Penguin.

Levinson, Nancy Smiler. (1988) *Clara and the Bookwagon*. New York: Harper & Row.

Numeroff, Laura Jaffe. (1981) *Beatrice Doesn't Want To*. New York: Franklin Watts.

Radlauer, Ruth Shaw. (1988) *Molly at the Library*. New York: Simon & Schuster.

Rockwell, Anne. (1977) *I Like the Library*. New York: Dutton.

Shay, Arthur. (1971) *What Happens at the Library*. Chicago: Reilly and Lee Books.

Tester, Sylvia Root. (1985) *A Visit to the Library*. Chicago: Childrens Press.

Weil, Lisl. (1990) *Let's Go to the Library*. New York: Holiday House.

West, Dan. (1988) *The Day the TV Blew Up*. Niles, IL: Albert Whitman and Co.

## OTHER GOOD RESOURCES

Bauer, Caroline Feller. (1991) *Read for the Fun of it: Active Programming with Books for Children*. New York: H. W. Wilson.

MacDonald, Margaret Read. (1988) *Booksharing: 101 Programs to Use with Preschoolers*. Hamden, CT: Library Professional Publications.

McInerney, Claire Fleischman. (1989) *Find It! The Inside Story at Your Library*. Minneapolis: Lerner Publications.

Sierra, Judy, and Robert Kaminski. (1989) *Twice Upon a Time: Stories to Tell, Retell, Act Out, and Write About*. New York: H. W. Wilson.

# Lumberyard/
# Building Center···········

Have you ever wondered why blocks and those wonderful old wooden toys are so expensive? A trip to the lumberyard will enlighten both you and the children about what has caused the demise of so many wonderful old hardwood toys. You can see why some cheaper wooden (soft wood) blocks tend to splinter and not last as long. In an age of plastic, however, it feels good to spend time in the world of wood. On a trip to the lumberyard, the children can

- learn how lumber is stored, measured, and cut;
- collect wood samples, wood shavings (curls), and sawdust;
- learn about the different kinds of lumber and the uses of each type; and
- compare lumber and other building materials.

While shopping for building materials, consumers have come to expect that bigger is better; many enormous building materials centers are available. When visiting a place with children, however, smaller is better. Look around for a small lumberyard, which will be more manageable and may allow you to get closer to the stacks of wood. A smaller lumberyard may also have people around to answer your questions—something that does not always happen in larger facilities. Ask parents or anyone you know in construction for recommendations or look in the yellow pages and previsit a few likely sounding places. Some lumberyard/building centers advertise display and showroom areas and help for the do-it-yourselfer. Lumberyards tend to be in outlying or suburban areas so you might want to look around for a neighboring park for a snack, pit stop, and play stop.

## Before the Trip

### WORDS TO LEARN AND USE

lumber ● board ● plank ● plywood ● veneer ● two-by-four ● paneling ● unfinished ● pre-finished ● stain ● cupboards ● cabinets ● hinges ● handles ● molding ● millwork ● woodwork ● trim ● Formica ● sink ● door ● stair tread ● beam ● carpet ● tile ● linoleum ● wallpaper ● railing ● window frame ● wallboard ● Masonite ● pegboard ● lathe ● plane ● sawdust ● siding ● hardwood ● softwood ● grain ● knot ● rough ● smooth ● post ● forklift ● maple ● pine ● oak

### TALK ABOUT IT

Look around your own room or a kitchen area and notice the cabinets and wood items, such as doors and woodwork. Ask the children where those items came from. Were they already made or did someone build them? Plan to go someplace where you might find wood to use for building or for cabinets that have already been built.

### SHOW AND TELL

Look up *lumber* and *forest* in an encyclopedia and show the children the pictures of large trees and logs cut from trees. Show pictures of how trucks transport lumber. Look for pictures of sawmills where logs are converted to board lumber or thin veneers. Show the children pictures of the lumber being transported to the lumberyard. Ask if they would like to see where the boards are now. Point out that not all trees are used for lumber. Explain that companies can only take lumber from forests that need to be thinned out. After cutting, many lumber companies plant new trees and allow the forest to grow again.

### THINGS TO BRING

paper and a pen or pencil to record measurements and other observations ● tape measure ● large container to hold sawdust ● plastic or paper bag for collecting things ● a camera

## On the Trip

### OBSERVE

Notice the stacks of lumber and the various sizes and shapes it comes in. Think about what the different types of lumber might be used for. Name as many different kinds as you can.

Look for other available building materials. Do you see wood trim materials, cabinets, concrete blocks, bricks, roofing materials, linoleum, ceiling tile, carpet, pre-finished paneling, wallpaper, or other items? Are there samples people can take home to help them decide what they want? Point out the different materials by name and ask the children if they have seen materials like these in their homes or schools.

Is there a work area with saws where employees are cutting lumber? If possible, watch this process and notice the pile of sawdust and wood curls accumulating on the floor.

Can you observe a forklift truck moving stacks of lumber? If not, wonder how the lumber gets moved onto the shelves and later onto delivery trucks.

### ASK

Ask the salespeople to explain the different kinds of lumber and what they are used for. Can they tell you about plywood, wood veneers, and different types and grades of wood boards they sell? Can they tell you about hard and soft wood and what those terms mean?

Ask about the cost of different kinds of lumber. Are some woods more expensive than others?

Can the salespeople tell you how various types of wood trims are made? Do employees do any of that work on the premises?

Ask about the work done at the lumberyard. Do employees cut wood to size for special orders? Do they make roof beams, cabinets, or other items? If not, do employees take orders and have them made someplace else?

How do the store employees deliver lumber? What machines do they use to help in their work? Can they show the machines to you, if you haven't already observed them in action?

### COMPARE

Look closely at the unfinished wood and notice the different grains and textures. Being careful to avoid splinters, touch the woods and feel the differences. Can you feel smooth, rough, hard, and soft surfaces? In what other ways do woods differ? Compare the grains and decide which ones look most interesting.

Compare unfinished and pre-finished wood.

If pre-finished paneling is on display, notice the grains in the panels and decide whether the grain shows up more before or after the wood is finished.

If small samples of finished woods are available, take them over to the unfinished wood stacks and see if you can recognize and match the grains.

Measure the different sizes of lumber with the tape measure. Measure in each direction so you can decide what one-by-four or two-by-four means. Ask the salesperson to help explain how lumber is measured and sold.

Measure other building materials as well, including concrete blocks, floor tiles, ceiling tiles, doors, and window frames. Talk about why measuring might be important in building.

### SENSE

Listen to the noises of the lumberyard. Do you hear saws buzzing or machinery moving? Are there grating noises from materials being cut?

Notice the smell of fresh-cut wood. Does it smell good? If possible, sniff around the different types of wood to see if they have different scents. Do finished and unfinished woods smell different?

### COLLECT

Ask for small samples of construction materials and pieces of wood to take back for various projects. Ask the salesperson to tell you the type of wood of each piece. Write the name on the wood someplace.

Ask to fill your large container with sawdust to take back with you. Also collect any wood curls and scrap lumber to add to your workbench area.

If the yard will cut the lumber for you, buy a hardwood two-by-four and have it cut into two-foot-long sections.

# After the Trip: Follow-up Activities

## TALK ABOUT IT

Let the children tell you the things they remember from the trip. Using the children's comments, make a list and title it "Things We Learned About Lumber and Building Materials."

Ask the children to tell you about things they noticed in their homes or at school that remind them of things seen on the trip.

## ALL ABOUT LUMBER BULLETIN BOARD OR POSTER

Design a bulletin board or poster that tells about lumber and how it is used. Start with the two types of trees and add pictures of plain lumber and then the things made from lumber. (See the Tree Walk chapter for more information about trees.)

*Conifers or evergreen trees* (such as pines, fir, hemlock, spruce, cedar and redwood) produce lumber called *softwood*. Softwood is used for siding, posts, planks, beams, doors, frames, panels, wood trim, pencils, and boxes.

*Deciduous trees* (such as maple, oak, birch, poplar, aspen, beech, and walnut) produce lumber called *hardwood*. Mahogany, ebony, teak, and rosewood are tropical hardwoods. Hardwood lumber is used for furniture, paneling, flooring, baseball bats, tool handles, and musical instruments such as guitars. Pieces of hardwood can be used for parts of furniture.

## SAMPLE MATCHING

See if you can find things in your room that look like the samples you collected on your trip. Do you have moldings, door frames, or trims that look like the samples? If you brought back Formica counter top samples, see if they match anything in your room.

## WOOD SHAVINGS

Collect samples of different woods and use a plane on them. Do the wood shavings look the same or different? Collect the wood shavings from each sample in a plastic bag and examine them to notice differences in color, size, texture, and so on. After you have finished examining the wood shavings, use them as hair for paper bag or paper plate puppets. Paint small bits of wood and use them for features on the puppets.

## WOODWORKING AREA

Set up a workbench or woodworking area. Provide saws, hammers, and nails. With supervision, let the children saw wood and use it to build simple items. *Closely supervise children when they use tools.*

As you and the children work with the wood, decide if it is hard or soft. Check the name of the wood sample to see if your guesses were correct.

Set up an area for painting and staining wood. Use light and dark stains as well as one and two coats of paint. What do you observe about how finishing changes the wood? Which finish allows you to see more of the wood grain? Which one do you like best?

For younger children, use plain water and water colors brushed onto the wood, instead of stains.

### WOODCUTS AND PRINTS

Use small wood scraps of different shapes for printing. Dip the wood samples in paint and press them onto large sheets of paper to design homemade wrapping paper.

Create wood blocks to use for printing or simple woodcut pictures by making indentations in soft wood. Using the point of a scissors blade or pen, make a design pattern on the wood. Cover the wood with tempera paint. Place a small piece of paper over the block and press gently so that the paper picks up the print. Since paint won't stick to the indented areas, those areas will remain clear to reveal the design.

### BLOCK AREA

Look at your blocks and see if the children can figure out how they relate to the lumber you have just seen. Take out the two-foot-long pieces of wood and decide what you need to do to turn them into blocks. Measure the sizes you want, saw, sand, and stain the wood for your own homemade blocks. Add them to your other blocks.

Turn your block area into a dramatic play lumberyard. Measure the size of the blocks, organize them by size, and put up signs to tell the board length. Children can come and purchase blocks with play money and have them delivered to a place in the room to use for building.

### WOOD PRODUCTS SORTING GAMES

Have the children cut out pictures of wood products from magazines, newspaper ads, and catalogs. Include everything from wood toys to pictures of paneling and cabinets. Use the pictures to play a variety of games, sorting them into different categories to illustrate certain concepts. Some examples include:

- things we can buy at a lumberyard and things we can't buy there;
- things we use for building houses and things we just use for living or playing;
- things our parents would buy and use and things we would use;
- things that are finished products and things we need to finish ourselves.

Each concept creates a different game. Make and use different sorting boxes or master boards, or use the pictures in small group discussions and have the group sort them.

### HOW A TREE BECOMES A BLOCK

Make up your own picture book telling the story of lumber. Collect pictures illustrating trees in forests, lumberjacks or loggers cutting down the trees, logs being transported to the sawmills, sawmills in operation, lumber being transferred to lumberyards, and the two-by-four you bought and had cut up. Add pictures of people planting new trees in the forest to complete the cycle. Have the children dictate comments for each picture. Put the pictures together into your own book. Collect pictures the lumberyard may have, and take some of your own.

### SAWDUST MODELING MATERIAL

Mix together 5 cups sawdust, 1 cup wheat paste, and 4 to 5 cups water in a large bowl. (The mixture should feel like dough.) Shape the mixture around a foundation, such as a Styrofoam craft foam ball or puppet head. Allow several days to dry, then paint. Use this lightweight material in a variety of modeling projects such as paperweights, decorative ornaments, busts or statues of favorite animals or people, or other gifts made by children.

### WOOD AND GLUE

Glue several curlicues of wood together to see what happens. Talk about how plywood is made by gluing several thin strips of wood veneer together. Try staining your own homemade bits of plywood.

Glue a thin curlicue of wood into a thicker piece of wood to explain how a veneer of one type of wood is added to another. Think about when and why people would make and use wood that had a veneered finish.

## Related Trip Ideas to Explore

carpenter's workshop ● woodworking or craft shop ● furniture or window factory ● cabinet shop ● gravel or sand pit ● stone quarry or brick yard ● lumber or paper mill

## Songs, Poems, and Finger Plays

### THE LUMBER SONG

*(to the tune of "I'm a Little Teapot")*
First you find a tree that's big and tall,
(hands curved over heads to form a tree)
Watch the lumberjack make it fall. (pretend to cut down tree)
Off to the sawmill the logs will go,
(pretend to lift and load on trucks and drive off)
And turn into boards that look just so.
(spread hands wide apart to indicate long boards)

### THE LUMBER STORE

Wooden boards called two-by-fours;
Wooden cabinets and doors;
Wood for walls and stairs and floors;
Paint for fences and so much more—
We will find at the lumber store.

### TREES AND WOOD

Each tree is very special,
And has a special name.
And when it turns to lumber,
Its name will stay the same.
The pine trees give us knotty pine,
That's used for walls or doors.
The oak tree gives us solid oak
For tables, chairs, or floors.

### WOOD WE USE

The trees that grow in forests
Where people camp and play,
Will someday be so many things
That we use every day.

(Have children think of things they use that are made of wood.)

### SAWDUST

Buzz—Buzz—Buzz, the saw works so hard (imitate sawing)
Cutting up the boards at the lumberyard.
Little mounds of sawdust are piling up high. (point to the floor)
We'll take some home and mix it, (scoop up and make mixing motions)
To use by and by.

## Resources

Alley, R. W. (1988) *The Clever Carpenter*. New York: Random House.

Appelbaum, Diane. (1993) *Giants in the Land*. Boston: Houghton Mifflin.

Black, Algernon D. (1973) *The Woman of Wood—A Tale from Russia*. New York: Henry Holt.

Burnie, David. (1988) *Tree*. New York: Knopf.

Dyson, Sue. (1993) *Wood*. New York: Thomson Learning.

Emberley, Barbara. (1963) *Story of Paul Bunyan*. Englewood Cliffs, NJ: Prentice-Hall.

Florian, Douglas. (1991) *A Carpenter*. New York: Greenwillow.

Miller, Cameron, and Dominique Falla. (1995) *Woodlore*. New York: Ticknor & Fields.

Mitgutsch, Ali. (1981) *From Tree to Table*. Minneapolis: Carolrhoda Books.

Scarry, Richard. (1968) *What Do People Do All Day?* New York: Random House.

Thompson, David. (1981) *Easy Woodstuff for Kids*. Beltsville, MD: Gryphon House.

Wade, Harlan. (1979) *Wood*. Milwaukee, WI: Raintree.

## ANOTHER GOOD RESOURCE

Kurelek, William. (1974) *Lumberjack*. Boston: Houghton Mifflin.

# Museum ···························

Museums offer wonderful educational experiences for young children, but ensuring a successful trip requires careful advance planning. There are usually too many interesting things to see, so you must choose ahead of time the particular areas you want to visit. Since children learn by doing, you may want to concentrate on active learning exhibits and plan shorter periods of time for just looking. You can make looking an active experience by having the children search for particular things in the display or imitate or imagine something related to the exhibit.

A trip to a museum offers children an opportunity to

- learn what museums are and how they help people learn about topics from assembling dinosaurs to painting pictures;
- see how materials are organized and displayed in museums and the special events or programs they offer;
- observe what the people who work in museums do; and
- try out or experiment directly with materials that explain or illustrate specific information related to science, history, art, diverse cultures, nature, or the many aspects of daily life.

To find museums that will interest your group, look in the phone book—it might reveal museums in your city you never realized existed. Don't overlook unusual museums such as car, train, aviation, doll, or musical instrument museums; living history museums; and outdoor restoration or ethnic museums.

Plan to previsit the museum to decide what would be most interesting for your group. Unless the museum docents or educational staff are knowledgeable about preschool children, it usually works best to lead your own tour, keeping the explanations short and the group moving. During your previsit, notice the best places to park, where to enter and put coats, bathroom and snack facilities, and other logistical details that will help make your trip run smoothly.

The activities in this chapter focus on museums in the generic sense and not on any specific museum type. Certain features are common to most museums and similar exhibits (for example, grinding grain) can be found in four or five different types of museums in different locations. Adapt the ideas and suggestions in this general trip to the specific museums you visit, adding site-specific vocabulary words and activities.

## Before the Trip

### WORDS TO LEARN AND USE

exhibit ● collection ● curator ● display ● case ● glass ● label ● laboratory ● workshop ● statues ● objects ● pictures ● treasures ● pottery ● jewelry ● weapons ● carvings ● paintings ● rare ● beautiful ● unusual ● valuable guards ● science ● nature ● history ● habitats ● audiotapes ● theater information ● docent ● guide ● designer ● restorer ● build ● repair ● catalog ● gift shop ● souvenir ● sample ● classify ● banner

### READ AND DISCUSS

Read *Museums*, by Jason Cooper, or the book of the same name by Janet Papajani. Talk about the different kinds of museums discussed in these books. These types range from the single topic museum, such as a baseball museum, to the living history museums of historic houses and villages with actors in costume. Ask the children what museums they have been to and what they liked in that museum. If the children have something to show from a museum trip, encourage them to bring it in and tell which museum the item is from. Set up a display of items from museums with information about the museum.

### LET'S FIND OUT

Collect information about the museums in your area from the phone book, tourist information, friends, or parents. Compile a list of the ones you find and their type. Discuss what things the children are most interested in learning about and plan to visit museums that match those interests throughout the year. Are all the museums indoors? Talk about what types of museums can be found outdoors (for example, sculpture gardens, military forts, and restorations of pioneer or western towns). Make your museum trip plans to fit your curriculum planning and the weather during the year. When you make plans to visit a specific type of museum (such as art or natural history), read one of the books about that specific type of museum in preparation for your trip and list specific questions to ask at the site.

### THINGS TO BRING

paper and a pen or pencil to record observations ● list of questions ● plastic or paper bag for collecting things ● a camera

# On the Trip

## OBSERVE

Notice the museum building. Is it an imposing, old building that has always been this particular museum, or a new or remodeled one adapted for this museum? What signs, decorations, or clues outside the building tell you something about what kind of museum it is (for example, sculpture works outside an art museum, or a banner with dolphins by an aquarium)? Point out the name of the museum and signs about special events. Does the building look large, and can you guess how many floors it has?

Inside the building, notice the desk and information areas, coatroom or checkroom, and signs about things you can and cannot do. Are there turn-stiles to go through? Do you need to buy tickets? If so, explain that process and why your group needs to stand in line. Look for maps and diagrams of the building, and point out the many different exhibit areas indicated on the map. Is there a video that tells about things in the museum?

Look around. Can you tell from the general entry area what kind of museum you are in? Talk about special features in that area that are unique to this museum (for example, a large sculpture, a big dinosaur, a pendulum swinging, a state map), and guess why it's there.

Notice the guards in each area, guides showing people around, and the people who were at the desks when you came in. Are they wearing special clothes? Do they wear ID cards? If the children have any question to ask the guards, let them do so. Explain that the guards are there to help people and protect the things in the museum from damage.

Walk into one of the exhibit areas that you plan to visit and notice all the things there. Talk about the things in each exhibit case, the labels on the side that tell about the items, and pictures on the wall or other items in the room.

Try to look in the laboratory or work areas where people may be assembling exhibits or repairing items. Observe the people working there.

Notice the signs in empty cases or where items have been removed for some reason and tell the children about that, explaining where the item has gone or what will be put in the empty cases.

Notice how the rooms are decorated and how that relates to the type of museum. Are there natural habitats around with displays in them, white walls for paintings, or murals on the walls depicting a culture or industry?

Watch video presentations, live theater presentations, or demonstrations that are of interest to your group (since you probably only have time for one or two short ones, choose carefully). Plan to talk about them later since there are so many things to see the group must keep moving on. Are there mechanical exhibits to watch?

### SENSE

Close your eyes and listen. What sounds do you hear? Is it a busy place where you hear general people sounds? Is it quiet? Do you hear sounds from any of the exhibit areas and can you tell what they are (for example, TV monitors, announcements, water rushing, ball falling into a mechanical machine, bird sounds on a tape)?

Let the children explore the touch and feel or hands-on areas of the museum to manipulate items, feel textures, and try out whatever experimental exhibits the museum has. If appropriate, ask questions or help explain the items as the children are involved with them. Read labels or procedures to them to help facilitate learning from the exhibit.

### COUNT

Count the number of exhibits in the areas you visit and think about how much time your group should spend looking at each one. Count the number of pictures on the wall, the benches in the room, and the number of doors or doorways (entrances and exits) in each room. Think about why there are so many doorways.

Count how many items may be in some of the exhibits—especially the diorama or habitat ones. See how many birds, swords, people, or other items the children can find as they look at a specific exhibit. Notice if items are numbered in any way, and then look at the descriptions and explain what matches each numbered item.

Try counting footsteps to measure large exhibit areas. Try to judge how high tall exhibits might be. Notice any signs that give heights or dimensions, and tell the children how heavy or tall something is.

## WONDER

Wonder how all these things got put together in this museum. Ask an employee how the museum takes care of the exhibits to make sure parts don't break off; what they do when something like that happens.

How did some of the really big items get into the museum—especially things that are bigger than the doors?

Do they ever change things around or have different displays? Who decides that and does it take long to make new exhibits?

## COLLECT

Bring back brochures, maps, or other information about the museum. Stop in the gift shop and see if there is any specific souvenir your group might choose (budget allowing) to take back. Sometimes postcards showing special parts of the museum are nice to have as a reminder of your trip. Museum shops usually have interesting items and especially good books. If there is anything you have been searching for to add to your resources, you may find it in this type of shop.

## After the Trip: Follow-up Activities

### TALK ABOUT IT

Talk about the trip and let the children tell you the things they remember and particularly enjoyed. Encourage them to ask questions about things they saw. There's so much to absorb and notice so the follow-up discussions become important tools for expanding learning. Write down the children's questions and comments to use in other activities. Look at some of the books in the Resources section to see if they help answer questions. If your follow-up discussions and study still leave many unanswered questions, write them down and send them to the education staff at the museum or plan a later return trip to get the answers.

### OUR MUSEUM BOOK

Start writing a big book about the museums you visit. Write up a few pages on each museum and include the museum's name, its type, the children's favorite activities, and the kinds of exhibits it had. Let the children add pictures and attach museum maps or brochures. Visiting museums and adding to the book could be year-long projects. Your book will become a scrapbook of your year and a great item to share with parents at holiday or year-end get-togethers. Review the book with the children to reinforce the memories and learning.

### LEARNING ABOUT EXHIBITS

Read *Dinosaurs, Dragonflies, and Diamonds: All About Natural History Museums*, by Gail Gibbons. This book uses a snake exhibit to tell in detail how museum exhibits are designed. *Let's Go to the Museum*, by Lisl Weil, is a good book to read in stages. It provides an overview of the work museum employees do to prepare collections for display.

After discussing these ideas, encourage the children to prepare an exhibit about something they have studied or collected. You can choose anything for an exhibit from matchbox cars to seashells. The key elements in setting up an exhibit are thinking about how things are organized, classified, labeled, and displayed.

Help the children put labels on the things they collect with the information they know or find out. For example, with a car display, labels might state: Joe's ambulance, from his birthday last year. Tom's Army Jeep, from his grandfather's World War II set—1945.

Then help the children decide how to arrange the display. For example, should the cars be organized by types of vehicles, by color, by age of the models, or another way? Perhaps the children will decide to keep changing the way they display the cars; they can make new signs or directions for them or set up roads or garages to add to their display. They may even want to make up a story about their display or shoot a video.

All these imaginative and changing uses would be fine and are related to the new hands-on learning exhibits popular in museums today. The only caution would be to keep track of who the display items belong to so they can be returned. The curators of traveling exhibits would be mighty unhappy if things couldn't get back to the original owners. Keeping a list of all the items and their owner is a good way to illustrate how real museums work.

### FRAME IT

Use a piece of construction paper to make attractive frames for pictures to hang in or for items to be displayed on tables. You can use any size of paper, but make sure the picture or item to be mounted is smaller than the finished frame size.

To make the frame, fold each of the paper's four sides down, approximately 1 inch. Open up the folds and pinch each of the corners so the adjacent edges form a point. It is not necessary to glue the frames in any way; the pinched corners will cause the folds to stand up loosely to form a frame.

Mount pictures in the center or put items in each frame with a label or description. Use contrasting colors for attractive displays.

### MUSEUM SORTING GAME

Collect pictures of various items from magazines, catalogs, or brochures. Cut out pictures such as people in costumes from long ago, toys, paintings, old cars, and tools. Label shoe boxes with the names of the types of museums you have visited, such as *Children's, Art, Science, History*; use picture clues on the boxes to represent the museum. Let the children sort the pictures according to the museum where they think the pictures belong. Try this activity after you have visited several different types of museums. If you have extra brochures from the museums, use them to label the boxes.

### EXPLORING ART

Read the books *Lines*, *Places*, and *Stories*, all by Philip Yenawine. Talk about how the children can use their imagination as the artists do to think of different places or stories to show in paintings or drawings. Another wonderful story to use as inspiration is *The Legend of the Indian Paintbrush*, by Tomie de Paola. Encourage lots of drawing and painting and save some works for an art show. Display paintings, artworks, and sculptures. Invite parents and others to visit your model art museum.

### FAMILY HISTORY MUSEUM

Choose an area to set up as a museum center and plan to collect things to display in this area each month. A book shelf or a table and bulletin board area would work. You could launch this idea with a Family History display. Tell parents about your plans and ask them to send in items they are willing to share, such as pictures of family members (including grandparents and great-grandparents), pets, houses, former residences, places families have lived; artifacts that are part of holiday celebrations; ethnic cooking items; and mementos from family traditions.

Label everything carefully as it comes in. Write up short descriptions to accompany each group of items. Let the children tell you about all the things they bring and what they know about them. Include their information in your labeling and description. Look at the things in your museum center often and let the children tell you and others about their parts of the display. Encourage the children to tell parents and other visitors to the classroom about the museum center display. They will be acting like museum tour guides.

After everyone who wants to has had their things on display in your Family History Museum, plan for other uses of your museum center. Maybe the children have collections of things they would like to display in the center (such as doll collections, stuffed animals, toy soldiers, or funny creatures). Or the group could decide to use the museum center for items collected on walks or in some area of study, or to display things made of clay or Lego building blocks.

In each case, your group will use some form of labeling and description to tell about the items on display. Encourage the use of nonbreakable items for this activity (displaying a glass animal collection is risky around preschoolers). If such things should come in, write up information that tells about the items and their owner. Include a note that the items are in a safe-keeping area and can be viewed by special request only (meaning with adult supervision).

## Related Trip Ideas to Explore

individual collections such as doll collections ● international institute or ethnic displays ● special exhibits or craft shows in malls ● restaurants or hotels that have items on display ● displays in a place of worship ● clock shops ● artist's studio ● photographer or frame shop

## Songs, Poems, and Finger Plays

### THE MUSEUM
*(to the tune of "My Darling Clementine")*
In the museum where I often go
You can watch a video.
About trains and boats and airplanes
And a lot of things that go.

There are telephones that will tell you
Many things you did not know.
And exhibits with some buttons
That will start a special show.

You can experiment, read a story,
Travel to the moon and more.
You can see that the museum
Has so much we can explore.

### OUR CHILDREN'S MUSEUM

Our children's museum is the most fun;
It has something special for everyone.
You can try what it's like to be on TV,
Or look at some creatures that live in the sea.

There's a grocery store that is just my size;
And a place to dress up in a fancy disguise.
You can play with water or make cars race.
It's great to go to this special place.

### THE SCIENCE MUSEUM

What did we see at the museum today?
A lot of dinosaurs on display.
Some are over ten feet tall,
But the baby ones were pretty small.

Another exhibit showed air doing tricks
And we used magnets to play pick up sticks.
Then we saw a special show
About the world long ago.

## THE ART MUSEUM

What did we see at the museum today?
Sculptures and paintings on display.
Paintings were hanging on every wall
And one sculpture looked like a waterfall.

One painting had very funny faces
With eyes and noses in the wrong places.
A lot of paintings seemed to show
What people looked like long ago.

# Resources

Agee, Jon. (1988) *The Incredible Painting of Felix Clousseau*. New York: Farrar, Straus & Giroux.

Alexander, Lisa. (1987) *A Visit to the Sesame Street Museum*. New York: Random House.

Brown, Laurene Krasny and Marc. (1986) *Visiting the Art Museum*. New York: Dutton.

Cohen, Miriam. (1983) *Lost in the Museum*. New York: Dell.

Cooper, Jason. (1992) *Museums*. Vero Beach, FL: Rourke.

de Paola, Tomie. (1988) *The Legend of the Indian Paintbrush*. New York: G. P. Putnam's Sons.

Delafosse, Claude, and Gallimard Jeunesse. (1993) *Portraits* (A First Discovery Art Book). New York: Scholastic (also in this series *Paintings*, *Landscapes*, *Animals*).

Florian, Douglas. (1993) *A Painter*. New York: Greenwillow Books.
————. (1993) *A Potter*. New York: Greenwillow Books.

Gibbons, Gail. (1988) *Dinosaurs, Dragonflies, and Diamonds: All About Natural History Museums*. New York: Four Winds Press.

Howe, James. (1990) *Pinky & Rex*. New York: Atheneum.

Kellogg, Steven. (1987) *Prehistoric Pinkerton*. New York: Dial Books.

Lionni, Leo. (1991) *Matthew's Dream*. New York: Alfred A. Knopf.

Mayhew, James. (1992) *Katie and the Dinosaurs*. New York: Bantam Books.
———. (1989) *Katie's Picture Show*. New York: Bantam Books.

Papajani, Janet. (1983) *Museums*. Chicago: Childrens Press.

Rey, Margaret, and Allan J. Shalleck. (1989) *Curious George and the Dinosaur*. Boston: Houghton Mifflin.

Rohmann, Eric. (1994) *Time Flies*. New York: Crown Books.

Ross, Pat. (1985) *M & M and the Mummy Mess*. New York: Viking Kestrel.

Strand, Mark. (1986) *Rembrandt Takes a Walk*. New York: C. N. Potter.

Tropea, Judith. (1991) *A Day in the Life of a Museum Curator*. Mahwah, NJ: Troll Associates.

Vincent, Gabrielle. (1986) *Where Are You, Ernest and Celestine?* New York: Greenwillow.

Weil, Lisl. (1989) *Let's Go to the Museum*. New York: Holiday House.

Yenawine, Philip. (1991) *Lines*. New York: Delacorte Press.
———. (1993) *Places*. New York: Delacorte Press.
———. (1991) *Stories*. New York: Delacorte Press.

# Restaurant· · · · · · · · · · · · · · · · · · ·

A great many preschoolers frequently eat out and visit restaurants, especially fast food restaurants. They are familiar with the special children's meals as they cross the fast-food counter. They are much less familiar with what happens on the working side of the counter, since many of them can barely see over the counter. Knowing this, many fast food restaurants have special tours available for preschool groups. Take advantage of this resource, but also plan to visit a different type of restaurant for comparison.

A trip to a restaurant provides opportunities for children to

- see how food is stored, prepared for cooking, and cooked;
- see the variety of ways food is served to people from carry-out to elegant table service;
- observe all the different jobs the restaurant staff members do;
- learn how different types of restaurants work; and
- gain self-assurance for future restaurant visits, which familiarity, knowledge, and prior experience provide.

For a first restaurant excursion, take your group to a familiar place. Later on, venture to different types of restaurants—perhaps ethnic or more adult-oriented places. If you will be eating unfamiliar foods or snacks at the restaurant, provide similar types of food for the children to try out in advance. Help them see how that food may be similar to something they are used to (for example, a fortune cookie is like a wafer cookie in a different shape).

## Before the Trip

### WORDS TO LEARN AND USE

menu ● waitress ● waiter ● hostess ● maitre d' ● chef ● salad bar ● booth ● counter ● place setting ● place mat ● tablecloth ● centerpiece ● busboy ● cafeteria ● fast food ● family style ● uniform ● entree ● a la carte ● beverage ● dessert ● appetizer ● dining room ● grill ● order ● tip ● check ● powder room ● award ● seafood ● cafe ● coffee shop ● buffet ● take out ● drive-through ● gourmet ● ethnic

Ask the children if they have eaten at restaurants. Make a list of the ones they mention and let them tell you their favorites. Talk about the different kinds of restaurants they mention. Are they fast food, family style, or restaurants featuring foods of a specific nationality?

Think of the kinds of foods the children have eaten in the restaurants you have listed. Wonder how those foods are prepared. Do they prepare a few things very quickly using special equipment (as in fast food restaurants), or do they have a full kitchen and cook things to order?

Generate a list of questions from the children about how foods are purchased and prepared in the restaurant. Plan to ask those questions on the trip.

### FOODS AROUND THE WORLD

Show the children pictures from *A Taste of Italy*, by Roz Denny (or one of the other Foods Around the World books). Show them what people eat in that country. Ask if there are restaurants that serve Italian food here. What other ethnic restaurants do the children like? Pick the two most popular types and plan to visit that type of ethnic restaurant sometime during the year.

### THINGS TO BRING

paper and a pen or pencil to record observations ● questions to ask the restaurant employees ● plastic or paper bag for collecting things ● a camera

## On the Trip

### OBSERVE

Notice if the building that houses the restaurant is unique or if it looks like several others of the same type. Is it part of a chain with special identifying characteristics? Notice the color of the roof, style of construction, shape of the building, and so on.

Are there construction features that suggest a particular ethnic identification for this restaurant? Does its appearance suggest a particular type of restaurant such as a fancy supper club or a truck stop? Talk about what gives the building this special appearance.

Notice the area around the building and how it is adapted for the needs of the restaurant. Is there parking space, a special drive-up arrangement, an identifying sign, and so on?

Notice the entryway into the restaurant. Do you come right into the table area, or is there a lobby or reception area? Notice what's in that area. Do you seat yourself, or is there someone to take you to your table? How do you know what to do when you enter? Are there signs, or does the building's style tell you?

Are there booths, tables and counters, or just tables? Are there special settings on the tables? Notice the type of table setting. Does it look plain or fancy? Do they use paper place mats or tablecloths? What things are on the tables, such as salt and pepper shakers, napkin holders, ashtrays, sugar bowl, or centerpiece? How do the things on the tables contribute to the restaurant's appearance?

Notice the lighting in the room and what effect it has on the atmosphere. Is it bright daylight or dark? What makes it that way? Is there a bar? Does that look the same as the rest of the restaurant? Are there room dividers for different areas? Are there smoking and nonsmoking sections?

Notice the way in which the room is decorated: floor covering, wall covering, lighting fixtures, decorations on the wall, and so on. Are there plants or other decorations that contribute to the atmosphere? Notice the type of tables and chairs. Is there a salad bar or are there cases that display desserts or special food items? Are there pictures of any foods to tempt you? Name and identify all the different things you see in the room.

Notice the clothes employees wear. Do their clothes tell you anything about their jobs? Are all the people wearing the same kinds of uniforms? Does the uniform style contribute to the atmosphere in the restaurant? Talk about the types of jobs people do in restaurants and use the names for those positions.

Observe the people at work. How do the tables get cleared and reset? How is the food carried to the tables? Is it a self-service or cafeteria style restaurant, or does someone take the customer's order and bring the food and drinks to the table? Do you see signs of food preparation, or is it all done in the kitchen area? Can you see where the kitchen is?

Look at the menus. Are they plain or fancy? Is it a long menu with many different things on it, or is it a short piece of paper? Are there pictures on the menu or funny or special names for things? Is there a children's menu? Look at the way the menu is organized and talk about the different sections of the menu, which list things by courses, such as appetizers, main courses, desserts, beverages, and so on. Talk about the meanings of *a la carte*, *complete*, and *full course dinner*. Point out the prices for different items.

Observe customers getting their checks and paying their bills. Notice if they leave money on the table. Talk about tips or gratuities and what that means. How do the customers pay their bills? Does the waitress or waiter take the money or credit card, or does the customer pay a cashier?

### Ask

Ask the receptionist or cashier to show the cash register and explain how they ring up items. Ask about credit cards and how they deal with those kinds of charges.

Ask the waitress or waiter to show you an order book and the system for conveying orders to the kitchen. How does he or she know when an order is ready?

Ask to see the service and supply areas and how the dishes are bussed. How are supplies maintained and what system does this restaurant use? Are there individual stations with silverware, dishes, and napkins for specific areas, or is there one central supply area? How does that work, and who keeps stocking the supply areas? Who fills pitchers, sugar bowls, coffee pots, and so on?

Ask to see the kitchen, and ask how the food is prepared. How is the kitchen organized? Are there special areas of the kitchen for different items such as a salad area where all salads are prepared? Who does the cooking? Are things cooked to order or reheated? How do the employees keep from getting in each other's way? Who is in charge? What do you call the person in charge of preparing food in a restaurant? Do the cooks wear special hats? Can you tell from the hats which person is the chef? How is food ordered and who does that? Ask all the questions you had prepared in advance. Ask to see refrigerators, freezers, and stoves, as well as pots and pans. How does this kitchen compare to a home kitchen? Notice the clothes worn by people in the kitchen area and signs of special health practices used in the kitchen. Do employees wear or use special clothing items to help keep things sanitary?

## COUNT

Count the tables and number of seats at the tables. Estimate how many people the restaurant can serve at any one time. Notice the different-sized tables and any arrangements for expanding tables to hold larger parties. Count the number of tables for parties of two, four, and larger groups. Which size table do they have the most of? Count the number of booths and seats at counters as well.

Count how many people work in the restaurant, the number of different jobs, and the number of people in each job.

Count the number of items on the menu in each of the sections. Which things do they have the most of?

Count light fixtures, the number of rooms in the restaurant, and architectural features that lend themselves to counting, such as windows or doors.

Count the number of highchairs or booster seats. Wonder what would happen if they ran out. Make guesses about whether this restaurant serves many families with children, based on how many children's seats you see.

## COLLECT

Take back as many things as the employees will give you, such as order books, place mats, menus and children's menus, paper chef or kitchen hats, plastic mitts or hair nets (if they use them).

Take pictures to use later. If possible, photograph the kitchen and table areas of the restaurant and the personnel who work there.

## SENSE

Notice all the smells in the restaurant. Can you recognize particular smells such as coffee, chocolate, hamburgers on a grill, or bread baking? Identify as many different aromas as you can. Are there ones that dominate?

Be aware of the different textures in the environment. Is it a hard, smooth, plastic environment, or a warm wood, soft texture environment?

Is the feeling of the place busy and hectic or calm and relaxing? Are people smiling?

Listen to the noises of the restaurant. Do you hear people chattering and laughing, dishes clattering, water pouring, food sizzling, fire crackling? What other sounds are you aware of?

Where do all the sensations come from? Are you aware of noises or activities outside the restaurant as well, or does the outside world seem far away?

# After the Trip: Follow-up Activities

## TALK ABOUT IT

Talk about the trip and write down all the children's impressions. Use their comments to send a thank-you letter to the restaurant. Find out if any of the children have eaten in that restaurant and if so what things they like to eat there.

Talk about the differences in eating at home and in a restaurant, and list the things the children say they like about eating out and the things they don't like about eating out.

Look over the pictures you took and make up a story about your trip to the restaurant, using your pictures and the children's comments.

## MAKE MENUS

Look at the sample menu you brought back and review the different sections of the menu, noting what kinds of foods go in each section. Find pictures in magazines of all different kinds of foods. Use those pictures to make menus to use in a play restaurant. Print the section headings and a few names of foods to go with the pictures. Put these together into a little booklet to resemble the type of menu you saw. If you wish, make a cover for your menu from construction paper. Print a restaurant name and the word *menu* on the cover.

## RESTAURANT COLLAGE

Collect ads, parts of coupons, and pictures of food items and fast food or local restaurants. Let the children make collages. They might make collages for particular types of restaurants, using the kinds of foods found in that restaurant. For example, a collage for Burger King or McDonalds would have foods that are found there; and one for an Italian restaurant or pizza parlor would have all those types of foods.

## DRAMATIC PLAY

Set up a dramatic play restaurant. Bring in a few small tables, menus (from restaurants or homemade), table setting supplies (place mats and plastic silverware), centerpieces, and other table items. Have the children pretend to be the chef, waitresses or waiters, hostess, and customers. You can use pretend food if you have some, or make things that look like various food items out of paper, playdough, felt, and other scrap materials.

If you wish, vary the type of restaurant from a family style, sit-down restaurant to a fast food restaurant or a pizza parlor. You could also prepare some actual specialties for a day. Using items such as individual pizza on English muffins, tacos, or home-baked cookies, serve lunch or snack in the pretend restaurant. *Fun Food*, by Sara Lynn and Diane James, has wonderful things to prepare as snacks to serve in your restaurant.

If you want to make this an ethnic restaurant, you can get some ideas of things to cook from *The Kids Around the World Cookbook*, by Deri Robins, or books in the Food Around the World series. You can cook the food in the kitchen or a separate area and bring the food to the restaurant area to be served. Let the cooks wear their chef hats, and remember to wash hands before cooking just as employees do in real restaurants.

## A LIFE-SIZED SORTING GAME

Make large master boards using 9-by-12-inch tagboard, and put a picture of a different kind of restaurant on each board. Include a delicatessen and different types of franchise restaurants from ice cream parlors and donut shops to steak houses. Also include ethnic restaurants. On 3-by-5-inch cards, paste pictures of different foods found in those restaurants. Make one card for each food item, including everything from hamburgers, tacos, and donuts to several types of ice cream cones.

Lay the master boards on a table and have a child pick a card and place it on the master board where that food would be found. You can play this game with a group, or with a few children who keep picking cards and sorting them to the appropriate master board.

## CHEF HATS

Cut a strip of white tagboard about 2 inches wide and almost long enough to go around a child's head. Staple a small rubber band to each end of the band (this will make the hat adjustable). Find a white paper bag with about the same circumference as the circle band. Staple the open end of the bag to the headband. You can also use tissue paper, but it is not as sturdy as a paper bag.

## DESIGN A BULLETIN BOARD

Divide a bulletin board into two areas, the kitchen and the dining room. Put pictures of large kitchen equipment, chefs, and food being prepared in the kitchen. In the dining room area, put pictures of tables and chairs, people being served and eating, stands for trays of food, and so on. Draw a counter area on one side and add display cases with pictures of fruits, cakes, pies, donuts, or muffins. Pictures of food taken from boxes of packaged foods would be useful for the bulletin boards.

## PLANNING BALANCED MEALS

Using pictures of food cut out from magazines, plan pretend balanced meals. Include pictures of appetizers, main courses, vegetables, fruits, and dessert items. Use a paper plate and have the children tell you what to order for breakfast, lunch, and dinner. Put those pictures on your plate. Discuss those choices and whether they make a balanced meal.

Let the children make balanced meal pictures on the paper plates, choosing pictures of foods to eat and pasting them on their plates. Look up the calories for some foods. On some display paper plates, write the number of calories for different foods next to the picture of the food. Write the calories for items such as potato chips, donuts and pies, cookies and cakes, as well as fruits and vegetables.

Explain to the children what the word calorie means. Talk about how many calories they need and about extra calories making fat. The next time you let the children plan the foods they choose, see if they make any changes in the things they choose.

### FLANNELBOARD ACTIVITY

Make felt cutouts for various food items and let the children put them together. Some sample items would be white circles for buns, brown ellipses for hamburgers, little green circles for pickles, red and yellow drops for ketchup and mustard, and various shapes to use for hot dogs, hot dog buns, pizza, and other common foods.

## Related Trip Ideas to Explore

specialty food stores ● cooking supply stores ● department store's housewares section that features cooking demonstrations ● ice cream factory ● caterer

## Songs, Poems, and Finger Plays

### THE HAMBURGER
*(to the tune of "I'm a Little Teapot")*
(use with flannelboard cutouts)

First you take a hamburger on a bun.
Then you start to have some fun.
Add a little ketchup and some cheese,
Lettuce and tomato, if you please.
Then you get to take a little bite.
Umm, delicious! Tastes just right!

### AT THE RESTAURANT
*(to the tune of "Frere Jacque")*
At the restaurant, at the restaurant,
There's a menu, there's a menu.
Menu tells us what to eat,
Menu tells us what to eat.
Yum, yum, yum.

At the restaurant, at the restaurant,
There's a chef, there's a chef.
Chef who cooks the yummy food,
Chef who cooks the yummy food,
We can eat, we can eat.

At the restaurant, at the restaurant,
There's a waitress, there's a waitress.
Takes our orders and brings the food,
Takes our orders and brings the food,
We can eat, we can eat.

### THIS LITTLE HAMBURGER

This little hamburger has ketchup. (hold up thumb)
This little hamburger has none. (hold up next finger)
This little hamburger has pickles. (hold up next finger)
And this little hamburger has cheese. (hold up next finger)
But this little hamburger has everything— (hold up little finger)
And that's for me, please! (move little finger toward mouth)

### FIVE LITTLE CHILDREN

(Hold up five fingers to start; with the other hand touching one
finger at a time as you say each line. You can also use props: attach
pictures of foods to wooden craft sticks and let children hold them
up in sequence.)

Five little children at the restaurant today.
The first one said, "I'll have steak if I may."
The second one said, "What's this I see?
Barbecued ribs, now that's for me!"
The third one said, "What should I eat?
I guess fried chicken would be a treat."
The fourth one said, "I'm not hungry,
A hamburger is enough for me."
The fifth one said, "I don't want that stuff,
But a great big pizza would be enough."
Along came the waitress
And what do you think!
They all ordered pizza,
As quick as a wink!

### A SONG FOR ALL RESTAURANTS

(to the tune of "Old MacDonald had a Farm")

Old MacDonald had a hamburger,
E-I-E-I-O.
And on his hamburger he had some cheese
E-I-E-I-O.
With some cheese, cheese here,
And some cheese, cheese there,
Here some cheese, there some cheese,
Everywhere some cheese, cheese,
Old MacDonald had a hamburger,
E-I-E-I-O.

Old MacDonald had a hamburger,
E-I-E-I-O.

And on his hamburger he had some pickles
E-I-E-I-O.
With pickles here, and some cheese there,
Here a pickle, there some cheese,
Everywhere pickles and cheese,
Old MacDonald had a hamburger
E-I-E-I-O.

Additional verses:
Ketchup, mustard, onions, and whatever else the children add

Variations:
And with his hamburger he had French fries
(a milkshake, onion rings, and so forth.)

Old MacDonald had some pizza
And on his pizza he had some cheese
(sausage, mushrooms, green pepper, tomato sauce, and anything else.)
(Use with flannelboard food cut outs.)

## Resources

Bang, Molly. (1985) *The Paper Crane*. New York: Greenwillow.

Barbour, Karen. (1987) *Little Nino's Pizzeria*. San Diego: Harcourt Brace.

Berbesson, Fanny Joly, and Brigette Boucher. (1989) *Marceau Bonappetit*. Minneapolis: Carolrhoda Books.

Buehner, Caroline. (1993) *A Job for Wittilda and Mork*. New York: Dial Books.

Calmenson, Stephanie. (1991) *Dinner at the Panda Palace*. New York: HarperCollins.

Davis, Maggie. (1988) *The Rinky Dink Cafe*. New York: Simon & Schuster.

Day, Alexandra. (1988) *Frank and Ernest*. New York: Scholastic.

Egan, Tim. (1994) *Friday Night at Hodge's Cafe*. Boston: Houghton Mifflin.

Florian, Douglas. (1992) *The Chef*. New York: Greenwillow.

Gibbons, Gail. (1989) *The Diner*. New York: HarperCollins.
———. (1989) *Marge's Dinner*. New York: Crowell.

Greenberg, Melanie. (1991) *My Father's Luncheonette*. New York: Dutton.

Hunter, Sarah Hoagland. (1995) *Miss Piggy's Night Out*. New York: Viking.

Kelly, True. (1989) *Let's Eat*. New York: Dutton.

Kovalski, Maryann. (1991) *Pizza for Breakfast*. New York: William Morrow.

Krementz, Jill. (1986) *Benjy Goes to a Restaurant*. New York: Crown.

Loomis, Christine. (1993) *In the Diner*. New York: Scholastic.

Lynn, Sara, and Diane James. (1992) *Fun Food*. New York: Bantam Books.

Moss, Marissa. (1994) *Mel's Diner*. Mahwah, NJ: Bridgewater Books.

Oxenbury, Helen. (1983) *Eating Out*. New York: Dial Books.

Pillar, Marjorie. (1990) *Pizza Man*. New York: Crowell.

Pinkwater, Daniel. (1993) *Space Burger*. New York: Macmillan.

Robins, Deri. (1994) *The Kids Around the World Cookbook*. New York: Kingfisher.

Roffey, Maureen. (1989) *Mealtime*. New York: Four Winds Press.

Rylant, Cynthia. (1992) *An Angel for Soloman Singer*. New York: Orchard Books.

Shaw, Nancy. (1992) *Sheep Out to Eat*. Boston: Houghton Mifflin.

Stadler, John. (1986) *Animal Cafe*. New York: Aladdin.

Sun, Chyng Feng. (1994) *Mama Bear*. Boston: Houghton Mifflin.

## OTHER GOOD RESOURCES

Denny, Roz. (1994) *A Taste of Italy* (Food Around the World Series). New York: Thomson Learning (also in series: *A Taste of India, A Taste of France, A Taste of Japan*).

Sobel, Harriet. (1979) *Cosmo's Restaurant*. New York: Macmillan.

Watson, Tom and Jenny. (1982) *Evening Meal*. Chicago: Childrens Press.

# School ·························

Schools are a microcosm of the larger community and as such can offer a glimpse into parts of that larger community. Student government, team sports, musical and artistic endeavors, student publications and activities, and academic and vocational pursuits illustrate similar activities in the larger world—and they are all under one roof. Trips to junior or senior high schools allow preschoolers a chance to

- see what older students do in school and compare it to their own school or their parent's work;
- observe what is inside a large school building and learn how it works;
- visit the school's special rooms, such as band, home economics, and science labs, and learn about what is in each;
- visit the people who work in school and observe what they do; and
- see the large group spaces, such as the auditorium, library, media center, gymnasium, and playing fields, and find out about their uses.

This trip is designed around a junior or senior high school because not as many preschoolers have visited those buildings, and they are usually much larger and more diversified than elementary schools. Many elementary schools now have special programs for preschoolers or parent-child programs so those sites are more familiar. If many of your children have never been to an elementary school, then by all means visit that school. If your program is located in a junior or senior high, then explore your own building, but also visit a different type of school—perhaps a building designed for preschool where the scale of everything will be so different. College campuses, vocational schools, and technical schools can also be exciting places to visit with many interesting things to see.

Arrange your visit with appropriate people in the school and bring extra help. Often, schools will assign student tour guides to show you around, which can be fun for your children.

# Before the Trip

## WORDS TO LEARN AND USE

office ● gym ● basketball hoop ● auditorium ● stage ● cafeteria ● band room ● instruments ● clarinet ● flute ● trumpet ● drum ● science lab ● home economics room ● locker ● hall ● combination lock ● classroom ● principal ● teacher ● students ● custodian ● bell ● hall monitor ● trophy case ● trophy ● cheerleader ● team ● textbook ● backpack ● bicycle stand ● parking lot ● school bus ● desk ● counselor ● media center ● study carrel

## TALK ABOUT IT

Ask the children where their older brothers and sisters go each morning. Discuss different levels of school. Ask the children what they think the big children do in school, and if they would like to go to see. Ask the children if adults go to school. Ask them why people go to school.

## FLANNELBOARD STORY

Make some flannelboard figures of different-sized children and school buildings and different-shaped buildings. Match the size of the child to the size of the building as you talk about the figures and buildings. Make up simple stories using names of brothers and sisters in the group and names of the school buildings. For example, "Each morning Susie's sister, Jane, gets dressed, packs her books, and goes to Sunnyside School. Keisha's sister goes to Madison Junior High." If you wish, add a felt school bus or bikes to embellish your story. Add pictures of colleges or vocational schools and parent-sized figures also. Many children's parents may be going to some type of school or working in schools.

**THINGS TO BRING**

paper and a pen or pencil to record observations ● plastic or paper bag for collecting things ● a camera

## On the Trip

### OBSERVE

Notice the general construction and materials used in the building. Notice the grounds around the school. Is there anything outside or on the grounds to suggest that this is a school building, such as sports fields, bike racks, flag, students, playground equipment?

After entering the building, take a look around and notice the general features of the building: the long hallways lined with lockers, the central hall area with pictures or other items on the wall, the general office area, and trophy cases.

Walk into the office and observe the people coming and going there. Look for faculty mailboxes, telephone and intercom systems, clocks, and other equipment. Talk to people who work in the office: student aids, secretary, principal, and counselors. Find out what they do.

Look carefully at the trophy case and notice the different kinds of trophies and what they say on them. Can you tell from looking at the trophy what sport it represents?

If there are pictures of classes or teams from years ago, examine them and notice differences in style of clothes, sports uniforms or equipment, hair, or general appearances.

Notice study carrels in the halls or other areas and talk about how they are used.

Visit the specialized areas of the school such as the gym, cafeteria, auditorium, library and media center, band room, home economics room, shop area, and science lab. If possible, let the children go on the stage in the auditorium and sing some songs to see how it feels to be on stage. Let them run around the big gym or on any outdoor playing fields. Notice the materials used in these room and any special construction used to make the rooms suitable for their special purposes.

Visit the heating plant and maintenance area of the building and ask the custodians to tell you about their work.

Do you see any evidence of student government, such as pictures of school or class officers, student council meetings in session, or announcements of student-run events. Are groups selling anything to raise money for a school-related activity? Point out such activities and talk about it with the children. Also point out announcements of upcoming sports events or other posters you may see.

### IDENTIFY AND DEMONSTRATE

Ask some students to show the children how the lockers look inside and how the locks work. Be sure to explain to the children the way combination locks work, if those are the types on the lockers. Have the students show the children the number and size of the books stored in the lockers. Discuss why the students need lockers.

If possible, arrange to have students demonstrate items found in the school's specialized rooms. Be sure to tell the children the names of the different items they see, including musical instruments; gym and sports equipment; and office, laboratory, or audiovisual equipment. Look for other signs of student activities or interests, such as signs on the walls, special displays, and bulletin boards. Talk about the information they convey.

If there is a computer center in the school, ask a student to demonstrate some of the computer graphics and explain how the students use the computers in school.

### LISTEN AND SENSE

Notice the sounds of musical instruments played separately and together. Be sure to point out the different sounds of instruments in the same family such as the strings (from violin to double bass), woodwinds, brass, and various percussion instruments, if they have any. Wonder if the size of the instrument is related to the sound. Make some generalizations about that relationship. Ask the music teacher if your conclusions are correct.

Talk about the general sounds you hear in the building as you walk along. Are there bells ringing for changing classes? Do you hear clanging lockers, singing, running, talking, clicking keyboards, or other sounds of students and teachers at work?

Do announcements come blaring out from time to time? Wonder where those voices come from and if you wish, go and find out how the public address system in the school works.

Notice the sounds in the gym area. Can you tell what sport is going on from the sounds you hear?

Are there any special aromas you find in some parts of the building, such as cooking smells from the home economics area, food smells from the cafeteria, coffee near the teachers' lounge, or cleaning materials or fuel smells in the maintenance or shop areas?

### COMPARE

Make some comparisons between things you see in the school you are visiting and your group's own school or room. Talk about the older students' lockers and your children's cubbies, the home economics room and your housekeeping corner, the shop rooms and your workbench area. Include some of the more general items used in both situations: books, science materials, audiovisual materials, computers, and so on.

Make size comparisons concerning the equipment and features found in the school, such as tables, chairs, drinking fountains, and library shelves. Point out how your own school setting is suited to young children. Wonder if all types of schools are suited to the size of their students. Discuss what happens if students are very large or very small for their age or have a disability that makes it hard for them to use things in the building. How is the building adapted to help children with special needs?

# After the Trip: Follow-up Activities

## TALK ABOUT IT

Talk about the trip. Let the children tell you the things that really impressed them.

Discuss with your children any similarities in things they do in school with what they saw older children doing in their school. Relate these similarities and differences to the different ages and abilities of children as they grow (some samples might be power tools and big workbenches in high school shop compared to hand tools and small workbench in preschool; parallel bars and climbing ropes in school gym compared to climbing structures in preschool). Discuss items they saw that looked familiar, such as stoves in the home economic room and easels in the art rooms, and items they might not have seen before, such as trophies and microscopes.

## THANK-YOU NOTE

Write a thank-you letter to the school principal and the staff involved in rooms you visited or events you witnessed. Let the children dictate to you the things to include in the letter. Have the children make pictures about the trip and send them along with the letter.

## SORTING GAME

Make a sorting game using a schoolhouse shape as the master board and pictures cut from catalogs and mounted on cardboard as the pieces. Children match items to the appropriate room. Master board rooms should include a picture clue to show the type of room.

## DISPLAY

Set up a display table of items associated with junior or senior high (for example, trophies, combination locks, cheerleader pom-poms, sports items, textbook, gym clothes, sports letters, school newspapers, and yearbooks). Cut out pictures from your community newspaper that show sports teams or activities from the school you visited and add them to your display. Write down some of the comments the children made about the school in a small scrapbook. Let the children add pictures and keep the scrapbook on the display table for people to look at. Add the newspaper clippings to the scrapbook.

## CHEERLEADING

Make megaphones out of paper or pom-poms out of crepe paper, and learn the school's cheer or school song. Invite a cheerleader or other students to visit you and have them tell what they like about their school. Have your children sing the song or cheer. Invite students who play on school teams to visit and show the children the special equipment (including shoes) used in their sport. Fencing team members make a big impression if you can find any.

### DRAMATIC PLAY

Set up a school dramatic play area. Make lockers out of cardboard boxes and add pretend locks. To make a lock, cut a piece of cardboard into a lock shape; cut another piece into a number dial shape. Attach the number dial to the lock with a brass fastener. Attach the lock handle with a paper clip so it can open.

Bring in old backpacks. Use old school books to carry in the backpacks and store in lockers.

Dramatize going to different classes by ringing a bell, walking to a different area of the room, pretending to work, ringing a bell, marching to another area, working.

### OUR BOOK ABOUT SCHOOL

Put together a booklet about your trip to school, using pictures from school supply catalogs to tell about the different rooms in the school. Include in the book photographs of students or teachers at the school, especially if they are related to any of the preschool children. Include information about the school such as colors, symbols, school teams, and subjects studied.

### MURAL

Make a mural of the school and surrounding area. Use cut-paper shapes to make the school building. Draw or use cutout figures for the students. Add school buses, flag, and playing fields to create a school scene.

## Related Trip Ideas to Explore

college campus ● vocational/technical schools ● community center ● school affiliated with a place of worship

## Songs, Poems, and Finger Plays

### SCHOOL BELLS

Ding, dong, hear the school bells ring.
See the children hurry,
Don't want to miss a thing.

Down the hall they scurry,
Loaded down with books;
Isn't it amazing,
How busy their school looks!

### SEE THE STUDENTS

See the students all in a row, (hold up two hands)
Marching off to class just so. (make hands march)
They study hard and work all day, (turn hands to form book)
But after school they run and play.(wiggle fingers and move
 hands to opposite sides)

### THIS IS THE WAY WE GO TO SCHOOL
*(to the tune of "Here We Go Round the Mulberry Bush")*

This is the way we go to school,
Go to school, go to school.
This is the way we go to school,
So early in the morning.

Additional verses:
This is the way we open our lockers…
To put our things away.

This is the way we walk to class…
As the bell rings each day.

This is the way we go to gym…
To get our exercise.

This is the way we go to lunch…
To eat a meal each day.

### OFF TO CLASS

Slip off the backpack.
(make motions of removing something from shoulders)
Unload all the books.
Open up the locker, (pretend to work lock and open door)
Hang things on the hooks. (imitate hanging up coat)

Now we are all ready. (march around room)
Off to class we go.
We'll listen to our teachers, (sit down in front of teacher)
There's a lot to learn, you know! (pretend to read a book)

## Resources

Allard, Harry, and James Marshall. (1985) *Miss Nelson Has a Field Day*. Boston:
 Houghton Mifflin (other books are available in the Miss Nelson series).

Arnold, Caroline. (1982) *Where Do You Go to School?* New York: Franklin Watts.

Birnbaum, Bette. (1990) *My School, Your School*. Milwaukee, WI: Raintree.

Carlson, Nancy. (1990) *Arnie and the New Kid*. New York: Viking.

Cazett, Denys. (1987) *A Fish in His Pocket*. New York: Orchard Books.

Cohen, Miriam. (1989) *Will I Have a Friend?* New York: Aladdin Books.

Crews, Donald. (1984) *School Bus.* New York: Greenwillow.

Delacre, Lulu. (1989) *Time for School Nathan.* New York: Scholastic.

Elliott, Dan. (1982) *Grover Goes to School.* New York: Random House.

Feder, Paula K. (1979) *Where Does the Teacher Live?* New York: Dutton.

Hoofman, Phyllis. (1990) *We Play.* New York: Harper & Row.

Howe, James.(1994) *When You Go to Kindergarten.* New York: William Morrow.

Jabor, Cynthia. (1989) *Alice Ann Gets Ready for School.* Boston: Jay Street Books.

Lindgren, Astrid. (1987) *I Want to Go to School.* New York: R & S Books.

McCully, Emily Arnold. (1987) *School.* New York: Harper & Row.

McDonald, Maryann. (1990) *Little Hippo Starts School.* New York: Dial Books.

Myers, Bernice. (1990) *It Happens to Everyone.* New York: Lothrop.

Oxenbury, Helen. (1983) *First Day of School.* New York: Dial Books.

Powers, Ellen. (1986) *Our Teacher Is in a Wheelchair.* Niles, IL: Albert Whitman.

Rey, Margaret. (1990) *Curious George Goes to School.* Boston: Houghton Mifflin.

Solomon, Chuck. (1989) *Moving Up (From Kindergarten to First Grade).* New York: Crown Publishers.

Stadler, James. (1993) *The Adventures of Snail at School.* New York: HarperCollins.

Tenaille, Marie. (1988) *The Day the Dragon Came to School.* New York: Aladdin Books.

Wells, Rosemary. (1981) *Timothy Goes to School.* New York: Dial Books.

# Service Station ············

As noted in the Car Dealership Trip, the care and maintenance of cars gets a lot of adult attention, so most young children have been to a gas station. Most often, however, they are told to stay in the car because of the hazards of cars coming and going. A service station, therefore, is a place children may have visited frequently, and yet they may know little about it—except that it is a place to get gas for the car. In fact, many children may not even see these places as many gas stations have been turned into miniature stores and video rental stations. But the old fashioned service station with auto mechanics who repair cars is still a fascinating place for children—as are specialized stores where brakes are repaired or oil changed. In all of these businesses, children can

- look underneath a car's hood—and under the car itself;
- learn how mechanics figure out what is wrong with a car, and what tools they use to help them diagnose the car's problems;
- observe people at work changing and fixing tires, changing oil, and cleaning parts of the engine;
- watch gas pumps in operation and learn where the gas is coming from; and
- learn about how various things work in the service station—from the air pump to the car hoist—and what parts are used to fix cars.

Take small groups of children to a working garage because the service areas and other spaces are small and there are not many other things to see on the premises. *Supervise the children closely* and keep them out of the way of the traffic, which is easier to do in small groups. If you have a larger group than can comfortably observe at one time, divide up the group. Send one group on a walk in the area and then switch places (you will need more adult supervision in order to split up a large group).

## Before the Trip

gas pump ● nozzle ● hose ● air pump ● motor oil ● gasoline ● antifreeze ● mechanic ● hoist ● tire ● air jack ● battery ● oil filter ● lubricate ● grease ● tow truck ● wrecker ● car wash ● wax ● gallon ● leaded ● unleaded ● diesel ● regular ● premium ● credit card ● self-serve ● full service ● hood ● tire iron ● windshield wiper fluid ● oil change ● dipstick

### TALK ABOUT IT

Ask the children if they know anyone who works in a garage or service station. What happens at a service station? Ask them what their parents do when something is wrong with their car. Where does gasoline come from? Have they heard their parents talk about the price of gasoline? Do they talk about getting good gas mileage? What does that mean? Plan to ask at the service station. Can they tell you which cars get good gas mileage?

### LIST

Make a list of questions resulting from the discussion. Include questions such as, "Where is the gas stored?," "How do the mechanics get under the car to fix it?," and others. Plan to go to a service station to find answers.

### THINGS TO BRING

paper and a pen or pencil to record observations ● a list of questions to ask the employees ● plastic or paper bag for collecting things ● a camera

## On the Trip

### OBSERVE

Notice the gas pump area and point out the different types of gas at the pumps. Show the children the words that tell people which pump has regular, unleaded, premium, or diesel fuel. Call their attention to the beginning letters of the words and then give the pumps nicknames by type of gas, such as the "S" gas, or the "P" or "D" gas, to help them identify which one is which. When a car arrives to get some gas, see if the children can tell which kind that car is getting.

Watch the numbers whirling on the pump and explain what each set of numbers means. Show them the dollar sign on one row so they know that one tells how much the gas will cost. If there are self-serve and full-serve areas, look at the gas prices in each area and talk about why one costs more. Ask the children what the difference is between full-service and self-service.

Look at the building on the grounds and notice how it is suited to the work that is done. Is there a garage area as well as a cashier's area? Notice the doors into each area and talk about the door for people and the doors for cars. Do mostly cars come to the service station or are there places for trucks as well? Talk about what is needed for trucks to come to a service station.

Look for the name of the station and any signs or use of its logo.

If there is an automatic car wash, try to observe that in operation. When it is not in use, look at the size of the brushes and the moving sections.

## IDENTIFY

Notice all the items around the garage and name as many as you can. Ask the mechanic to tell you about some of the items. Some things to watch for and talk about are the credit card machine, cash register, cans of oil, funnels, window cleaner, antifreeze, fan belts, tires, headlights, fuses, and other spare parts. There may even be a computer called a *diagnostic analyzer* that mechanics use to tell what's wrong with a car.

Notice the tools the mechanics use and ask them to show you how some work, such as the air jack, the hoist for the cars, air gauges, air pump, and tire irons. If a car is in for repair or service, try to watch it being elevated and see if you can take a peek under it.

## COUNT

Count the gas pumps and the number of hoses at each pump. Count the number of pumps for each type of gas.

Count the number of rows or service areas. How many cars can fit in each area?

Count how many people work in the service station, the number of work spaces in the garage, and the number of doors.

Count how many cars you see at the station or how many tires you see in the garage.

## LISTEN AND SENSE

Listen to the clicking sounds of the gas pumps and the sounds of the gas being pumped into the car tanks.

Try the air pump and listen to the sound it makes. If a mechanic will demonstrate the air jack, prepare the children for the very loud noise that machine makes. Talk about why the air makes noise when it is being pumped. Have the children practice blowing and see if they can hear that. Does it make any difference in sound when they vary how hard they blow?

What other sounds do you hear, such as traffic, car horns, bells when cars drive in and out, radio, or power tools? Is it a quiet or noisy place?

Notice all the smells in the garage such as smells from fuel, exhaust, new tires, and special hand-cleaning soap in the bathroom. Ask the children if they like the smell of gasoline. Notice the smells in the car wash area as well.

## WONDER

Wonder where the gas comes from to get into the pumps. Ask someone to tell you where the storage tanks are located. If possible, find out when the tankers deliver fresh supplies and plan to visit at that time (or tell the children when it is, if it's at a time you can't visit).

Wonder why the mechanics wear special overalls and how they get their hands clean.

Talk about where the oil, grease, and general dirt in the garage come from and wonder how employees clean up the garage each day. Ask the mechanic if you can't decide.

Wonder how mechanics fix tires. How can they find a hole in a tire to patch it? Ask a mechanic to demonstrate how they find the hole. Do they inflate the tire and feel where the air is coming from, or do they submerge it in water and watch for bubbles? Ask the mechanic to explain or demonstrate how they repair the tire.

Wonder if it would be fun to work in a service station. What would you have to like to do to work there?

## After the Trip: Follow-up Activities

### TALK ABOUT IT

Talk about the trip and have the children tell you all the things they can remember. Discuss what causes tires to become flat and how they can be fixed. Let the children use a bicycle pump to inflate balloons. Stick a pin in a balloon to demonstrate how tires get punctures. How do they fix tires?

Talk about the clothes mechanics wear. Why do they need heavy coveralls? Wonder how to remove grease from hands and clothes. Take some rags with grease stains on them and experiment with ways to get them clean. Does plain water remove heavy dirt? Does soaking them in soapy water work? What happens when you scrub them?

Follow up on your discussion of where gas comes from. If you have not found out yet, look in an encyclopedia for an explanation to give the children. *Automobiles*, by Sylvia Wilkinson, also has a section that discusses gasoline and gas mileage.

### THANK-YOU LETTER

As a group, write a thank-you letter to the station that includes statements of what the children saw on the trip. If appropriate, include pictures the children drew after the trip.

### GAS PUMPS, LARGE AND SMALL

Make small gas pumps out of tall, thin, cartons. Use plastic tubing or telephone cords for the hose and pump spray handles from cleaners for nozzles. Place in the block and truck area.

Make a large gas pump out of large cartons and use it with trikes and wagons. Use pieces of garden hose attached at either side or make two gas lines to encourage interaction. Use the pumps in the dramatic play area or outdoors. Set up a pretend air pump for the tires.

## For the Sandbox

Build a pretend garage out of small cartons. Use tow trucks to tow small cars needing repairs to the garage

## A Picture Story

Have the children look for magazine pictures of things they saw at the service station. Use the cutout pictures and descriptions dictated by the children to tell the story of what the group saw on the trip or what work is done at service stations.

## Matching Game

Make a matching game using service station logos cut out of magazine advertisements.

## Dramatic Play

Set up an outdoor car wash for trikes and wagons. Provide a hose with a nozzle and lots of rags for wiping and pretend waxing.

Set up a service station dramatic play interest area with cartons, gas pumps, air pumps, tools, and a few small cans, such as small watering cans or empty oil cans. Have children bring cars and trucks to be checked and fixed, and take turns being customers or station mechanics. Include self-service pumps, full-service pumps, and a repair shop. Let the children decide on prices for the different kinds of gasoline. Mark the pumps with the different types of gas: regular, unleaded, diesel. Talk about which vehicles use which gas. Remind the children to use the diesel pump for the trucks.

## Display

Set up a display of gears and talk about how they work. If you can, find old small engines that can be taken apart to add to the display. What does oil do for old gears?

## Service Station Diorama

Use shoe boxes to hold dioramas of service stations, using small boxes for pumps and the thick plastic connection frames from toy packaging for car hoists. Attach small strips of paper folded like a spring to raise and lower the pretend car jack. Use small plastic cars in the diorama. Make small gas pumps out of a toothpaste pump, and cover the pump with colored paper. Tape a cap from a ball-point pen to the pump with the opening pointing up. Tape one-half of a shoelace to the pump as the gas hose. Leave the stiff part of the lace loose to use as the nozzle to fill small cars. When not in use, the hose can rest in the cap as its holder.

### A Visit with a Mechanic

Invite a mechanic, perhaps from the service station you visited, to visit the children and see the service station you have set up. Have the children ask the mechanic questions they have, including how they get their hands and clothes clean again and how they fix tires.

## Related Trip Ideas to Explore

auto parts store ● tire dealer ● hub cap store ● auto body shop ● scrap yard ● salvage yard

## Songs, Poems, and Finger Plays

### WHEN WE GO TO THE STATION
*(to the tune of "Here We Go Round the Mulberry Bush")*
This is the way we pump the gas, (pretend to be filling gas tank)
Pump the gas, pump the gas.
This is the way we pump the gas,
When we go to the station.

Additional verses:
This is the way we check the oil... (pretend to check the oil)
When we go to the station.

This is the way we wash the car... (pretend to wash a car)
To get it nice and clean.

This is the way we change the tires... (pretend to change tire)
When we have a flat.

This is the way we wash the windows... (pretend to wash windows)
And make them sparkly clean.

### PUMPING GAS
See the gas pumps all in a row.
(imitate the actions described)
Lower the hose, push the crank,
Put the nozzle in the tank;
Squeeze the handle,
And hear the gasoline flow.

S—s—s—s
Watch the pump,
Look at those numbers go!

### THE GAS STATION

The gas station now is a whole lot more,
It's turned into a little store,
And while our car sits at the pump,
We'll run inside and then explore,
The food and games and things galore.
And while our car gets gas to eat,
We often get a different treat.

### AT THE STATION

*(to the tune of "Down by the Station")*

Down at the station,
Early in the morning.
See all the cars,
Waiting in a row.
See the mechanics,
Moving them around.
Life up the hoists,
They're off the ground!

## Resources

Cole, Joanna. (1983) *Cars and How They Go*. New York: Crowell.

Gibbons, Gail. (1985) *Fill It Up*. New York: Crowell.

Ludlow, Karen. (1994) *Benny the Breakdown Truck*. New York: Crown.

Pomerantz, Charlotte. (1987) *How Many Trucks Can a Tow Truck Tow?* New York: Random House.

Santori, Chris. (1993) *Lift the Hood*. New York: Random House.

Scarry, Richard. (1974) *Cars and Trucks and Things that Go*. New York: Golden Press.

Schaefer, Margaret. (1990) *Let's Build a Car*. Nashville: Ideals Children's Books.

### OTHER GOOD RESOURCES

Hobbs, Laura. (1977) *Cars*. New York: Franklin Watts.

Parker, Steve. (1992) *The Car* (Inventions in Silence). New York: Aladdin Books.

Steele, Philip. (1991) *Cars and Trucks*. New York: Crestwood House.

Wilkinson, Sylvia. (1982) *Automobiles* (A New True Book). Chicago: Childrens Press.

# Zoo••••••••••••••••••••••••••••••••

Many preschool children have been to the zoo—which is probably the number one destination for both families and groups. Many programs plan an outing to the zoo as a special celebration and invite families along. Visiting a local zoo with children and their family is an excellent way to use this valuable community resource. The excursion usually provides an opportunity to see the animals and have a fun group experience. This special visit, however, usually takes place at the end of the year, leaving little time for follow-up activities that could expand the learning opportunities. A trip to the zoo can provide more than looking at animals and watching the seal or dolphin show (although those are fine and enjoyable things to do). A trip to the zoo can also help children

- learn about how a zoo works and about the people who work at a zoo;
- find out about the different habitats and why they are designed in particular ways;
- see how employees prepare food for the animals, and what different animals eat and how they are fed;
- learn how the zoo gets its animals and cares for them while they are there; and
- find out about or participate in special educational programs and presentations the zoo offers.

Many communities have more than one zoo. This is particularly true in areas that have the large super zoos that are main tourist attractions. All zoos are worth visiting, and sometimes the smaller ones offer more accessible and intimate experiences with special petting or children's zoos.

Many zoos have special tours available that take groups behind the scenes into the kitchens and nurseries or provide special presentations and programs for visiting school groups. These tours and presentations require advanced registration and often fill up quickly.

You can visit any zoo on your own, however, provided you have enough help to have the children tour in small groups. These small groups allow you and the children to talk about the animals you are looking at.

Plan carefully; trips to the zoo can be exhausting so plan breaks and rest stops. One experienced director said she never went to the zoo without a blanket and lots of books for a relaxing story time. Breaks for snacks, lunch, or playtime in the park area also make for refreshed animal watching. Bring moist wipes for washing children's hands before eating snacks, since hand washing may not always be convenient and hands get dirty along the way. If the zoo has a train or tram that covers parts of the larger outlying areas, riding it will provide a nice break. Do not try to take in everything in an enormous zoo in one trip. Pick a few special areas to concentrate on and plan to come back another time.

## Before the Trip

### WORDS TO LEARN AND USE

wild animal ● exhibits ● captivity ● cages ● fence ● glass ● moats ● pools ● monkey island ● railing ● zookeepers ● trainer ● veterinarian ● curator ● lion ● tiger ● big cats ● den ● endangered ● mammals ● nursery ● incubator ● hospital ● enclosure ● natural habitat ● naturalist ● guide ● environment ● tropical garden ● forest ● conservation ● desert ● entrance ● ticket booth ● zoo train ● tram ● monorail ● vendors ● souvenir shops ● kit-chen ● commissary keeper ● feed ● seals ● dolphins ● shows ● species ● landscape ● gardener ● horticulturist ● wildlife safari

### TALK ABOUT IT

Ask the children if they have been to the zoo and what things they like to do at the zoo. What animals do they particularly like to see? From your discussion, try to generate lists of what each child wants to see at the zoo. Use the lists to form groupings of the children to determine which places each group will plan to visit. That way, the children will all get to see something they particularly want to see. Although there will be many things everyone wants to see, this preplanning system allows for meeting individual interests. If you are going to visit as one group altogether, use this discussion and listing to make a priority list of the order in which you will plan to tour the zoo so you can see the things of greatest interest to most of the children.

### READ

Read *Zoo*, by Gail Gibbons, *What's It Like to be a Zoo Worker?*, by Judith Stamper, *Zoos*, by Jason Cooper, or other books about zoos and how they work. The books mentioned above are excellent introductions and show a lot about the workings of a zoo. Write down questions the children have about the zoo and the work people do there. Plan to ask the zoo employees your questions.

## THINGS TO BRING

paper and a pen or pencil to record observations ● questions to ask zoo workers ● blanket ● books ● washcloths ● snacks ● visiting plans for each group ● plastic or paper bag for collecting things ● a camera

## On the Trip

### OBSERVE

Notice the entry area to the zoo. Are there special signs, banners, or decorations that tell you about the zoo? Do you have to buy tickets or is the zoo free? Show the children signs directing you to particular exhibit areas and maps or directories of the zoo.

Notice how the zoo is laid out and how the animals are housed. Are the animals in natural habitats, with landscaped areas divided by rock formations, moats, or water? Are there large open spaces where animals roam and people see them from a zoo train or tram? Are there large aviary areas that you can walk into where lots of bird are flying around, or do you view the animals more in caged areas that you walk around? Are there special buildings that house one kind of animal, such as all the large apes, with both indoor and outdoor viewing areas? Point out to the children how the animals can go from one place to another. Where do the animals like to be? What are they doing most of the time? How are spaces adapted to an animal's likes and comfort?

Try to observe several animals being fed. If possible, have the zookeeper show you the food for the animals and tell you a little about feeding the animals. How do they know if the animals are getting enough to eat? Do they have separate feeding dishes for the animals in the same habitats or cages and how can they be sure the animals are not eating each other's food? Can you tell what the zookeeper is feeding the animals? Notice which ones eat meat and what other things they eat. Do you see any special procedures the animals seem to follow themselves around eating? Do certain animals in the cage eat before others? Observe the monkey island to see if the senior animals eat before the children. Watch for a while and see how the animals behave in relation to food. Do any animals feed other animals? Do they play with their food when they are not so hungry? Do they eat fast or slow, eat everything quickly, or nibble at it and keep coming back to their food? Do the zookeepers leave food in the cage or remove it after awhile? What do they do if some animals are not eating very well?

What other animal behaviors can you observe? Do you see animals playing, grooming themselves or others, fighting, chasing, or exercising? Do the animals seem to communicate with each other and how do they do that? Do the animals notice you or other people? How can you tell?

Notice signs around the zoo and see if the children can read the symbols. What do the signs say about feeding animals or other things in relation to the animals? Are there signs posted about special demonstration or shows in some areas? Most shows at zoos are interesting to watch and teach a lot about the animals so try to time your visits to attend some. Find out if you have to get there early to be sure to get in.

Observe the animal nurseries, if you can. Notice how small some of the very young animals are and how different they look. Can the children tell what type of animal the baby is in all cases?

## IDENTIFY

Tell the children about sections of the zoo, such as ocean world, rain forest, and jungle, and discuss what animals they might find in those areas. Read information about each animal to the children, specifically their common name (forget the scientific ones), how old they are, where they come from, what they eat, and other things the children would find interesting. Call attention to how big animals are even when they are only two years old and how very young the small animals are.

Call attention to animals in the same families, such as the large cats, and the monkeys and apes, where there are several different sizes of full-grown animals, leading up to the largest ones in the families. Notice the markings and coloring of animals within the same family, as with leopards, panthers, and tigers. See how many animals the children can identify as you come to them and then give them added information about the animal or tell them the specific name of the type of animal. For example, jaguars, leopards, and some cats can be confusing, as can many types of apes or wolves. The children may be better at identifying the animals than the adults—especially if there were no information cards about the exhibits.

In general, try to call attention to identifying characteristics as you see them: whether an animal can climb trees and jump, the shape of its head, and whether it has whiskers or claws. Observe all the zoo employees. Talk about the jobs that are necessary to take care of the animals and keep the zoo clean and nice for people. Watch for any people working to build new exhibits.

### COUNT AND COMPARE

There are many opportunities for counting and comparing at the zoo. Count the number of enclosures or cages in an area, and the number of animals in each one. Finding the animals can be tricky because they sometimes sleep curled up in hard-to-spot places and blend into the setting. Talk about why the animals sleep that way and if it is helpful to the animal.

Compare sizes of animals and see if you can tell if males are larger than females. Compare the sizes of different animals of the same general family type to find the biggest and smallest as from baboon to gorilla. Play games while at the various areas such as: Find the biggest (or smallest) animal; which is bigger—lion or tiger? baboon or monkey? Which bird has the longest beak?

Count the number of limbs on various animals and how many they usually walk on. Are all the limbs the same size on each animal? If not, which ones are bigger? Talk about how different animals use their limbs. Count horns, antlers, tusks, humps on camels, and other animal features.

Count cars on the zoo train, trees, vendor booths, balloons, zoo vehicles, park benches, walkways, or anything else you see as you are waiting in various places.

### SENSE

Listen to the sounds of the zoo wherever you are. Notice sounds in the aviary areas. Can you find the birds making the sounds? Which are the noisiest? Listen to sounds made by the monkeys, seals, and other animals that tend to be rather noisy. Which animals are the quietest? Do you hear sounds from an animal's moving or eating as well as the sounds it may make chattering? Do you hear the zookeepers talking to the animals? Do you hear announcements, loudspeaker sounds, music, vehicles, or any other sounds?

Is there a dark, enclosed exhibit of night creatures? How does it feel in that area? Is it quiet? What sounds do you hear, if any? Notice how your sight adapts to being in the dark and how bright things seem outside afterward.

Visit the children's zoo or petting area, or any touch and see exhibits. Talk about how various things feel, from the hard shells or tusks of some animals to the soft downy feeling of others. Let the children pet different animals. If the zoo has a baby llama, touch it and compare how soft the llama's coat feels compared to other animals. Can you feel the difference in feathers and fur and in long silky coats and heavy curly ones? Notice how much the animals like to be petted.

Probably the sense of smell gets the most exposure at the zoo. Notice which areas of the zoo tend to be the smelliest. Are they indoors or out? What different kinds of things do you smell: the animals themselves, food smells, waste smells, straw, disinfectants or cleaning supplies? Are there nice smells coming from the vending areas? Notice how your sense of smell adapts in certain places—the smells may seem very strong at first and lessen as you are in the area for a while.

### WONDER

Wonder what happens to the animals in bad weather. Where do they go if it is too hot or too cold or in bad storms such as blizzards or hurricanes? Do animals ever get frightened?

Do the animals show feelings? Do they like some animals better than others? How do they show their feelings? What makes them sad or happy? Do they get angry and what do they do in all these cases? Do they fight?

Where do the unusual animals come from? How does the zoo find them and get them to the zoo? How do they find out what things different animals like so they know what to put in their environment? Wonder what it feels like to walk into the cage with some of the big animals. What happens at night at the zoo? Does anyone stay to watch the animals? How do they find out if there are any problems?

Try to find someone who can answer these questions. There may be people or resources in the education building to help. The zoo gift shop may have some good books or recommendations on resources. There are some excellent magazines for children, such as Zoobooks, which are sold in zoo gift shops and available at libraries. These magazines have specific information on animal behavior.

Collect as much free information as you can to take back with you. Buy postcards to remind you of your visit and use in follow-up activities.

## After the Trip: Follow-up Activities

### TALK ABOUT IT

Talk about the trip and ask the children to tell you the things they remember and liked at the zoo. Ask them about things they learned that they did not know before or things they did not like. Write down the things they tell you on separate sheets of paper by topic, such as "Things We Liked at the Zoo," "New Things We Learned at the Zoo," "Things We Did Not Like at the Zoo," and "Funny Things We Saw at the Zoo." As you talk about different topics over the next few days, such as the work you saw people doing at the zoo or how food was prepared, add an information sheet on that topic. Put all these together in a homemade book and title it "Our Big Book about the Zoo."

## ZOO MURAL

Make a large group mural of the zoo. Let the children divide up the spaces on the mural for various parts of the zoo; for example, the water sections, bird areas, and large animals. Use cut paper for items such as large rocks, walls, and ponds. Use pebbles, pieces of bark, leaves, grass, and small branches for landscaping. Rick-rack or dark rope works for monkey bars, climbers, and swinging ropes. Use bird and animal stickers for the animals or cut them out of wallpaper sample books. Let the children decide other items they want in their zoo such as a train or vending booths. Wallpaper books may have other pictures they might want to add to the scene. Use the mural as a backdrop for a zoo display or in a zoo dramatic play area.

## LOOKING AT BOOKS

Set out several books that feature pictures and information about zoo animals. *Giraffe*, by Peter Anderson, and other books in the See How They Grow Series have great pictures and descriptions of how much each animal grows in its babyhood and youth. *A Children's Zoo*, by Tana Hoban, and *A Visit to the Zoo*, by Sylvia Root Tester, also have wonderful pictures. *Blizzard at the Zoo*, by Robert Bahr, tells the true story of rescuing and caring for zoo animals in a blizzard.

Create your own book about animals using a small scrapbook. Devote a page or two to each animal and encourage the children to describe it and tell as much as they know about it. Look in books to find out such facts as what it eats and where it is from. Include the children's impression of the animal as well. Was it pretty, scary, funny, or sleepy? If the animal belongs to a family and the children mention it, fine, but do not work too hard on scientific classifications at this stage. Treat each animal on an individual basis. Include pictures that the children draw or that you took at the zoo. At the end of your book, include generalizations about the animals, such as which ones eat meat, which animals are the best climbers, and which ones like water.

## SAWDUST-DOUGH ZOO ANIMALS

Create a sawdust dough to make animals. You'll need 2 cups sawdust (from a lumberyard); 3 cups flour; 1 cup salt; about 1 cup water; a large bowl; and a mixing spoon.

Mix together the sawdust, flour, and salt in the bowl. Slowly add the water as you knead the dough until it is a good modeling consistency. Use more or less water as needed.

Use the dough to form zoo animals. When the dough dries, the models will be lightweight (and may break if dropped on the floor). Have the children paint the animals and use them for a table top zoo display and to play with. Build environments for the animals using blocks or other construction sets (such as Lincoln Logs), or make cages using small shoe boxes placed on their sides. Cut an insert from the shoe box cover and use electrical tape to make bars or cover the covers with onion bags to resemble screening. By taking the covers off the shoe boxes, you can open or close the cages. Make many animals to use in your zoo and add plastic or rubber animals.

### ANIMAL LION PUPPETS

Paint the outer rim of a paper plate yellowish brown. Let the children fringe the edge of the plate (with single scissors slices all around). Draw a face in the middle of the plate or glue on features. Tape or staple a wooden craft stick to the back of the plate for a handle. Use the puppets with the lion songs and finger plays.

### LET'S PLAY ZOO

Make a variety of animal head bands and costumes. Use a strip of heavy paper or tag board to make a band that almost fits around the children's head. Staple a rubber band to the ends of the headband. One size fits all and the stretchy band can go on or off easily. Staple on animal ears or antlers.

For elephant ears, use two pieces of gray 8 1/2-by-11-inch paper. Round three edges of each piece. Fold the fourth edge on the diagonal and staple to the headband.

For an elephant's trunk, wrap a long strip of gray paper around a pencil to curl it. Unroll and tape it to a child's nose.

You can make animal ears by cutting ear shapes out of paper, gluing the shapes onto lightweight fabric in the animal's coloring and stapling them to the band. If the ears need to stand upright, use tag board instead of paper.

To make a lion's mane the children can wear, cut the center out of a large paper plate. Attach yarn and fringed orange paper (yellow or brown paper also works) or crepe paper to the plate's outer rim. The children wear the plates around their faces. Make sure the holes are large enough for the children's faces. Use braided nylons to make lion's tails and attach them with a safety pin.

You can also make animal costumes by painting large-sized paper bags. Cut a hole for the head in the bottom of the bag and make armholes on either side. Paint with stripes or other animal patterns or in plain colors, depending on the animal. Attach flaps to the shoulders to resemble seals or penguins. Use large boxes for animal cages.

Some children can be the zookeepers and some the animals. The zookeepers will need to make food to feed the animals, such as paper fish or shredded paper mixes. If you wish, put on a trained seal show using hula hoops and balls or other props.

## PLAY GUESSING GAMES

Give clues describing an animal and let the children guess what it is. Some examples might be: "This animal is very tall and runs very fast." "It has a very long neck." (giraffe) "This animal has a thick fur coat and lives where it is very cold." "It is white." (polar bear)

## MAKE ANIMAL HABITATS

Decorate boxes or pieces of paper to look like an ocean, rain forest, and grassland area. Cut out many pictures of animals, fish, and birds and let the children sort them by where they live.

## DRAMATIZE ANIMALS STORIES

Read several of the stories in the Resources section and act out the stories. *Happy Lion,* by Louise Fatio (and all of the Happy Lion stories), offer dramatic possibilities. *The Great Zoo Hunt,* by Pippa Unwin, is set up like the "Where's Waldo" books. It might be difficult to search for things in the book, but it has good dramatic potential. Some children can act as the hiding animals and other children can be the zookeepers trying to find them. Children can also make up their own zoo animal stories and choose others to help them act out.

# Related Trip Ideas to Explore

mall petting zoo ● aquarium ● bird sanctuary ● animal safari

# Songs, Poems, and Finger Plays

## I'M A GREAT BIG LION

I'm a great big lion;
You can hear me roar. (all roar!)
I've had my dinner;
But I want some more. (pretend to eat)

### LEO LION

I'm a little bit afraid
When I hear Leo Lion roar; (children roar)
But I like him when he's sleeping,
'Cuz he doesn't even snore. (drop heads to sleep)

### THE TIGER

The tiger is a ferocious beast (act fierce and stalk like a tiger)
His stalking makes me hide (hide behind hands)
I'm glad he's locked up in a cage (pretend to lock cage)
And we are all outside! (fold hands and smile)

## THE CAMEL

Mr. Camel ate some grass,
He opened his mouth so wide;
instead of chewing up and down,
He chewed from side to side!

## THE ZOO

The elephant has a great big nose, (hold arm in front of face like a trunk)
And up and down is how it goes. (move arm up and down)
The buffalo is shaggy and fat,
With two sharp horns for a hat. (extend two fingers on each hand up from
     forehead for horns)
The hippo with his mouth so wide,
Shows you all his teeth inside. (put hands together and open and close them)
The tall giraffe walks all around, (put hands over head and walk around)
And never, never makes a sound.
But the monkeys jumping as monkeys do, (jump like monkeys)
Are the funniest animals in the zoo.

## OH, DO YOU SEE

*(to the tune of "The Muffin Man")*
Oh, do you see the elephants go? (walk like
     an elephant)
The elephants go, the elephants go?
Oh, do you see the elephants go?
They stomp around just so!

Oh, do you see the monkeys go?
     (jump like monkeys)
The monkeys go, the monkeys go?
Oh, do you see the monkeys go?
They jump around just so!

Oh, do you see the dolphins go? (move arms as if swimming)
The dolphins go, the dolphins go?
Oh, do you see the dolphins go?
They swim around just so!

Additional verses:
giant turtle, crawls; tiger or lion,
stalks; ask children to name other
animals seen and show how they
moved.

# Resources

Ancona, George, and Mary Beth Miller. (1989) *Hand Talk Zoo*. New York: Macmillan.

Anderson, Peter. (1993) *Giraffe* (See How They Grow Series). New York: Dorling
     Kindersley (there are many other books in this series).

Arnosky, Jim. (1994) *Crinkleroot's 25 Mammals Every Child Should Know*. New York:
     Bradbury Press.

Ashabranner, Brent. (1988) *I'm in the Zoo, Too!* New York: Dutton.

Bahr, Robert. (1982) *Blizzard at the Zoo*. New York: Lothrop.

Blades, Ann. (1989) *Spring*. New York: Lothrop.

Brandenberg, Franz. (1988) *Leo & Emily's Zoo*. New York: Greenwillow.

Brennan, John. (1989) *Zoo Day*. Minneapolis: Carolrhoda Books.

Carle, Eric. (1982) *1, 2, 3 at the Zoo*. New York: Philomel.
———. (1987) *Have You Seen My Cat?* Natick, MA: Picture Book Studio.

Cooper, Jason. (1992) *Zoos* (Discovery Library of Great Places to Visit). Vero Beach, FL: Rourke.

Dowell, Philip. (1991) *Zoo Animals* (Eye-Openers Series). New York: Dorling Kindersley.

Fatio, Louise. (1954) *The Happy Lion*. New York: McGraw Hill (there are many Happy Lion books).

Florion, Douglas. (1992) *At the Zoo*. New York: Greenwillow.

Gelman, Rita Goldman. (1992) *I Went to the Zoo*. New York: Scholastic.

Gibbons, Gail. (1987) *Zoo*. New York: Crowell.

Hoban, Tana. (1985) *A Children's Zoo*. New York: Greenwillow Books.

Irvine, Georgeanne. (1990) *Let's Visit a Super Zoo*. Mahwah, NJ: Troll Associates.

Lerner, Mark. (1980) *Careers at a Zoo*. Minneapolis: Lerner Publications.

Machotka, Hana. (1990) *What Do You Do at a Petting Zoo?* New York: William Morrow.

Ormerod, Jan. (1991) *When We Went to the Zoo*. New York: Lothrop.

Parker, Nancy Winslow. (1992) *Working Frog*. New York: Greenwillow Books.

Rey, Margaret, and Alan J. Shallack. (1985) *Curious George Visits the Zoo*. New York: Houghton Mifflin.

Roffey, Maureen. (1988) *I Spy at the Zoo*. New York: Four Winds Press.

Rothmann, Peggy. (1994) *Good Night, Gorilla*. New York: Putnam.

Rowan, James P. (1985) *(I Can Be A) Zookeeper*. Chicago: Childrens Press.

Shay, Arthur. (1988) *What Happens at the Zoo?* Chicago: Reilly and Lee Books.

Stamper, Judith Bauer. (1989) *What's It Like to be a Zoo Worker?* Mahwah, NJ: Troll Associates.

Tester, Sylvia Root. (1987) *A Visit to the Zoo*. Chicago: Childrens Press.

Unwin, Pippa. (1990) *The Great Zoo Hunt*. New York: Doubleday.

Weiss, Ellen. (1988) *A Visit to the Sesame Street Zoo*. New York: Random House.

Whithead, Pat. (1985) *Let's Go to the Zoo*. Mahwah, NJ: Troll Associates.

## OTHER GOOD RESOURCES

Barton, Miles. (1988) *Zoos and Game Reserves*. New York: Gloucester Press.

Jacobson, Karen. (1982) *Zoos* (A New True Book). Chicago: Childrens Press.

*At the Zoo* (video). (1993) Goldsholl Learning Videos.

*The Zoo Crew—What Do You Want to be When You Grow Up?* (video). (1995) Big Kids Productions.

# Trips in Reverse

# Resources That Come to You ● ● ● ● ● ● ● ● ● ● ● ● ● ● ● ● ● ● ● ● ● ● ●

Every community boasts a large number of untapped resources, including people who are willing to share their experience with young children. Use these resources to enhance follow-up activities or to use in the place of a walk or trip. To find out what is available in your community, all you have to do is ask.

## USE FAMILY RESOURCES

Parents, grandparents, siblings, or friends may be able to demonstrate a variety of activities in the following areas:

- hobbies (anything from handicraft activities to cooking special foods or sharing collections)
- talents (musical instruments, singing, dancing, magic performances)
- ethnic costumes or cultural items, slides from travels
- pets
- occupations
- babies
- sports activities and accompanying uniforms or equipment (from fencing to football).

## CONTACT COMMUNITY RESOURCES

Many agencies have public relations departments that can arrange for a visit or demonstration, such as:

- dairy council, county extension service agent;
- firefighter with fire engine;
- police officer with police car;
- hospital or health personnel (nurse, lab technician, dentist, doctor);
- repair people (electrician, plumber);
- community service group (scouts);
- arts group (theater, music);
- librarian;

- reporter and photographer (newspaper, television);

- pet store personnel;

- park naturalist, forest ranger;

- service people (parcel delivery person, mail carrier).

### TECHNIQUES FOR FINDING NEW RESOURCES

- Use a questionnaire or talk in person to parents about what they would be willing to share (work, hobbies, special interests). Include inquiries about grandparents or siblings who may also have things to share.

- Write to or call the school personnel in your area.

- Write to or call the people who work in community agencies mentioned above.

- Write a letter to the editor or an article for your local paper, asking people in the community to donate their time. Place a notice on the bulletin board at the grocery store or local community center.

Once you have people interested, arrange a short orientation for them. Let them know what to expect from preschoolers and confer with them about their presentation. Make sure their presentation is at the right level and is not too long, complicated, or scary for a group of young children.

# Appendix

# General Permission Slip

Dear Parent:

    An important part of our regular program includes walks in the neighborhood and a few field trips into the community. These are an excellent means of expanding children's knowledge of the world around them. Children are always well supervised on excursions. Please sign and return the enclosed permission slip for our records.

Sincerely,

_____

_____ has my permission to go on

neighborhood walks and community field trips while attending

_____ program.

_____    _____

Date                Parent Signature

# Notification and Permission Slip

Dear Parent,

We are planning a trip to the Community Nature Center on Thursday, May 15. We will be leaving at 9:30 a.m. and returning at 11:30 a.m. Several parents have volunteered to accompany us, so we will have enough supervision for the children to explore the center in small groups. Please dress your child in old clothes suitable for exploring woods and dirt. Be sure your child is wearing a long-sleeve shirt, long pants, and an old sweater or jacket. Please do not send any money with your child. We will provide a snack while at the center. We thank you for your cooperation.

We hope to see many of the early blooming shrubs and sapping of the maple trees. There are also many small animals and birds on view at the center. If we are lucky, we will see beavers at work in the pond area, as well as frogs and toads. We hope this information will help you interpret any comments your child may bring home, since children often give graphic, but confusing, reports—such as having seen, "tree milked" or "some jumping things!"

Sincerely yours,

_____

Please sign and return the field trip permission slip below.

- - - - - - - - - - - - - - - - - - - - - - - - - - - - - - - - - - - - - - - - - - - - -

Date _____

_____ has my permission to participate
in the field trip to _____ on _____

_____
Parent Signature

_____
Phone number where I can be reached in case of emergency

# Field Trip Planning Form

Type of Walk/Trip _____

Purpose _____

Words Associated with the Walk/Trip

_____

_____

Introductory Activity or Question

_____

Things to Watch for or Collect on the Walk/Trip

_____

_____

Anticipated Problems

_____

Follow-up Activities

● _____

● _____

● _____

● Songs _____

● Books _____

● Poems or finger plays _____

Is a Revisit Appropriate? ❑ yes ❑ no

Purpose _____

Activity _____

# Field Trip Checklist for Staff

| Field Trip Site | Phone No. | Date | Time | Schedule |
|---|---|---|---|---|
| A | | | | |
| B | | | | |
| C | | | | |
| D | | | | |
| E | | | | |

**Transportation Arranged/Extra Help Secured**

**(Name and Phone No.)**

Trip A

Trip B

Trip C

Trip D

Trip E

**Special Needs**

Trip A

Trip B

Trip C

Trip D

Trip E

| | Trip A | Trip B | Trip C | Trip D | Trip E |
|---|---|---|---|---|---|
| Parent notices complete | | | | | |
| Site arrangements complete | | | | | |
| Name tags organized | | | | | |
| Planning forms complete for all adults on trip | | | | | |
| First-aid kit ready | | | | | |
| Bag of tricks ready | | | | | |
| Snack for trip | | | | | |
| Permission slips returned | | | | | |

# Orientation List for Volunteers

1. Thank you for helping make this exciting experience possible.
2. Familiarize yourself with the information sheet for this trip. It will give you the purpose of the trip, the logistics of the trip, points of interest to talk about en route, and special words to explain to the children.
3. You will supervise five children. Their tags and yours are the same color and you have a list of their names. You might play a little game with the children to help you learn their names. Try to relate personally to each child, making sure each one feels comfortable.
4. Some children may feel unsure in new situations. Comfort them, hold their hands, smile. Talk about how fun it is to go away for a little while and then return and tell others about it.
5. During the course of the field trip, talk with your group of children about what they are seeing. Frequently repeat the names of things, and also repeat or retell information that may be given by a guide. Encourage questions and stimulate curiosity with your own questions. For example: "I wonder how that works?" or "Why do you think she is doing that?"
6. Anticipate situations such as puddles, mud, or obstacles in the path. Prepare children so impending difficulties may be avoided. Tell the children what to do, such as "Take a big, big step over the puddle," instead of saying "Don't step in the puddle." Practice mooing like the cows before entering a barn so the noise won't startle anyone.
7. Each class and group should stay together. Watch for children who may need individual attention and supervise them closely.
8. Children must be with adults at all times! They should not be left alone or sent alone to find another group or teacher. Getting lost is a frightening experience and should be avoided. Go to the bathroom as a group, if necessary, or find another adult to supervise the children who are waiting.
9. Stay calm and relaxed. Your calmness will reassure children in any situation. Remember, most problems can be solved with a few moments of calm thinking. Play little games such as "I Spy Something Red" or "What Do I See?" in situations where children have to wait and are growing restless.
10. Have fun. Enjoy what you're doing and share your enthusiasm—then the children will share your enjoyment.

# Information Sheet for Volunteers and Staff

The list of children you will supervise is attached. Thank you for helping us make this a wonderful experience for our children.

Site to be visited: _____

Phone: _____ Address: _____

Name of our contact person at the site: _____

Directions to the site (map attached). Special drop off/pick up/parking arrangements made:


Things to note and talk about on the way:


Concepts and words to emphasize or explain:


Things to point out:


Things to collect and bring back:


Timetable for trip:


Suggested meeting spots:


Procedures in case of emergency:


Anticipated problems/suggestions to prepare for or avoid:

# Suggested Resources

## CURRICULUM PLANNING/CHILDREN'S LEARNING

Broad, Laura Peabody. (1991) *The Playgroup Handbook.* New York: St. Martin's Press.

Cherry, Clare. (1987) *Nursery School and Day Care Center Management Guide.* Columbus, OH: Fearon Teacher Aids.

Herr, Judy, and Yvonne Libby. (1994) *Creative Resources for the Early Childhood Classroom.* Albany, NY: Delmar Publishers.

Katz, Lillian, and Sylvia Chard. (1989) *Engaging Children's Minds.* Norwood, IL: Ablex Publishing.

McCartney, Susan. (1991) *Active Learning in a Family Day Care Setting.* Glenview, IL: GoodYear Books.

Peterson, Rosemary, and Victoria Felton-Collins. (1986) *The Piaget Handbook for Teachers and Parents.* New York: Teachers College Press.

## FINGER PLAYS/ MUSIC

Bayless, Kathleen, and Marjorie Ramsey. (1990) *Music: A Way of Life for the Young Child.* New York: Macmillan.

Cole, Joanna, and Stephanie Calmenson. (1991) *The Eentsy Weentsy Spider: Fingerplays and Action Rhymes.* New York: William Morrow.

Cromwell, Liz, and Dixie Hibner. (1983) *Finger Frolics.* West Bloomfield, IL: Partner Press.

Holley, Cynthia, and Jane Walkup. (1993) *First Time Circle Time: Shared-Group Experiences for Three, Four, and Five-Year-Olds.* Columbus, OH: Fearon Teacher Aids.

Redleaf, Rhoda. (1993) *Busy Fingers, Growing Minds.* St. Paul: Redleaf Press.

Scott, Louise Binder. (1984) *Rhymes for Learning Times.* Minneapolis: T. S. Denison.

Schiller, Pam, and Moore, Thomas. (1993) *Where is Thumbkin? 500 Activities to Use With Songs You Already Know.* Beltsville: Gryphon House.

Wilmes, Liz and Dick. (1995) *2's Experience Fingerplays.* Elgin, IL: Building Blocks.

## SCIENCE/SOCIAL STUDIES/DRAMATIC PLAY

Brokering, Lois. (1990) *Resources for Dramatic Play.* Columbus, OH: Fearon Teacher Aids.

Brown, Sam, ed. (1981) *Bubbles, Rainbows and Worms: Science Activities for Young Children.* Beltsville, MD: Gryphon House.

Mitchell, Ann, and Judy David, eds. (1992) *Explorations with Young Children: A Curriculum Guide from the Bank Street College of Education.* Beltsville, MD: Gryphon House.

———. (1992) *Social Studies: A Way to Integrate Curriculum for Four and Five Year-Olds.* (A companion video tape to *Explorations.*) Beltsville, MD: Gryphon House.

Sherwood, Elizabeth, Robert Williams, and Robert Rockwell. (1990) *More Mudpies to Magnets: Science for Young Children.* Beltsville, MD: Gryphon House.

Williams, Robert, and Robert Rockwell. (1987) *Mudpies to Magnets: A Preschool Science Curriculum* . Beltsville, MD: Gryphon House.

## GENERAL REFERENCE GUIDES

(1995) *The World Book Encyclopedia.* Chicago: World Book, Inc.

Gillespie, John T., and Corinne J. Naden, eds. (1994) *A to Zoo: Subject Access to Children's Picture Books,* 4th ed. New York: R.R. Bowker.

———. (1993) *Best Books for Children,* 5th ed. New York: R.R. Bowker.

———. *Subject Guide to Children's Books in Print.* New York: R.R. Bowker, Annual.